Stubborn Children

Medicine and Society
Series Editor: Andrew Scull

'STUBBORN CHILDREN,

Controlling Delinquency in
the United States, 1640–1981

JOHN R. SUTTON

UNIVERSITY OF CALIFORNIA PRESS
Berkeley · Los Angeles · London

University of California Press
Berkeley and Los Angeles, California

University of California Press, Ltd.
London, England

© 1988 by
The Regents of the University of California

Library of Congress Cataloging-in-Publication Data

Sutton, John, 1949–
    Stubborn children.
    (Medicine and Society)

    Bibliography: p.
    Includes index.
    1. Juvenile corrections—United States—History.
2. Reformatories—United States—History.
3. Juvenile delinquents—United States—History.
4. Juvenile justice, Administration of—United
States— History.   I. Title.
HV9104.S88 1988   364.3′6′0973   87–10850
ISBN 0–520–06093–8 (alk. paper)

Printed in the United States of America
1 2 3 4 5 6 7 8 9

To the memory of
Benjamin R. Morales
1915–1983

CONTENTS

LIST OF TABLES AND FIGURES

ACKNOWLEDGMENTS

My primary debt for this study is to Gary Hamilton, who taught me most of what I know about historical sociology and who offered unflagging encouragement and inspiration at every stage of the research. Most of the theoretical arguments presented here were germinated in our ongoing collaborative dialogue on American conceptions of authority and obligation. I also want to note the special contribution of Edwin Lemert, who has exerted a diffuse, but nonetheless pervasive, influence on my thinking about the social construction of deviance.

A number of other scholars read part or all of some version of this study and contributed valuable critical comments. Bob Liebman and Marsha Witten gave particularly detailed and comprehensive readings and corrected many errors of reason and exposition. Thanks are due also to Marvin Bressler, the late Forrest Dill, George Downs, David Garland, Bruce Hackett, John Meyer, Cliff Nass, Ann Orloff, Ann Swidler, David Tyack, Walter Wallace, and Robert Wuthnow. I am also grateful to a small group of colleagues who enthusiastically shared their knowledge of the methods of event-history analysis: Terry Amburgey, Chuck Denk, Mike Hannan, Michal Tamuz, and Larry Wu. All these friends did their best to save me from my own worst excesses; any gaffes that remain are undeniably my own responsibility. Finally, very personal debts are owed to Meyer Rothberg, for exercising his calling; and to Beth Berlese, for being herself.

Funding for this project was pieced together from a variety of sources. Early research was supported by a dissertation fellowship from the Regents of the University of California. Subsequent analysis and writing was done while I was a fellow of the NIMH Research Training Program on Organizations and Mental Health at Stanford University; special thanks to Dick Scott, program director, for exceptional creative ambience. Loose ends were tied up with the aid of a faculty research grant from the Princeton University Committee on Research in the Humanities and Social Sciences.

Some of the results from this analysis have been published in a series of journal articles. Much of Chapter 1 appeared as "Stubborn Children: Law and the Socialization of Deviance in the Puritan Colonies," *Family Law Quarterly* 15 (1981): 31–64. An earlier version of the quantitative analysis in Chapter 3 was published in "Social Structure, Institutions, and the Legal Status of Children in the United States," *American Journal of Sociology* 88 (1983): 915–947. Most of Chapter 5 appeared as "The Juvenile Court and Social Welfare: Dynamics of Progressive Reform," *Law and Society Review* 19 (1985): 107–154.

INTRODUCTION

Delinquency is the vengeance of the prison on justice. It is a
revenge formidable enough to leave the judge speechless. It is at
this point that the criminologists raise their voices.

Michel Foucault

The American system of juvenile justice is a loosely articulated collection of laws and institutions that govern our official responses to
misbehaving and dependent children. The fate of that system is
woven deeply into the history of the nation. It originated in the early
legal experiments of the Massachusetts Bay colonists, and it grew
through bursts of reform that coincided with watershed social and
political crises—the rise of Jacksonian democracy, the administrative
consolidation of the Progressive era, and the civil rights revolution of
the 1960s and 1970s. Perhaps more than any other people, and
certainly earlier, Americans have treated children as a lens through
which to view the future and as a means by which to control it. Thus
policies concerning deviant children have been at the moral center of
debates over crime, poverty, and education—indeed, over the political growth of the nation.

This book is a historical account of how Americans invented and
elaborated this specialized system of control. The empirical focus
throughout the study is on the laws and institutions that define
legally actionable forms of youthful deviance and prescribe official
sanctions. But I intend to use this focus to illuminate a much broader

1

issue: the turn from punitive justice to an avowedly therapeutic style of social control. This turn has implied a reconceptualization of the nature of deviance and a wholesale reorientation of the social control machinery. As Foucault puts it, modern states have replaced the legal conception of the responsible criminal actor with the psychological conception of the morally inept delinquent, and control agencies now claim to repair damaged selves rather than to punish.[1] In the last two centuries the therapeutic model has made its way into a variety of control settings throughout the Western world. But it is telling that the concept of delinquency is now conventionally associated with the crimes of youth, signifying that in the social control of children the therapeutic ideal survives in its purest and most stubborn form.

Any attempt to explain the therapeutic approach to child control must confront a difficult historical paradox. American juvenile justice since the 1820s has been the target of constant public skepticism and occasional public outrage. Frequently, attacks have come from sharply opposed ideological positions: humanitarian critics have deplored the routine brutality and arbitrariness of the official system, and conservatives have criticized its perceived tendency to coddle young criminals. Few on either side would argue, now or in the past, that official strategies successfully prevent deviance or rehabilitate offenders. Yet if we measure the system's success in terms of its ability to garner resources, to survive, and to expand, rather than its ability to achieve stated goals, juvenile justice in the United States is a flourishing enterprise. Successive generations of reformers have approached the problem of delinquency with renewed aspirations, sought more detailed legislative mandates for their discre-

---

1. Foucault was not, of course, the first to recognize this phenomenon. There is a rich sociological literature on the "medical model" of deviance, but until recently most studies focused on microlevel processes rather than on the historical origins of the therapeutic model. For a particularly germane study in the microsociological tradition, see Cicourel (1968).

tionary authority, and progressively expanded the size and scope of the official institutional system.[2]

Conventional theories of social control offer only partial solutions to this paradox. On the one hand, systems theories—whether drawn from a Durkheimian "consensus" perspective or a Marxian-inspired "conflict" perspective[3]—contain persuasive accounts of the ways in which formal, specialized control systems emerge in modern societies. But these accounts tend to be abstract and instrumental. They say little about why a specifically therapeutic style of control may appear in a particular context or why it persists when it serves no discernible general or class-specific social interests. On the other hand, models focusing on the agency of moral entrepreneurs (e.g., Becker 1963; Gusfield 1963; Platt 1969) often capture the noninstrumental, even ad hoc, nature of many control reforms. They fruitfully emphasize the marginal social location of reformers, the parochialism of their moral perspectives, the self-serving character of their therapeutic discourse, and the socially constructed—hence arbitrary and symbolic—nature of the policies they advocated. But the most conspicuous weakness of the entrepreneurial model is that it slights the larger political context in which reformers operated. Thus it does not yield generalizable inferences about long-term patterns of institution building.

This study explores both systemic and entrepreneurial influences on American strategies of child control in a comparative and longitu-

2. For example, U.S. Census publications show that, in 1880, Americans incarcerated 67,972 children in various kinds of public and private institutions, or 577 per 100,000 children age ten to twenty. By 1923, that number had climbed to 168,360 (773 per 100,000) (U.S. Census Office 1895, 882; U.S. Bureau of the Census 1927, 19, 291, 346). In 1974, 76,671 inmates were reported in official detention and correctional facilities (U.S. Department of Justice 1977, 32). This last figure does not include the large number on probation or parole supervision or children held in mental hospitals for juvenile offenses (see Lerman 1980).

3. For reviews of these approaches, see Hopkins (1975), Chambliss (1976), Hagan et al. (1977), Hagan (1980), and Meier (1982). Humphries and Greenberg (1981) offer a more comprehensive critique of systems and agency theories.

dinal perspective. I begin with the assumption that social systems do not invent deviant labels, enact laws, or sanction offenders; rather, people do, but they do so in the context of collectively held norms that lend transcendent significance and authority to their actions. American child control reformers were motivated by a set of inherited institutional patterns that lent internal coherence to social movement activities, gave marginal social movements access to a more broadly legitimate tradition of political discourse, and provided ideological continuity from one wave of reform to another. These patterns have many sources, but here I emphasize two main models for the enterprise of therapeutic justice: (1) myths of social order and deviance that were gradually incorporated in the rationalized ideologies of the helping professions and (2) the peculiarly American view of the state as moral exemplar rather than coercive authority. These are broad cultural motifs with common roots in the civil ethos of Calvinism, but they have practical implications for the distribution of political power and the trajectory of legal change. The solution to the paradox is that American juvenile justice is not an expression of an instrumental concern for children, or even deviance, as such; rather, it is an outgrowth of the purely political process of constructing a welfare state.

My causal argument can be stated briefly. I am interested in three distinguishable aspects of reform: the *timing* of key institution-building reforms, the *content* of those reforms, and the *process* by which local innovations were adopted to become national patterns of control. My most general argument is that the historical development of a rationalized system of child control has been driven by tensions and paradoxes that are inherent to the enterprise of therapeutic justice. Tensions between formal law and discretionary action, between public order and private morality, and between the state and the family threaten to erupt when the system is exposed to external criticism. Thus the *timing* of successive waves of reform is affected by larger crises of legitimation. Major changes in the laws affecting deviant children have typically been inaugurated at historical intervals when struggles over broader issues of governance and social order were pronounced. These struggles induced strain on existing patterns of control and created opportunities for reformers to propose moral solutions to political problems in the form of institutional cures for crime and poverty. A large part of my task in this analysis is to describe how children became a focus of a more general state-building program.

Second, I argue that the *content* of the reforms cannot be explained either in terms of system imperatives or the purely self-serving ambitions of reform entrepreneurs. Instead, the logic of reform is historical: reformers in each generation worked from a set of assumptions inherited from the generation before and sought to achieve their own local interests within those assumptions. Jacksonian asylum reformers developed a penal discourse informed by Calvinist predestinarian theology and Enlightenment rationality, and later Progressives distilled the concept of the juvenile court as a means both to correct and to protect the reformatory system developed in the previous century. Yet there is a pattern of reform that has repeated itself over time and that shaped these situational responses into a long-term developmental process. Reformers sought to adapt an inertial institution to a changing social environment by seeking out new sources of legitimacy. The tendency in juvenile justice was to move in two different directions simultaneously: to seek legal sanction from the state and to synthesize a therapeutic program from the ideologies of the helping professions. This unstable partnership between formal law and substantively oriented criminology and child welfare did not eliminate the tensions inherent in therapeutic justice, but rather institutionalized and perpetuated them within an expanding edifice of legal rules and administrative agencies. Thus each wave of reform emerged as a corrective response to previous reforms and carried within itself the seeds of the next round of innovations.

Finally, the study explores the *process* by which local innovations were adopted as national models of reform. Here the legislative autonomy of the American states provides an interesting opportunity for comparative analysis: I address this process empirically by analyzing the rates at which the states adopted reforms. The evolutionary logic of systems theory suggests that reforms would spread gradually from urban core states to the rural periphery and that all states would eventually converge on a similar set of innovations at some threshold level of modernity. We know from a variety of studies that innovations in social control and child welfare emerged first in areas where the stresses of modernization were greatest in successive historical periods: colonial New England (Erikson 1966), the urban centers of the Eastern seaboard in the mid nineteenth century (Rothman 1971; Mennel 1973), Progressive era Chicago (Schlossman 1977; Platt 1969), and California after 1960 (Lemert 1970; Scull 1977). These studies do not directly support a linear modernization argument, however; rather, they imply that innovations arise from urban-industrial frontiers where institution building is still a dynamic process. Moreover, few studies have examined the ways in which reforms have diffused beyond these centers. The institutional approach adopted here suggests that the diffusion of specialized agencies for managing childhood is driven by ideological processes that operate independently of functional need. Empirical research has identified processes of this sort operating within both the United States (Meyer et al. 1979) and the larger world system (Boli-Bennett and Meyer 1978; Ramirez and Boli-Bennett 1981). In this study I use dynamic quantitative techniques to specify the limits of systemic factors and to suggest where alternative interpretations would be more fruitful.

The organization of the narrative follows the episodic pattern of reform. Chapters are structured around crucial stages in the expansion of juvenile justice institutions, and the focus shifts from microlevel discussions of the origins of reform innovations to macrolevel analyses of the diffusion of reforms within each stage. Chapter 1 sets the tone for the rest of the book by analyzing the Massachusetts Bay "stubborn child" law of 1646, which represents the first formal provision for public child control in the Western world. The discussion places the statute in the larger context of Massachusetts Bay law and politics, draws comparisons with other colonies, and identifies themes that influenced subsequent juvenile law in the United States. These themes are taken up again in Chapters 2 and 3, which are concerned with the establishment of special penal institutions for children in the nineteenth century. In Chapter 2, I examine the first such institutions, the houses of refuge established in the 1820s. I argue that the prototypical decline "from care to custody" that occurred within their first few years resulted not from simple bureaucratic inertia but from internal philosophical and political conflicts that reflected the larger divisions of Jacksonian society. Chapter 3 employs quantitative data drawn from legislative histories to describe the legal implications of juvenile reformatories and to test hypotheses about their diffusion nationwide.

Chapters 4 and 5 repeat this basic sequence in the context of the juvenile court reforms of the early twentieth century. In Chapter 4, I take up the neglected question of what the juvenile court really was as a legal entity. Documentary sources suggest that it was not—and was never intended to be—a practical innovation in the treatment of children but was rather an attempt to preserve established reformatory methods in a more rational, bureaucratic context. Chapter 5 again takes up the issue of diffusion. Here I am particularly interested in the role of the charity organization movement in the passage of juvenile court legislation. The analysis suggests that the role of these moral entrepreneurs was not to invent new forms of deviance or impose new strategies of control, but rather to dramatize ideological linkages between child welfare and more broadly legitimate programs of state building.

Chapter 6 jumps ahead some fifty years to the next major wave of legislative activity, the decarceration reforms of the 1960s and 1970s. Again developments in juvenile law are found to be at the center of a broad set of trends encompassing several institutional sectors, particularly mental health, social welfare, and criminal justice. And again actual reforms turn out to be more symbolic than substantive. Not surprisingly, the dynamics of reform in the second half of the twentieth century are decisively altered by the growing participation of the federal government, but the analysis shows that federal influence is exerted in unexpectedly indirect ways. Finally, in Chapter 7, I draw together the findings from all three reform waves, identify connecting themes, and suggest some theoretical inferences about the three-hundred-year history of child control reform in the United States.

Before moving on, I want to mention some issues that are not addressed in the study and thus identify its attendant limitations. First, I am concerned with the formation of juvenile justice policy, not implementation or practice. At many points I rely on and refer to a growing body of historical and ethnographic studies of reformatories, juvenile courts, mental hospitals, and social welfare agencies. These studies show with depressing regularity that reforms were not implemented in the way reformers intended and did not have the expected effects. I do not attempt to add to this literature here. To plough the same ground again is pointless and would only divert me from my main interest in the long-term dynamics of change.

My exclusive concern with policy innovation suggests a second limitation. The analysis focuses primarily on the activities of elites—including middle-class professionals and government officials—because the creation and transformation of child control policy appears to be an elite domain. Recent social histories have shown convincingly that lower-class and immigrant clients have had an insurgent effect on the evolving character of social control institutions (see, e.g., Katz 1983; Brenzel 1983). On an everyday level, institutional managers and social workers struggled to maintain control of their agencies and to resist clients' attempts to use existing institutions for their own purposes. But lower-class voices were systematically excluded from settings in which policies were generated, except when reformers quoted them in sentimental paraphrases; and their impact came after fateful decisions had been made. Reformers were aware of, and sought to block, client strategies of self-help by building rings of legal defenses around their institutions. This book is in part an account of those defenses; that, I think, justifies a top-down approach.

The third caveat concerns gender. This study focuses on a succession of major innovations—the first institution of a specific type in a given state, the first law to establish jurisdiction over certain kinds of deviance, and so on—and where the changes I examine are not indifferent to gender, they are explicitly directed at males. For example, after 1850, states built reformatories for boys before they built reformatories for girls; in the empirical analysis I am concerned only with the first institution of any kind. Yet the social control of women clearly has a history of its own. Freedman (1981) and Brenzel (1983) have shown that the drive for women's institutions was not a residual process, but rested on a distinct conception of female deviance. Schlossman and Wallach (1978) and Chesney-Lind (1978) show further that juvenile courts respond differently to male and female delinquency because of the perceived predilection of lower-class girls to sexual deviance.[4] Nonetheless I argue that the generic concept of delinquency is logically and historically prior to a gender-specific one. I hope that this study offers useful insights for more fine-grained analyses to follow.

4. For a good overview of social control directed at women, see Schur (1984).

1

Inventing the Stubborn Child

In November of 1646, the governing General Court of Massachusetts Bay passed a barrage of legislation designed to codify a unique legal structure for the colony. These laws formalized the rights and responsibilities of colony members, proscribed a variety of criminal acts, and clarified the legitimate domain of official authority. Among the laws passed at this time was a statute that made it a capital offense for a child to disobey his parents:

> If a man have a stubborn or rebellious son, of sufficient years and understanding (viz.) sixteen years of age, which will not obey the voice of his Father, or the voice of his Mother, and that when they have chastened him will not harken unto them: then shall his Father and Mother being his natural parents, lay hold on him, and bring him to the Magistrates assembled in Court and testify unto them, that their son is stubborn and rebellious and will not obey their voice and chastisement, but lives in

sundry notorious crimes, such a son shall be put to death. (Farrand 1929, 6; Shurtleff 1854, 101)

The Puritans took the text of this statute almost verbatim from Deuteronomy 21:20–21. Taking it at face value, the "stubborn child" law (Sidman 1972) was legally distinctive in three ways. It defined a special legal obligation that pertained to children, but not to adults; it defined the child's parents as the focus of that obligation; and it established rules to govern when public officials could intervene in the family and what actions they could take. It was the first statute of its kind in North America, and probably in the modern world.

Two interpretations of the meaning of this statute have been presented. One suggests that the stubborn child law is the progenitor of modern child regulation laws—"not only the root but also the trunk of many current laws governing parent-child relations" (Teitelbaum and Harris 1977, 32). It was copied into the colonial codes of Connecticut, Rhode Island, and New Hampshire, and it remained in force in Massachusetts in substantially amended form until 1973. It served as a direct or indirect model for legislation enacted by every American state making children's misbehavior a punishable offense. It appears to foreshadow the 1838 case of *ex parte Crouse,* which legitimized state supervision of troublesome children on the basis of the medieval doctrine of *parens patriae,* and which has never been entirely repudiated.[1]

But the bare words of this statute belie any sense of legal continuity between colonial and modern means of child control; indeed, they suggest an enormous gulf between the Puritans and ourselves in attitudes toward children's misconduct. Modern policies are framed

---

1. In its original form *parens patriae* had more to do with property law than with the behavior of children: it was a means for the Crown to administer landed orphans' estates. The Pennsylvania Supreme Court invoked it in the *Crouse* case to deny a writ of *habeas corpus* to a child incarcerated for delinquency. The court justified this ruling on grounds that delinquency is not a crime and that the Philadelphia House of Refuge "is not a prison, but a school" (4 Whart. 9, 11 [1839]).

in the language of secular experts, not Old Testament prophets; they emphasize discretion rather than dogmatic judgment and ameliorative treatment rather than punishment. The statute contains no hint of mercy, let alone of the modern notions of prevention and rehabilitation; and the fact that the penalty was never actually imposed,[2] indeed was reduced by subsequent amendment, further obscures the meaning of the statute.

Thus a second interpretation suggests conversely that there is no continuity between colonial and modern means of child regulation. According to this view, the stubborn child law was a product of an economically tenuous authoritarian society, a futile and atavistic attempt to enforce traditional authority relationships on the doorstep of the New World. The statute is seen as being primarily of instrumental significance in supporting parental control over children's labor, and more generally in assuring rigid conformity of thought and action in future generations (Teitelbaum and Harris 1977, 10–11, 33; Sidman 1972, 44). Such a law, it is suggested, has no such instrumental role in a modern, pluralistic society.

In both of these interpretations, the stubborn child law is conceived narrowly, either as legal precedent or economic instrumentality; from either perspective it appears to be a slightly absurd historical curiosity. In this chapter I argue that beneath the archaic language of the law lies a distinctively, precociously modern approach to social control. Seen in the wider context of colonial society, the statute exemplifies two tendencies in colonial Puritan law that presaged the emergence of a rational therapeutic model of control in the nineteenth- and early twentieth-century United States. The first of these tendencies is toward the socialization of law and the family. By this I mean that formal law chartered the family as an agent to further the values of the commonwealth. Law in Massachusetts Bay developed as a response to perceived disorder and as an affirmative statement of public policy. Its substantive goal was to sustain a community of saints through the

2. A number of authors make this point. See Haskins (1960, 81), Hutchinson (1936, 372–373), Wertenbaker (1947, 166).

rational allocation of responsibilities among appropriate spheres in the social order, of which the family was the most fundamental.

A second tendency of Puritan law was toward the normalization and universalization of deviance. In Puritan thought no individual, not even those of the saved elect, was immune from sin; its seeds were perceived to lie in everyone, especially untutored children. Thus the survival of the commonwealth as a moral enterprise demanded the development of formal means of surveillance and self-regulation. In short, the argument here is that the stubborn child law can best be explained not as a means to control children's misbehavior, but as part of a larger strategy for limiting conflict and maintaining established authority.

I elaborate this argument in four steps. The first is to address the economic explanation for the emergence of formal-legal child control in Massachusetts Bay through a brief comparative analysis of data on the colonial labor market. Next I turn to the distinctive legal and political transformations that occurred in the commonwealth during the seventeenth century and place the stubborn child law in the context of these larger events. The third step is to substantiate this argument with a survey of legal development in other colonies. Finally, I return to the topics of socialized law and normalized deviance and suggest the impact of Puritan thought on the development of juvenile law in the United States.

Law, Labor, and Colonial Child Control

In the view of some scholars, the impetus for the stubborn child law was to protect a valuable source of labor. Teitelbaum and Harris (1977, 10) maintain that economics "accounted for" this and other statutes that reinforced the patriarchal family in colonial Massachusetts: "Labor in the colonies, even more so than in England, was a family enterprise. . . . Farms and small businesses predominated, for which patriarchal family organization was particularly well-suited." They argue that children were valuable as a labor resource and that laws enforcing parental authority assured the dependence of children on parents until long after what would otherwise have been the case (Teitelbaum and Harris 1977, 33). Sidman (1972, 44) advances a complementary argument, noting that many New England child control laws included both children and servants: "That grouping indicates a possible interchangeability of children and servants in the Puritan socio-economic system. Thus, it can be argued that early stubborn child legislation fulfilled a major economic objective—to control disobedient servants."

However, the labor-supply argument is weak because it suggests differences between New England and other colonies where they do not exist. In particular it implies a stereotyped distinction between northern and southern colonies: in the South, it is assumed, larger families and the availability of slaves made labor more abundant and easier to control, and large plantations permitted economies of scale that could not be achieved on small New England farms. Yet the historical evidence suggests that the labor situation in New England was not notably different from that in the other colonies for most of the seventeenth century. Labor was in short supply and commanded high wages everywhere (Handlin and Handlin 1950, 218; Morris 1975, 44–46). In all the colonies, indentured servants were widely employed as an alternative to free and family labor, so much so that bondsmen accounted for more than half of all English immigrants in the seventeenth and eighteenth centuries (Stampp 1956, 16). Moreover, the large-scale plantation economy of the South did not develop until well after the legal patterns we are concerned with were established. In the Chesapeake colonies as well as New England, it was rare in the mid seventeenth century for farms to exceed ten acres (Ver Steeg 1964, 57).

Nor does slavery appear to have been a uniquely southern institution at this time. Population estimates reported by the U.S. Census Bureau (1965, Series Z 1–19) show that the black population in the colonies was not disproportionately concentrated in the South until late in the century. If we assume that colonial blacks were primarily slaves or servants—a distinction that was not clear in the seventeenth century—census data show that New Hampshire had roughly the same per capita availability of black bonded labor as Virginia through 1660, and Rhode Island kept pace until 1680. As the Handlins (1950, 218) conclude, in the seventeenth century "none of the elements that conspired to create the slave were peculiar to the productive system of the South." Nor, conversely, are there any signs of dependence on child labor peculiar to New England.

If the availability of extrafamilial labor was about the same in all the colonies, it is still possible that a smaller average family size led New Englanders to perceive their children as a relatively scarce resource and to seek extraordinary legal means to bind them to parents. But again there is no evidence of significant differences in family structure, including numbers of children and relative importance placed on the family unit, among the colonies. Although statistical data are incomplete, Seward (1978, 38–39) suggests that southern colonies were generally similar to New England in this regard. New England families were nowhere near as large as once thought, but they tended to have more children than modern American families; and, more important, they enjoyed significantly lower infant mortality rates than were common in Europe at the time (Seward 1978, 45–62). Thus even if we assume that New Englanders regarded their children primarily or even largely as economic assets, they were unlikely to have seen them as conspicuously scarce ones.

Instrumental explanations of this sort not only misconstrue the New England labor market; they also misunderstand Puritan law. Even if the Puritans had been in a disadvantaged labor market relative to the other colonies, they are unlikely to have resorted to statutes like the stubborn child law to solve their labor problems. They frequently sought to legislate a planned economy, but they did so straightforwardly and in plain language, not through arcane scriptural exhortations. New Englanders established wage and price controls, actively recruited skilled laborers to emigrate from Europe, and provided for the compulsory impressment of persons of all social strata into labor of general public import, such as harvesting and road building (Morris 1975, 6–7, 55–84). They were not embarrassed to specify children's economic obligations with equal frankness.

Although there is a generally conservative thrust to both colonial economic and family regulations, the laws are far from unanimous in supporting parental domination. According to Haskins (1960, 240–241), the law instituting partible inheritance in Massachusetts Bay was motivated by a desire to provide children of a parent who died and left no will with opportunities for economic independence. Seward (1978, 57–61) notes several studies showing that parental power was used to delay children's marriages, allowing parents to maintain control over them. Formal law appears to support this parental prerogative to some degree: the 1648 legal code, the *Laws and Liberties,* required that parental approval be sought and given before a daughter could be courted. Yet the law also supported the autonomy of children in this matter by giving them express rights of legal redress when marriage was "willfully" and "unreasonably" denied (Farrand 1929, 12, 37).[3]

It appears in general that children in Massachusetts Bay were no more subordinated to their parents than those in other seventeenth-century families. On the contrary, Puritan law is notable for the degree to which it specified the responsibilities that inhered in the exercises of parental authority (Labaree 1979, 76). Puritan families were required not just to feed and clothe their children, but also to educate them and train them in a calling. Again, the requirements of the law defy a merely instrumental interpretation. The calling was more than just an occupation; it was the earthly form in which the drama of salvation was acted out. "It raised the ordinary work of one's profession . . . and the ardour with which secular work was prosecuted to the level of a religious duty in itself" (Troeltsch 1960, 609). The parent's duty in this regard transcended the mundane requirements of control over labor. Child raising had direct implica-

---

3. For general summaries of Puritan child regulation laws, see Haskins (1960, 81) and Powers (1966, 442–446).

tions for the collective mission of the commonwealth. Accordingly, the law did not simply enforce obedience; it specified and regulated mutual responsibility.

It is relevant in this regard to address Sidman's contention that children, because they are so often mentioned in New England law in conjunction with servants, were regarded primarily as such. The correct interpretation is just the reverse: neither offspring nor servants were viewed in the law as simple objects of adult will. Servants and apprentices were often the children of neighbors; both children and servants were members of the family unit, and masters and parents alike were required to see to the moral and educational upbringing of their wards (Haskins 1960, 81). "Puritanism held that the family was not merely a handy social organization to provide for material considerations but primarily a spiritual center, and the layman was frequently admonished for being 'very careful for the shine, and take[ing] no care for the foot' " (Ver Steeg 1964, 59–60). Thus it appears that, in the eyes of the law, servants were raised to the level of children rather than children lowered to the level of servants.[4]

I have dwelt at some length on the issue of whether child control can be reduced to labor control because it is characteristic of the problems that beset scholarly inquiries into Puritan life. Earlier generations of scholars created a stereotype of the Puritans as dour fanatics bent on establishing a theocratic paradise on a rocky and altogether inhospitable shore. Based on this stereotype, "it was possible for writers to say that the seventeenth century was 'a period of rude, untechnical popular law' and that 'the Scriptures were an infallible guide for both judge and legislator' " (Haskins 1965, 18; quoting Reinsch 1907, 367, and Hilkey 1910, 68). Recent revisionist historians have suggested a review of this stereotype, and, in the area of law, a much more complex view of New England institutions has emerged than was previously available.

4. Puritan law explicitly provided for means of redress to servants and children when masters and parents failed in their obligations. See the *Laws and Liberties*, chapters entitled "Children," "Masters, Servants, and Laborers," and "Schools" (Farrand 1929, 11–12, 38–39, 47).

Colonial law must be seen not as a set of crude means to short-run ends, but as a distinct legal culture, deliberately and rationally drawn from a variety of sources and designed for long service in a biblical commonwealth. It is certainly true that the Puritans placed a high value on labor and on the family, and it may be true that a latent function of their child control laws was to assure a minimum labor supply. But this tells us little about what the law meant or was intended to achieve. To reduce the colonial preoccupation with duty, work, and established authority relationships—all deeply rooted Calvinist ideals—to the level of economic instrumentality is to impoverish our understanding of the Puritan mind and set an artificial barrier between the Puritans and ourselves.

Any direct explanation of the adoption of the stubborn child law in 1646 is probably impossible, given the lack of detailed records—such as printed reports of hearings and debates[5]—that could be used to illuminate the passage of a law in more recent times. We can, however, set the law in the context of broader legal developments that were taking place around the time of its adoption. In the next two sections I discuss the process of legal codification in Massachusetts Bay and compare developments there with contemporaneous events in other colonies. The point is to show that a great deal of statutory innovation in the colony, including the stubborn child law, arose not from a dogmatic blueprint for a Puritan utopia, but from a process of political conflict and pragmatic compromise.

The Legal Transformation of Massachusetts Bay

The chronology of legislative events in the years immediately before and after the passage of the stubborn child law in 1646 is now fairly well established. The law itself was passed in the midst of a general movement to codify the laws of the Massachusetts Bay Colony. Agitation for a comprehensive written code began in the General Court

---

5. For example, the Commonwealth's legislative *Records* (Shurtleff 1854) contains only finished legislation. It is, in effect, a collection of session laws.

(colonial legislature) in 1634. The next year a codification committee was appointed and dissolved without agreeing on a draft. In 1636, a second committee was appointed. John Cotton, a clergyman and member of the committee, submitted a working draft of a code—called by Governor Winthrop in his *Journal* "Moses his judicialls"—that drew heavily from scriptural sources. It was here that the stubborn child law first appeared (Haskins 1960, 123–125).

Cotton's draft never became law (Haskins 1960, 25; Morison 1930, 228). A succession of committees was appointed, and in 1641, the General Court adopted and published the *Body of Liberties*, which was "less a code of existing laws than it was a compilation of constitutional provisions" (Haskins 1960, 129). Several criminal and civil liberties provisions of Cotton's draft were enacted as part of the *Body of Liberties*, but the stubborn child law was not among them (Haskins 1960, 125 and n. 67).

The law was enacted in 1646, subsequent to a General Court resolution calling for a more comprehensive code, and in the midst of a flurry of committee activity and a general examination and revision of existing laws in preparation for the new code (Haskins 1960, 36; Farrand 1929, vii; Shurtleff 1854, 90–101). Based on evidence from General Court records, Haskins (1960, 135) suggests that the laws passed in the period 1646–1647 were based on recommendations made by codification committees and that "the [General] Court then enacted all or part of them with the understanding that they would form part of the proposed Code." The code, entitled *The Book of the General Laws and Liberties Concerning the Inhabitants of Massachusetts*, was passed in 1647 and published the following year. The law requiring death for the "stubborn or rebellious son" appears therein as capital law number fourteen (Farrand 1929, vii, 36).

Thus the stubborn child law was not enacted in a vacuum. It was adopted as part of a larger project of legal codification that forced authorities for the first time to be explicit about the structure of rights and responsibilities in the commonwealth. The code was, in turn, the product of a broader political ferment that came to a head in the 1640s. In that decade, leaders reassessed their goals and normative strategies, creatively blended their past experiences with new conditions, and spawned institutions that persist as irreducible elements of the American experience of government. The new code was, in part, an aggressive statement of a utopian agenda, but it was also in part a defensive response to potentially destructive conflict. Thus in order to understand the meaning of the stubborn child law, we must first explore the kinds of strains to which Massachusetts Bay authorities addressed themselves.

These conflicts had both internal and external sources. First, colonial leaders sought to maintain internal control against the demands of increasing numbers of nonelect residents—those who were not members of the dominant Congregationalist church—for a right to participate in colonial government. At the same time, the colony's very survival depended on a stable relationship with the Crown. Membership in the British empire brought with it a legal charter, military protection, and an economically vital trade relationship, but also a potentially undesirable degree of interference in colonial affairs (Wertenbaker 1947, 293). Internal and external strains exacerbated each other: if leaders could not stifle internal dissent, they risked greater scrutiny from England.

Internal dissension appeared in both religious and political forms. Religious dissent was rooted in Puritan theological controversies over the autonomy of the local church congregation, relations with the Anglican church, and the degree of religious toleration that would be entertained within the colony. The Congregationalist wing, which was dominant, favored internal reform of the Church of England and opposed both an ecclesiastical administrative hierarchy and political participation by the nonelect (Ver Steeg 1964, 76–77). The colony included significant minorities of Presbyterians, who favored a centralized church structure, and Anglicans, who resented exclusion from the political affairs of the colony. Their protests were to have political implications both for relations with England and for the degree to which power could be centralized within Massachusetts Bay itself.

The overtly political cleavage within the colony emerged gradually from the process of transition from a formally chartered trading company to a commonwealth. The original charter of the Massachusetts Bay Company vested judicial as well as legislative authority in officers of the Bay Company (the Assistants), who were designated colonial magistrates. They quickly established an extensive system of courts for resolving disputes between individuals and hearing criminal cases. The Assistants initially controlled the General Court as well, but in 1634, the colony's freemen were given the right to elect their own representatives, or Deputies.[6] As the Deputies gradually evolved into a lawmaking body coequal with the Assistants, and as they began to question the Assistants' discretionary power, the stage was set for overt conflict—between oligarchic Assistants and more popularly elected Deputies, between judge-made law and positive law, and between arbitrariness and the rule of law—that was to eventuate in the 1648 code (Haskins 1960, 36–37; Morison 1930, 88–94; Labaree 1979, 42).

Just as the Puritans were divided over the structure of authority within the colony, they were ambivalent about the nature of their relationship with the Crown. Unlike Plymouth, the Bay Colony was established by royal charter, and the autonomy the colonists sought for their holy commonwealth required that they stay on good terms with the Stuart monarchy. The English Puritans were neither schismatics nor revolutionaries; they sought to adopt certain separatist practices and institutions while still claiming political loyalty to England. Colonization appeared to offer the best opportunity for both legitimacy and autonomy from direct political control (Haskins 1960, 14–16).

6. Church membership was a prerequisite for status as a freeman, hence for voting in colonywide elections. Because the franchise was limited in this way, it may appear that the creation of the House of Deputies did not broaden the foundation of citizenship, but merely shifted its focus from company to theocracy. At this early stage at least, however, voting was probably no more restricted and authority was no more oligarchical than in the average English borough at the time (Haskins 1960, 29; Davis 1970, 4). Ver Steeg (1964, 41) has suggested that "most if not all" of the nonservant adult males were freemen.

The colony's formal autonomy was increased by the fact that the charter of the Massachusetts Bay Company did not contain the requirement, customary to the charters of other joint-stock companies, that the charter itself and thus the meeting place of company stockholders remain in England. Whatever the reason for the omission, its significance was not lost on the settlers. The charter was transported to Massachusetts, and with it the locus of control over the company, and hence the colony (Adams 1887, 192; Morison 1930, 65–79; Haskins 1960, 11; Ver Steeg 1964, 36).

Thus the Massachusetts colonists possessed unusual latitude in constructing their own political institutions. Possession of the charter in the New World effectively prevented merchants unsympathetic to the Puritan cause from gaining control over the colony. The only formal limitation on the colonists' lawmaking authority was the ambiguous charter provision that "No laws shall be made contrary to this our realm of England" (Morison 1930, 88). This clause was not taken as a requirement, but as a caution. Its effect "was less to deter the colonists from establishing laws contrary to those in England than to serve as a warning that they be circumspect about the methods they employed in so doing" (Haskins 1960, 190). Had the colony developed as the members of the founding oligarchy intended, it might have maintained its low profile on the Stuart horizon, and the unprecedented legal and political developments of the late 1640s might not have occurred. Instead, a revolt by a minority of colonists resulted in the formalization and rationalization of authority in the colony, and indirectly in the passage of the stubborn child law.

The rebellion came in the form of the Remonstrance of 1646, a petition presented to the General Court by a group of notables who were dissatisfied with the oligarchic structure of the colony's politics. In their petition the Remonstrants asked for civil liberties to be granted to all Englishmen in the colony and for political participation to be granted to Anglicans and Presbyterians. They further asked to be released from all taxes if all these conditions were not met and threatened to appeal to Parliament if redress was not forthcoming. To give teeth to their threat, the Remonstrants cited the lack of a body of laws in the colony as evidence that their traditional rights had been denied. The immediate response of the General Court was straightforward: members charged the Remonstrants with sedition, and, to rebut the charge that the colony had no legal structure, they drew up a clumsy document that claimed to show parallels between the laws of England and Massachusetts Bay (Adams 1887, 258–268; Morison 1930, ch. 8; Hutchinson 1936, 124–127; Wall 1972, 166).

The Remonstrance is less significant for its immediate outcomes than for its long-range implications as a political strategy. The petitioners sought to catch the Puritan oligarchy—the governor and the Assistants—in a pincers movement by seeking support from groups both inside and outside the colony that challenged their authority. On the one hand, they appealed to three overlapping groups within the colony: Presbyterians, who longed for a unified church hierarchy; the unenfranchised of every persuasion; and the Deputies of the General Court, who were struggling for equality with the Assistants. On the other hand, the Remonstrants invited parliamentary intervention by invoking the traditional standards of English common law as an antidote to arbitrary government (Wall 1972, 166). By demanding the realignment of the colonial polity with the traditional authority of English law, they implicitly attacked the founding premises and ideology of the Puritan movement in the New World and questioned the legitimacy of the colony's leaders as interpreters of the divine plan for the commonwealth (Ziff 1973, 98).

The Remonstrance was a failure in the short run, but the issues it raised demanded a long-term response by colonial authorities. The policy of ad hoc decision making by a small oligarchy could not continue indefinitely. Such a system would eventuate only in a full-blown theocracy that would incite further internal dissent and scrutiny from England. Nor could the colonists succumb to English law: to replace rationally interpreted scripture as the wellspring of legitimate authority would have destroyed the very purpose of the colony.

Puritan authorities instead took a third path that was both pragmatic and original. They issued two documents—the Cambridge Platform and the 1648 *Laws and Liberties*—that declared in nuclear form the principles of church-state separation and established constitutionalism as the basis of political authority.

Although it was not adopted by the General Court until 1651, the Cambridge Platform was directly precipitated by the Remonstrance. The Platform declared an uncompromisingly Congregationalist position on church government by rejecting the ideas of administrative hierarchy and toleration of the nonelect as church members. On the face of it, this appears to have been an audaciously conservative step to take: rejection of non-Congregationalists from church membership was a flat denial of the right of political participation to a significant minority of colonists, an act that seemed to invite English intervention. In fact the English government never intervened because in the interval between the Remonstrance and the adoption of the Cambridge Platform, the majority in Parliament had shifted from the Presbyterians to the Congregationalists (Adams 1887, 267; Wertenbaker 1947, 299–302; Bremer 1976, 119–121).

Yet the Platform did not aim at theocracy. Rather, it prohibited it by placing responsibility for enforcement of church discipline in the hands of civil authorities and by limiting the power of individual clergy within the local congregations (Ver Steeg 1964, 84; Labaree 1979, 70). By separating the spheres of civil and ecclesiastical authority in this way, the Puritans were both reacting against the conditions under which they had suffered in England—where, they felt, there had been altogether too little distinction between church and state—and elaborating a new ideological standard for the development of indigenous institutions based on the Calvinist idea of the calling. The secular government was authorized to punish heresy along with other crimes because, in the context of the commonwealth, heresy implied sedition; the church, by contrast, was limited in sanctioning power to persuasion, warning, and ultimately excommunication (Bremer 1976,

93–94). Individual conduct was the business of the collectivity as a whole because individual weakness was conceived as a threat to the whole society. Nonetheless, church, state, and family were separate institutions of social control, and individuals were expected to enact roles appropriate to their institutional calling. The Cambridge Platform declared formally that the clergy was not to act as a theocracy; in practice, "civil authorities . . . exercised far greater influence in religious affairs than did religious leaders in matters of state" (Labaree 1979, 73).[7]

Like the Cambridge Platform, the codification of colonial statutes in the *Laws and Liberties* was a creative political compromise. The original ruling oligarchy of Massachusetts Bay, as represented by the Assistants, resisted codification both because it would impinge upon their power of particularistic, discretionary decision making and because it would provide concrete evidence of their disregard for English laws.[8] Conversely, the Deputies supported codification as a weapon in their struggle with the Assistants. But ultimately, a code of some sort was required to meet the Remonstrants' charge that no body of laws existed in Massachusetts Bay (Adams 1887, 194, 198; Morison 1930, 225–227; Wall 1972, 231–232).

Although the *Laws and Liberties* claimed to represent English law, it was a decisive departure for two reasons. First, in an attempt to heal the breach between Deputies and Assistants and between free-

7. See also Davis (1970, 39) and Haskins (1960, 62–63). An interesting analysis of litigation in colonial Essex County supports this point. Konig (1979, 90–107) found that, in the second half of the seventeenth century, the courts were used not only to support the authority of the local church, but increasingly to protect personal liberties from the power of town meetings and congregations.

8. The colony's leaders were deeply suspicious of all types of legal formalism. This was not a unique attitude—many of the reforms they put into practice, such as a unified court system, had been called for by contemporary English reformers. But these antiformalistic tendencies were given added impetus by the substantive goal of commonwealth. Attorneys were not welcome in Massachusetts Bay, for example; initially, they were allowed to plead other men's cases only if they charged no fee. See Howe (1965, 4–5), Haskins (1960, 192), and Powers (1966, 528). On the conflict between substantive goals and legal formalism, see Weber (1978, 809–815).

men and the oligarchy, the code invoked the notion of the "covenant" as the source of political authority. Thus in place of the simple justification of divine right that had been abused by the Stuarts, the Puritans implicitly rehabilitated the long-standing English notion of the rule of law. Beyond this, however, they replaced the traditional authority of kings as the ultimate referent of law with an ideal of rational constitutionalism that arose directly from the concept of the calling: Puritan rulers ruled not by virtue of their person, but through their *position* as divinely appointed interpreters of biblical law (Haskins 1960, 56).

Second, in its attention to individual behavior—as expressed, for example, in the stubborn child law—the code sought to breathe life into the concept of the covenant. By exhorting moral concern for private behavior and by establishing a universalistic system based on public law for the enforcement of the morality of the commonwealth, the Puritans politicized private life, especially that within the purview of the family. As it was realized in the form of a legal order, then, the covenant became a true contract, divine in significance, which bound leaders and followers, officials and citizens, parents and children into an interlocking system of mutual obligation.

In summary, the compromises involved in the Cambridge Platform and the codification of Massachusetts law had two immediate goals: first, to maintain internal solidarity and, second, to deflect potential criticism from England. In defining various public and private rights and responsibilities, these documents are not simply indicators of issues salient to Puritan theology, but of issues that were salient because they arose from political crisis:

> Although these documents . . . have frequently been considered the high-water mark of the civil-ecclesiastical tie in Massachusetts, it is more valid to suggest that both documents should be interpreted as signs of weakness, that the civil-ecclesiastical relationship had, by this date, become seriously endangered. Conformity could no longer be assumed. (Ver Steeg 1964, 84–85; see also Rutman 1965)

In their response to dissent, the Puritan leaders did not overwhelm their opposition but rather coopted it. The formal separation of civil and ecclesiastical authority and the establishment of a comprehensive system of laws constrained dissenters to operate within the system; at the same time, "the triumphant culture was not to continue to grow without weaving into its fabric threads from the concepts of its opposers" (Ziff 1973, 99). The ultimate basis of political authority was publicly declared divine and placed beyond criticism, but its secular means of administration was from then on to be legitimately at issue.

The enactment of the stubborn child law cannot be understood apart from this process of conflict and pragmatic political compromise. We cannot connect it directly with any immediate precipitating incident, as we can, for example, Puritan legislation on rape.[9] But it is clearly of a piece with other contemporary legal developments. The family, along with the church and the state, was one of three institutional orders that the Puritans saw as fundamental to the exercise of authority within the colony. The stubborn child law was one of a variety of laws by which the mutual responsibilities of family life were prescribed. The Puritans sought to use law as an unequivocal statement of community norms intended to buttress authority where they considered it most vulnerable. To this end the doctrine of the covenant provided a useful bridge between public and private spheres of conduct: by enlisting parents as agents of the commonwealth, it allowed particularistic norms like the stubborn child law to be declared from the universalistic platform of public law.

The intimate connection between the adoption of the stubborn child law and the sequence of contemporary events in the life of the colony indicates that the law was not dictated either by the material

9. The General Court increased the severity of punishment for various kinds of rape, authorizing either mandatory or discretionary death penalties, when it was discovered that a prominent colonist's daughter had had sexual relations with her father's servants repeatedly between the ages of seven and nine (Haskins 1960, 150).

condition of the colony or by dogmatic application of biblical precepts to the regulation of conduct. Rather, it was part of a strategy for containing political conflict that was consistent with deliberate efforts to advance the goals of the commonwealth.[10] Insofar as the law was the product of a political process that identified noncriminal misconduct by children as a weak thread in the fabric of authority and thus as a target for civil intervention, it may have much more in common with current attitudes toward juvenile deviance than has otherwise been suspected. I return to this issue in the last section of this chapter. But to substantiate the argument that the stubborn child law was part of a general solution to a uniquely Puritan dilemma, some comparison is required to establish key differences between Massachusetts Bay and the other colonies in that regard.

Legal Development Outside New England

Virginia Law

The most fruitful approach to this problem is to compare Massachusetts with Virginia because the legal development of the other colonies was generally peripheral to one or another of these centers. These two cases may be discussed briefly in terms of the role of religion and the role of law in the formation of their respective social institutions.

Virginia settlers shared no reformist zeal and did not seek to establish a biblical commonwealth; yet in their consistency of outlook they brought with them the seeds of a common culture. As Boorstin (1958, 56) has put it, "If other colonies sought escape from

---

10. It is interesting to note in this regard that, according to the colony's legislative *Records*, the stubborn child law was passed the same day as capital laws against blasphemy, smiting parents, and denying scripture, along with lesser laws against pow-wowing Indians, heresy, missing church, swearing, and being a "wanton gospeller" (i.e., showing contempt in church), a series of economic provisions, and sedition charges against the Remonstrants (Shurtleff 1854, 90–101).

English vices, Virginians wished to fulfill English virtues. . . . If Virginia was to be in any way better than England, it was not because Virginians pursued ideals which Englishmen did not have; rather that here were novel opportunities to realize the English ideals." The ideals that the Virginians sought to fulfill were those of the English country gentleman, a cultural model that in the course of the seventeenth century came to include an amateur interest in and patronage of the arts and sciences, participation in the Anglican church, cultivation of leisure, and generous displays of hospitality. Immigrants to Virginia were not originally gentry, but migration opened a route to gentry status, an aspiration they shared with much of the English merchant class (Ver Steeg 1964, 68; Boorstin 1958, 99).

Religious life in Virginia was neither as vital nor as much a part of civil life as it was in New England. This is partly because Anglicanism was a taken-for-granted component of gentry culture, but also because of conditions inherent in the New World experience. In Virginia the church was disengaged from public life, and theological discourse remained static, even compared to that in England. One reason was that scattered landholdings in the Chesapeake region made the maintenance of a regularly attended parish church more difficult than in New England. This relative dispersion was not due to large landholdings, but to tobacco culture's voracity for new land and to the availability of waterways that made settlement of the interior more feasible than in New England. Furthermore, the distance from England and the English church prevented active supervision of the colonial church (no Anglican bishop was ever appointed for the colonies) or even recruitment of skilled clergy. The Virginia church, which began merely as a necessary ornament to a cultured way of life, entered a self-perpetuating decline into provincialism (Ver Steeg 1964, 88–89; see also Washburn 1965, 125–126).

In New England, by contrast, religion was the organizing principle of social life. The Puritans brought their church with them; they looked to the Bible, to its learned clerical interpreters, and to their own reason conjunctively for solutions to problems of living.[11] Religious inspiration did not consist, however, merely of prohibitions and rigid blueprints; it also encouraged idealism and creative problem solving. Haskins (1960, 17) observes that

> although the Bible . . . was believed to provide a complete and unamendable constitution, God's word as therein contained did not inhibit, but rather gave impetus to, progress and reform. The Puritan conception of the Kingdom of God was not a static one, confined by the injunctions of the Decalogue and the lapidary counsels of the prophets; it was equally inspired by the life of Christ and the spirit of the Sermon on the Mount. Thus, a zeal to reform both the individual and society is one of the very notable features of Puritanism, which was active rather than contemplative.

The implications of this distinction for the development of legal cultures in Massachusetts and Virginia are profound. The two colonies looked to different sources of legal authority: "In the case of Massachusetts, it was God. In the case of Virginia, the King" (Washburn 1965, 125). Administrative practices followed upon these basic assumptions: where the Puritans felt impelled to institute reforms, the Virginians were comfortable imitating traditional legal customs (Washburn 1965, 117). In New England the law was seen as an affirmative instrument of social policy—to cite a relevant example, in 1647, Massachusetts enacted a public school law that declared it a public responsibility that education be available free to all who were fitted (Haskins 1960, 110). In the Chesapeake region, education was a local affair, facilities were unevenly distributed, and often they were entirely informal (Ver Steeg 1964, 102).

In Virginia, as in Massachusetts, colonial maturation brought change, change brought conflict, and each colony's response to conflict was consistent with its founding purpose and social organiza-

11. Despite the emotional intensity of Puritanism, "the emphasis of the Puritan mind in New England was on reason" (Ver Steeg 1964, 79–80). Reason applied to biblical scholarship and disquisition was seen as a path to God. The alternative was the emotional heresy of, for example, Quakerism, which led to individualism and the potential ruin of the divine plan of the commonwealth.

tion. Virginia's relationship with the Crown began to sour by the end of the seventeenth century, and by this time the foundation of the plantation economy had been laid. To the Puritans the capitalistic organization of the colonial venture was a means to an end, but in Virginia it was an end in itself. Thus, as links with England began to weaken, Virginia government became less concerned with maintaining English ways than with sponsoring indigenous, individualistic agrarian capitalism. As localistic and patriarchal "government by gentry" developed, it became still less likely that law would be used as the tool of a centralized authority to orchestrate private conduct (Washburn 1965, 128–129; Boorstin 1958, 110–127).

Law in the Peripheral Colonies

In the late seventeenth and eighteenth centuries, the regional prototypes just discussed spread and deepened as new colonies were founded. Puritan child regulation laws rode on the back of Puritan culture throughout New England. In one way or another Massachusetts was responsible for the founding of the other New England colonies (Ver Steeg 1964, 42). Despite the fact that, for example, Rhode Island and Connecticut were founded by congeries of dissenters from the Massachusetts Bay regime, it is no mystery that they adopted the Puritans' more rigorous prohibitions on personal conduct. Dissenters such as Roger Williams were not primarily champions of religious freedom, but rather zealous separatists who felt that the Bay colonists had not gone far enough down the road toward reformation and purification (Ver Steeg 1964, 45–51).[12]

After 1660, a fundamental change occurred in the organization of colonial ventures that limited opportunities for deliberate legal innovation. Colonies established after that time were no longer seen by

12. Rhode Island was chartered in 1644 and Connecticut in 1662. In 1647, Rhode Island issued a preliminary legal code that was almost entirely adapted from Dalton's *Country Justice,* an English handbook for justices of the peace that was well known in the colonies (Howe 1965, 14).

the Crown as instruments for the export of mercantile capitalism, as Massachusetts and Virginia had been, but rather as "outposts of empire" established under proprietary grants to associates of the Crown (Ver Steeg 1964, 14, 44). The development of law in these colonies depended, initially at least, on the predispositions of the proprietors.

New York, New Jersey, and Pennsylvania were formed from a grant made to the Duke of York, who laid down their laws as well. New York's law was a combination of the Roman-Dutch law long used by the Dutch settlers in New Netherland, provisions from the "Bible codes" brought by migrating Puritans, and English common law (Johnson 1965, 74–76). The light political touch required for the coexistence of New York's heterogeneous population was hardly conducive to intense civil scrutiny of individual morals; at any rate this combination was discarded when New York adopted the common law exclusively in 1691.

The Duke of York's law for Pennsylvania, issued in 1676, contained one interesting provision regarding children. Chapter 19, entitled "Children and Servants," required parents to educate their children and prescribed that stubborn and unruly children might be whipped by a constable (George et al. 1879). This law was not a version of the stubborn child law that has been under discussion here, but of another Massachusetts law that provided that children and servants whose parents or masters were not fulfilling their obligation—thereby permitting them to become stubborn or unruly—might be taken from the home and apprenticed by selectmen. This law is a provocative example of a diffusion effect, but it is not characteristic of the Pennsylvania code and does not reveal any deeper trend toward a New England–style legal culture. The duke engaged in cafeteria-style lawmaking in Pennsylvania as he had in New York—the title page of the code contains the note, "Collected out of the several laws now in force in His Majesty's American colonies and plantations." In any event, the law was not of long duration because the code was in use only until 1682 (George et al. 1879, 3).

When Pennsylvania subsequently became a Quaker domain, it was administered so that Quakers maintained political and economic power. There was no attempt to attract or co-opt Puritan minorities by writing them into the legal system. Nothing in the spiritually individualistic Quaker doctrine—abhorred by Puritans and Anglicans alike—would have suggested the public regulation of private morality. Even if it had, the Quakers would not have written such a regulation into formal law because they rejected supra-individual authority whether in the form of religious hierarchies or political establishments.

Finally, New Jersey went through several changes of ownership, for a while owned in part by Quakers, and at one time having as many as twenty-four proprietors. This lack of stability led to political and economic chaos, from which New Jersey was rescued only when it became a direct royal colony in 1702 (Ver Steeg 1964, 116–118). Thus New Jersey, like Pennsylvania, showed none of the conditions one would expect to precipitate legal innovation.

Government and law continued along familiar paths in the southern proprietaries as well. In Maryland both the economy and the structure of proprietary power laid the foundation for an indigenous aristocracy resembling Virginia's. Power at first rested entirely in the proprietor, Lord Baltimore. The House of Burgesses eventually gained some of that power but kept it narrowly based by limiting franchise to landholders (Ver Steeg 1964, 42).

Carolina was established as a proprietary colony in 1663. Its articles of government were drawn up by one of the proprietors with John Locke's collaboration. This fundamental constitution probably would have been inappropriate to New World conditions even if it had been applied rigorously, but the colony's proprietors tended to disregard it and change it arbitrarily to gain advantage over the colonists. In any event, the combination of absentee legal authority and an early plantation system (Ver Steeg 1964, 121) obviously precluded the development of a system of social control based on a New England–style polity or legal culture.

Last and probably least interesting for our purposes, Georgia was established as a proprietary colony in 1733 and organized as a philanthropic enterprise intended both to rid England of its idle hands and to score an economic coup for English mercantilism by means of a harebrained scheme to corner the silkworm trade (Ver Steeg 1964, 161). Following a familiar pattern, the trustees attempted to administer the colony entirely from London; they set unrealistic goals and rules from which there was no appeal. Because there were no taxes, there was no representative assembly. The settlers were functionaries of a corporation, not members of a community (Boorstin 1958, 84–88).

In summary, the colonies established after 1660 fell into patterns of development that had been established earlier in Massachusetts and Virginia. These patterns were not dictated by either the geographic or economic conditions under which the early colonies were founded, but rather were suggested by the organization of political authority in the colonies and the colonists' goals. This is not to suggest that economics played no role in colonial development, only that it does not explain the apparent variation in legal development. Massachusetts and Virginia, as capitalist joint stock companies, and prosperous ones at that, had more in common in terms of economic organization than either had with the proprietary colonies. What differed in these two enterprises was the collective purposes that lay beneath their formal structure. In Massachusetts Bay the joint stock arrangement was a vehicle for the commonwealth ideal and the nucleus for an indigenous form of political authority. In Virginia the agenda was individual economic mobility. In each setting, patterns of institution building followed from these founding principles. Once decisive choices were made, economics confirmed them and encouraged their adoption elsewhere.

This is not a deterministic argument. I do not claim that the stubborn child law was a necessary outgrowth of the Puritan plan for the commonwealth, only that it was consistent with other features of their strategy for maintaining the moral integrity and solidarity of the community. The commonwealth was never fully realized, in part because of the very capacity for rational adaptation that gave it its distinctive character in the first place: as strict Congregationalism mellowed and gave way to Unitarian intellectualism, the reformist edge of the faith was blunted. During the eighteenth century and into the nineteenth, there was a corresponding change in expectations placed on children and in prescribed techniques of nurturance. As Chapter 2 describes, the old Calvinist orthodoxy was challenged in turn by Lockeian and Romantic theories, and new syntheses were achieved in both theological and secular arenas.

Of what significance, then, is an old law calling for the death penalty for disobedient children? Is it merely the fossilized spoor of an extinct system of law? If one speaks only of the letter of the law, and particularly its penalty, it probably is, and probably was when the Puritans enacted it. If one speaks instead of its spirit—how it was used and what it implies about deviance, law, childhood, and social control—it is not.

Conclusion

Erikson (1966, 198) suggests that the singular contribution of Puritanism to modern views of deviance is the conviction that, despite the rhetoric of environmentalism and rehabilitation that has dominated since the eighteenth century, deviance is a symptom of a characterological defect innate to the individual. For the Puritans that defect was damnation; in later visions it became hereditary inferiority or cultural debilitation. I suggest that the Puritans made a second equally important and complementary contribution, more subtle than branding and isolating the conspicuous deviant. This was their relentless vigilance, their "attempt to universalize . . . tension and repression" that followed on their realization that evil was ubiquitous (Walzer 1967, 44).

The Puritans' response to the ubiquity of evil was a practical adjustment of both the letter and the practice of the law to cope with everyday as well as egregious cases of deviant behavior. Even in the laws they drew from scripture, they seldom authorized penalties as harsh as those mentioned in the Bible (Haskins 1960, 151). In the law permitting the death penalty for the child who smites his parents, which immediately precedes the one in the *Laws and Liberties* for stubborn and rebellious sons, the penalty is expressly mitigated in cases where the parents are neglectful. In the administration of laws, a spectrum of penalties—from a mere remonstrance, to a referral for ministerial counseling, to wearing a visible symbol of guilt, on up to the more severe and stigmatizing stocks, brandings, and mutilations—was available. The severity of punishment was contingent on the offender's degree of repentance:

> Implicit in the battery of punitive devices . . . is an attitude of hopefulness for the wayward which, despite the endless sermonizing on the depravity of man, was among the most vital forces in Puritanism. If the Puritan magistrate abhorred the criminal act, he respected the offender to whom, no less than to himself, God's promise of grace was freely proffered, and whose soul, however disordered in its faculties, could not be regarded as hopelessly lost. (Haskins 1960, 210)

There are two reasons why the Puritans had to blur the fine edge between sin and virtue. The first was simple and humane—for example, what parent could nurture a child as Puritan society required and yet view that child as damned?[13] The other reason is political and ideological: how could Puritan authorities consistently require the application of their techniques of child training and also insist on the reality of the child's depravity and the inscrutability of grace? Maintenance of the commonwealth required one, while theology dictated the other.

Although the great minds of Massachusetts Bay generally avoided the implications of this contradiction as it applied to children, they faced it assertively in the Antinomian controversy of the 1630s. The

---

13. The full historical implications of the contradiction between parental love and belief in infant depravity are drawn by Slater (1977, ch. 1). I return to this issue in Chapter 2.

substantive issues at stake in this event were not clear even to the participants, but they are, as Erikson suggests, clearly political. The Antinomian crisis itself was a sign of the institutionalization of political authority in the colony. The position declared by the principal defendant, Anne Hutchinson, was strictly correct in terms of Puritan theology. She held that grace was a matter of divine contract and that the contract was met by the individual with an inner conviction of salvation. Moreover she made known her doubts about whether several noted Puritan leaders were in fact in a state of grace. The political threat in this accusation is obvious, but colonial leaders could not suppress these seditious accusations without altering the theological assumptions upon which they were based. Using the concept of commonwealth as their Archimedean lever, they insisted on their responsibility to assure the alignment of private consciences. "Thus the idea of the new theology was that an individual's relationship to God needed to be screened by some intermediate level of authority—a congregation, a government, an administration" (Erikson 1966, 73).

Walzer (1967) has written that the Puritan mind was conceived in anxiety and sustained by discipline. Anxiety in a period of rapid social change is not an unusual phenomenon, but the Puritan response was unique: they institutionalized anxiety and discipline as the guiding principles of collective authority. "Congregational discipline" was neither a retreat to Whig nostalgia nor an embrace of secular authority: "Their discipline would have established dramatically new forms of association" (Walzer 1967, 57). Walzer writes here about sixteenth-century English Puritanism; by the seventeenth century, that new form of association—one that was both voluntary and formal—had arisen in New England. The siege mentality implicit in Puritanism became in the New World an explicit and vital means of political mobilization.

Secular law in Massachusetts Bay played a crucial role in that transformation. According to Hutchinson (1936, 369–370), the perceived need for order within the colony, the absence of traditional hierarchical distinctions among men, and the rejection of ecclesiastical courts necessitated the codification of many offenses into formal, secular law that were not found in common law at that time. This development would not have occurred without the political and geographic characteristics that were unique to the Bay colony: while the ascendant Puritans in England were becoming more tolerant because of their minority status, the isolation of Massachusetts and the ideology of the commonwealth permitted the sect ideal to be transformed into a comprehensive, militant social ethic. Only in Massachusetts, then, did the "calling" become thoroughly socialized and supported by secular authority through law (Ziff 1973, 79–80).[14] The Puritan community was organized into a system of mutual surveillance and discipline on the presumed basis of shared values, and thus the most pressing political issues could be reduced to problems of management: "The father was continually active, warily watching his children; the elders of the congregation were ever alert and vigilant, seeking out the devious paths of sin; so also the godly magistrate" (Walzer 1967, 62). Thus individual salvation panic was raised to an organizing principle of collective life.

Erikson makes a persuasive claim that the Puritans were the first to regard deviant behavior as a sign of some innate flaw of the person. The point made here is somewhat the reverse: the Puritans were the first to universalize deviance on a programmatic basis. To them, grace was scarce and mysterious, temptation was constant, and sin was original; thus they were prepared to see misbehavior everywhere. They tried to control it systematically, as with the stubborn

14. According to Calvinist orthodoxy, the individual's calling was a sanctified vocation that was pursued in the secular world: the Christian was to be an *active* citizen. The church as the embodiment of the holy commonwealth served as the source of ethical authority in an essentially sinful society. This more assertive, yet tolerant, posture distinguishes English Puritanism from the generally more ascetic forms of continental Calvinism and Lutheranism (Troeltsch 1960, 598–602). The crucial point here is that, in the New World, toleration was no longer required. Secular institutions such as law could be established at the outset as aspects of the commonwealth, and the individual could fulfill a secular calling without ambiguity or compromise.

child law. When they felt that control had failed, they responded
with hysterical abandon, as in the witch trials. The witch trials represented the last gasp of the "old" Puritanism in the sense that political
stability required the routinization and formalization of responses to
ubiquitous evil. It is this combination of formalized law and substantive specificity that leads to the conclusion that Massachusetts Bay
law was a precocious development. Hutchinson notes that, particularly before the adoption of the *Laws and Liberties,* law was administered in the colony on a particularistic basis: civil cases were judged
by the rule of equity "according to the circumstances of the case,"
and criminal penalties were "adapted to the circumstances of a large
family of children and servants" (Hutchinson 1936, 367). This
particularism was not eliminated by the creation of a code of laws.[15]
It continued until the decline of the colony's political fortunes in the
late seventeenth century. The Puritans' socialized jurisprudence was
eclipsed by a more formalistic and less activist view of law, only to
emerge later, transformed, as a new legal doctrine.

Morison attests to the precocity of Massachusetts Bay law by
writing: "The nineteenth century was shocked by so wide a judicial
discretion, and endeavored by statute 'to make the punishment fit the
crime.' Modern social jurisprudence reverts to the puritan practice,
of making the punishment fit the criminal" (Morison 1930, 233).
But as we will see, the Puritan response to deviance, particularly
deviance among children, was never entirely eclipsed, even temporarily. Their influence on the development of juvenile justice in the
United States was direct, in both philosophical and legal terms.

The Puritan legacy as exemplified in the stubborn child law was
not theoretical, but rather technical and administrative. A fully developmental view of deviance and a concomitant theory of rehabilitation were the products of a later age and were in a strict sense

15. Powers (1966, 529–530) notes that magistrates had long fought the idea of
fixed legal penalties. In the *Laws and Liberties,* many penalties were fixed; nonetheless,
magistrates continued in practice to exercise wide discretion in sentencing.

precluded by the doctrines of original sin and predestination. But Massachusetts Bay made two contributions to modern American methods of legal domination that are the collective analogues to Walzer's themes of anxiety and discipline. First, they introduced the notion that morality is rational and calculable, even though, as an accompaniment of grace, it is ultimately inscrutable. Thus they could subdivide the black and white realms of sin and virtue into various shades of gray and suit the punishment not only to the crime but also to the imputed spiritual condition of the criminal. Second, they contributed an ideology and spiritual technology of community responsibility for individual moral conduct. Only in the New World could the formal legal system be used as such a disciplinary apparatus, because it was here that the commonwealth achieved political control over both public and private space, thus permitting the politicization of private as well as public conduct. The Puritan system contains the roots of what Foucault (1977) and Donzelot (1979) have identified as the major tendencies of modern means of controlling deviance. First, deviance is normalized:

> The art of punishing, in the regime of disciplinary power, is aimed neither at expiation, nor even precisely at repression. It brings five quite distinct operations into play: it refers individual actions to a whole that is at once a field of comparison, a space of differentiation and the principle of a rule to be followed. It differentiates individuals from one another, in terms of the following overall rule: that the rule be made to function as a minimum threshold, as an average to be respected or as an optimum towards which one must move. It measures in quantitative terms of value the abilities, the level, the "nature" of individuals. It introduces, through this "value-giving" measure, the constraint of a conformity that must be achieved. Lastly, it traces the limit that will define difference in relation to all other differences, the external frontier of the abnormal. . . . The perpetual penality that traverses all points and supervises every instant in disciplinary institutions compares, differentiates, hierarchizes, homogenizes, excludes. In short, it *normalizes*. (Foucault 1977, 183)

Second, social institutions such as law and the family are conceived as instruments of public policy in the control of normalized deviance—in other words they are socialized:

> From being the plexus of a complex web of relations of dependence and allegiance, the family became the nexus of nerve endings of machinery that was exterior to it. These new mechanisms acted on the family on the basis of a double game that eventually required its juridical conversion. On one hand, they penetrated it directly, turning family members . . . against patriarchal authority, organizing—in the name of hygienic and educative protection of these members—the depletion of parental authority under an economico-moral tutelage. On the other hand, they induced the reorganization of family life, by promoting the new norms as being so many advantages favoring a more complete realization of the family's goal of increased autonomy. (Donzelot 1979, 91)

Despite the crudeness of their formulation, the Puritans had laid the foundations of such a technology, most conspicuously as it applied to children. The goal of legal intervention was not simple repression, but the internalization of repression, to "transform repression into self-control" (Walzer 1967, 40). They "normalized" deviance by seeing its potential everywhere. By imputing the individual's state of grace—both a transcendent criterion and a stamp of the person's "nature"—from isolated acts of deviance, they began to rationalize the relationship between severity of offense and severity of punishment. Finally, in the ferocity of response of which they were capable when all other means had failed, they drew a line beyond which no rescues would be attempted.

The Massachusetts Bay colonists were only two steps short of having a "regime of disciplinary power" that we would recognize as fully modern. The first is the qualitatively different, more thorough notion of infinite gradations among offenders and offenses grounded in a theory of socialization; the second is a system of institutional control of deviants. The Puritans were held off temporarily from the former notion by their predestinarian theology, which maintained an ultimate ontological distinction between sinners and the saved. It took a century or more for them to overcome this doctrine as much in theory as in practice. Institutions were superfluous in the colonial context because the technology of surveillance in Massachusetts Bay was meant to sustain a therapeutic community, a panoptic society over a hundred years before Bentham invented the modern penitentiary. "Perpetual penality" for the Puritans, as to some degree for all salvation religions, was a quality of earthly life itself.

The Puritans' dream of commonwealth was never realized, and their technology of surveillance was largely dismantled by subsequent events in colonial history. But the stubborn child law itself stayed in force in amended form until 1973, and the Puritan notion of legal child regulation was never entirely extinguished. As I show in the next chapter, Calvinist-inspired reformers in the early nineteenth century resurrected the normalization of deviance and the socialization of law and the family in another context.

2

Moral Institutions

The first publicly funded and legally chartered custodial institutions for juvenile offenders were established in New York, Philadelphia, and Boston in the 1820s. These institutions—the Houses of Refuge in New York (1824) and Philadelphia (1826) and the House of Reformation in Boston (1826)[1]—mark the formal beginning of the modern juvenile justice system in the United States. The founding of the refuges was a historic watershed, not just as a method for controlling juvenile deviance, but also as the exemplar of a general reform impulse that gripped the entire society. In the three most populous cities of the United States, reformers surveyed the impacts of industrialization, immigration, pauperism, and crime,

---

1. These are the years in which the legislation that chartered the refuges was passed. The New York refuge was opened on January 1, 1825, the one in Boston in 1826, and the Philadelphia refuge in 1828 (Hawes 1971, 41, 53; Mennel 1973, 3–4).

seeking a focus for their energies that would not just provide a symptomatic solution to the problems of social disorganization, but would also reach to the very root causes of disorder. The refuges provided just such a focus.

More important, the refuges typified the Jacksonian era trend toward the physical confinement of deviants as a means of imposing moral order on society as a whole. Like many other movements of reform and reaction in that period, the refuges appeared in the cities that most clearly possessed "the necessary conditions of a conscientious middle-class, an adequate supply of funds, and social evils in need of attention" (Heale 1968, 161). The organization of the refuges betrayed a precarious conflict of ideals and objectives that characterized the period. On the one hand, their internal regimes were severe and militaristic. The emphasis on discipline within the institutions betrayed a profound fear of social disorder that was characteristic of postcolonial Calvinism (see Rothman 1971, 216–221). On the other hand, the refuges and the other asylums of the day strove in ideology at least toward a perfect future rather than a nostalgic past. The refuge reformers sought to employ rational methods of rehabilitation, free of prejudice and superstition; by curing delinquency, they hoped to nip future poverty and crime in the bud. Thus the moral order the asylums sought to impose was unmistakably Christian, but of a decidedly secular variety.

As the refuges typified the asylums, so the asylums characterized the conflicts of Jacksonian democracy. The Puritan-Yankee aristocracy had been put on the defensive by religious disestablishment and the decline of the Federalist party. These events, capped by Jackson's accession to the presidency, made it clear that the surviving ideals of the Puritan commonwealth would have to be adjusted to the new climate of liberalism. Thus old interests struggled for new alignments with a mixture of despair and millennial zeal.

The refuges are important not just as examples of the asylum movement, but as exemplars—as laboratories in which the most advanced techniques of penal treatment were first developed and put into practice. They set landmarks as both legal and organizational entities. Three legal innovations are associated with the refuges: first, refuge legislation explicitly recognized a distinction between juvenile and adult offenders. Second, the statutes inaugurated the indeterminate sentence long before adult penal reformers agitated for its use in the late nineteenth century (Hawes 1971, 41). Third and most relevant to this study, refuge legislation broadened the legal liability of children to include not just the lawbreaker, but also incorrigible and neglected children.[2] These powers were seen at the time as distinctive features of the institutions. Refuge chaplain and historian Bradford K. Pierce (1869, 67–68), for example, quotes the fifth annual report of the New York Society for the Reformation of Juvenile Delinquents, founders of the New York refuge:

> The legislature has very much enlarged the objects of our institution and intrusted to its managers powers that have not heretofore been delegated. These are essential to its beneficial action, and mark the great difference between it and other similar institutions that previously existed, however similar they may be in name. If a child be found destitute; or abandoned by its parents, or suffered to lead a vicious or vagrant life; or if convicted of any crime, it may be sent to the House of Refuge. There is in no case any other sentence than that it shall "there be dealt with according to law." That is, it may, if not be released by some legal process, be there detained, if the managers should think it unfit to be sooner discharged, until it arrives at age. Parents or guardians, from the time it is legally sentenced to the Refuge, lose all control of its person. . . . It is these

2. The laws did not at first explicitly extend jurisdiction over noncriminal juveniles. In Massachusetts, Connecticut, and New Hampshire, the colonial "stubborn child" laws discussed in Chapter 1 were carried into the national period. The New York and Pennsylvania statutes initially authorized the confinement only of criminal and vagrant youths; New York added neglected children in 1833 and "disorderly children" in 1865, and Pennsylvania added incorrigibles and neglected children in 1835. In the quantitative analysis presented in Chapter 3, these dates are used to identify the expansion of *formal* jurisdiction over noncriminal children, but it is clear that from the outset refuge legislation increased reformers' control over predelinquents: "The laws . . . provided a legal definition of juvenile delinquency. A juvenile delinquent was a child who broke the law, or who was in danger of breaking the law, and the community hoped to keep him from becoming an adult criminal by providing reformatory treatment in a house of refuge" (Hawes 1971, 57).

important features that mark the difference between our institution and all others that previously existed.

The refuges exemplified their time and set precedents for the future also as experiments in organizational form. They were typical of the asylum movement in that they were founded by voluntary reform associations, and these associations in turn sought public authority and financial support for the institutions. Thus, like other humanitarian reforms, they stood halfway between the private philanthropy of the colonial era and the professionalized penal and social welfare institutions of the late nineteenth century. They were ideologically more advanced than even the penitentiaries of the period in that they espoused a more advanced form of the preventive-rehabilitative treatment philosophy that recognized the social, rather than individual, nature of crime. The social nature of crime suggested a corollary obligation that the refuges gladly shouldered on behalf of society: "to train the neglected child and the unfortunate vagrant or drunkard for a more wholesome life" (McKelvey 1936, 13). Finally, the refuges typified the reforms of the time in the ambivalent way they practiced their treatment philosophy. They showed a "curious mixture of puritanical zeal and progressive education" in their attention to discipline on the one hand and uplifting moral education on the other (Teeters 1960, 166). In this sense the refuges were organizational microcosms of the society, where fear and optimism fought to dominate the public mind.

Despite the refuges' path-breaking role in the development of American juvenile justice, the original institutions were neither long-lived nor often imitated. After New York, Philadelphia, and Boston established refuges, a few more cities set up similar institutions, but the movement as a whole ran out of steam. The ideological enthusiasm that fueled the movement had failed by the late 1840s, in part because more pressing issues were competing for public attention (Pickett 1969, 156). Thus "the period from 1829 to the mid-1840s marked a period in which the Refuge system, at least in the eastern cities, consolidated its early gains and prepared for the day in which the reform school concept would replace it" (Pickett 1969, 163).

But most important, the refuges were superseded because, even in the eyes of some contemporary reformers, they had failed (Rothman 1971, 257–260). In the search for order, they veered too far to the side of egregious discipline and punishment and soon became nothing more than warehouses for troublesome children. Yet even in their failure they succeeded in establishing incarceration as the response of choice to all types of juvenile deviance, long after the goal of "moral education" had ceased to be taken seriously.

Rothman (1971, 262) suggests three factors that precipitated the refuges' declining effectiveness and prestige. First, he suggests that the institutions' basic environmental theory of deviance justified and even provoked harsh, coercive discipline. Second, the inmate population came to consist of youths more experienced in crime, as local officials shunted off their most serious cases and ignored the less serious offenders, who were considered most amenable to refuge discipline. Third, reform enthusiasm and legislative support waned as inmates came to be drawn more and more from the immigrant lower class. This argument, although persuasive as far as it goes, is too simple. It ignores many of the details of the critical first few years of the refuge system and minimizes the significance of those years in establishing a recurrent pattern of reform in juvenile justice.

I address myself to two issues in this chapter. First, how did the refuges acquire their unprecedented power of legal domination over the lives of children? The evidence suggests that many of the institutions' "preventive" powers were not part of the original reform agenda, but rather emerged from the political process of reform. Through that process, representatives of competing groups negotiated an organizational order for the refuges on the basis of their respective ideals and interests. One point on which all could agree was that the refuges should be modeled after the family. In the end the refuges enjoyed all the discretionary authority of the family, with the additional legitimation of formal law.

Second, how and why did the refuges lose their reformative luster and become mere warehouses for deviant children? There is substantial evidence to show that the decline of the refuges was not simply the result of a loss of institutional momentum, as Rothman suggests, but was accelerated by conflict among reform groups within the refuge movement itself. Although there was general agreement that the family would provide the organizational model for the refuges, there was protracted conflict over whose paradigm of family organization and child raising would prevail. The decline of the refuges was not simply the familiar organizational drama of systems requirements prevailing over goal attainment; rather, it implied the emergence of a negotiated model of family discipline that alloyed Calvinist moralism with more liberal notions of nurturance. The result was an institutional package—including an ideology, a treatment mode, and statutory power—that would suggest a pattern for future reforms in the treatment of juvenile offenders and simultaneously become an example of the conditions that subsequent reforms were designed to correct.

I will not recount the history of the refuges in detail but will instead draw on extant histories to construct a comparative framework through which to discuss the process of institutionalization that occurred in the first few years of the New York, Philadelphia, and Boston refuges. As other writers have observed (e.g., Mennel 1973, 11–12; Pickett 1969, 74–75; Schlossman 1974, 124; Teeters 1960, 166), the refuges in this period faced a problem of self-definition and of ambivalence about the internal regimes and public roles they would assume. Whether the refuge was a prison, a family, or a school and whether reformation would best be achieved through discipline and work or love and education were problematic for a time. The same writers have observed that this ambivalence led to conflict—not only between inmates and staff, but also at various levels of the staff and management hierarchy and with the community. That conflict was an argument between treatment and social control as competing paradigms of institutional development. The actors in the early years of the refuge drama did not participate as individuals, but as partisans of various reform impulses that were all prominent in the larger drama of Jacksonian reform. Their conflict was not simply over how a refuge should be run, but over how a society should be structured. This chapter describes the dimensions of that conflict and its implications for the early development of juvenile justice institutions.

I first describe a typology of three reform impulses that were represented in the early refuge movement (the Calvinist, Enlightenment, and Romantic approaches) in terms of four dimensions: social goals, social bases, views of deviance, and views of the child. The aim here is to typify these impulses rather than to generalize them, to cast into bold relief their areas not only of conflict but also of congruence.

Second, I apply this typology to the history of the New York, Philadelphia, and Boston refuges and identify key groups of actors by their reform sympathies and organizational roles in the refuges. I examine their behavior at various points in the institution-building process in order to discover how the logics of these reform perspectives were worked out historically. The goal of the analysis is to replace our present oversimplified, unilinear image of the "decline" of the refuges with a more systematic and sociologically sophisticated model of intrainstitutional conflict and negotiation.

The analysis shows that all three refuges coped in a roughly similar fashion with disparate demands placed upon them by society. On the one hand, the refuges' ideological legitimacy required an emphasis on reforming the inmate through moral education. On the other hand, political legitimacy required an increasing emphasis on security, discipline, and control. Three key features of the modern juvenile justice system emerged as the conceptual links between treatment and control paradigms: jurisdiction over noncriminal juveniles, informal commitments, and the indeterminate sentence.

A Typology of Jacksonian Reform Movements

In the early nineteenth-century United States, three fairly distinct views of human nature, society, and desirable social change existed in a mutual dynamic tension and informed the thought of refuge reformers. The first, Calvinism, formed the root stock of American culture, not only in New England, but in areas of Presbyterian influence in the South as well. Enlightenment thought provided the diffuse and plastic vocabulary of American liberalism, a rational framework within which a variety of disparate groups could negotiate their vision of the good life. Romanticism, still nascent in the 1820s and 1830s, was a revolt of the spirit carried out by disaffected intellectuals against the rationalistic strictures of urban, commercial society. What is most remarkable is not that these perspectives coexisted during the brief period under review here, but that they positively required each other.

Social Goals

The Calvinist contribution to early nineteenth-century reform was made through two not entirely distinct means: evangelical revival and benevolent reform.[3] Both were forms of "Protestant countersubversion" (Lewis 1970), reactions to disestablishment, deism, and popular democracy (Thomas 1965, 657). Both sought to achieve social order by paternalistic means, whether directly through conversions or through interdenominational Bible societies, Sunday School Unions, and tract societies. Humanitarian benevolence was a direct application of the Puritan doctrine of predestination, which held that the saved elect were moral leaders, responsible for the spiritual welfare of the nonelect (Lewis 1970, 69). In Griffin's (1960, 23) flowing terms, "For God's greater glory, society's greater stability, and the maintenance of certain Federalist principles, men believing themselves the trustees of the Lord and their brethren's keepers formed societies to make other people behave."

Benevolent reform was a two-pronged strategy on the part of conservative Protestant clergy. First, they sought a moral regeneration of society that they could no longer achieve through direct

3. For detailed historical analyses of these movements, see Miller (1965), Griffin (1957, 1960), Foster (1960), Bodo (1954), and Lewis (1970).

political means; second, they sought to contain the schismatic tendencies of revivalist enthusiasm (Lewis 1970). This strategy involved doctrinal compromises, however, particularly on the issue of predestination. To maintain interdenominational harmony and to provide a justification for good behavior, predestination—and its corollary, the unattainability of salvation by worldly activity—were gradually jettisoned. Calvinistic pietism was deemphasized in favor of social moralism, and the goal of benevolent reform became preparing the individual soul for the reception of grace (Lewis 1970; Griffin 1957, 424–425).[4]

The Calvinist benevolents espoused a conservative political philosophy informed by the Old Testament prophets: they predicted the destruction of the republic itself if its civil and religious institutions were not renewed through the individual purification of hearts (Miller 1965, 66–72). At their extreme they opposed all nonreligious efforts to reform society without reforming people. Communitarian and Fourierist societies especially were denounced as manifestations of "heartless deism, revolting socialism, blasphemous pantheism, and withering skepticism" (Griffin 1957, 439). Taken as a whole, however, the benevolent movement was not so obdurate. By whetting their adherents' appetites for millennial social change, the benevolent societies made them ripe for the more immediate and visible change possible through secular reform activities. For many individuals benevolence provided a transitional organizational context midway between pietism and humanitarian movements, such as the refuge movement, organized on a thoroughly secular base (Banner 1977). By about 1830, Protestant reform leadership had crested and given way to secular organizations (Lewis 1970, 90–91).

---

4. This reversal of means and ends in Calvinist benevolent reform is the direct analogue to Weber's (1958) account of the "Protestant ethic" in the economic realm. Calvinism, by insisting on both moral behavior and salvation by grace, invites the heretical response that, because grace is predestined, one might as well behave any way one chooses. That response demands in turn some rational justification for moral behavior. For the fatal effect of this conundrum on Calvinist child-rearing theory, see the discussion below of conflicting views of childhood.

Although Enlightenment thought may appear to be most compatible with the secular humanitarian movements that succeeded the benevolent societies, in fact its influence was diffuse and ubiquitous. It was not a rigid system: to late eighteenth-century Americans who saw themselves as "enlightened," this meant that "it had recently become possible, through the proper use of the human faculties, to understand the universe better than it had ever been understood before, and to make practical use of this understanding. . . . They were almost all Lockeians" (May 1970, 203). Americans were most receptive to the moderate Enlightenment views of Locke and Newton, who presented rational schemes of the moral and physical world that seemed to accord with constitutionalist principles (May 1970, 209–210).

The Enlightenment vision was not received in America whole and untransformed, however. Conservative Protestants claimed to be anti-Enlightenment, especially anti-Deist; Jefferson and Jackson were excoriated for pandering to American Jacobinism. But even the conservatives shared some of the key assumptions of the moderate Enlightenment: the idea of a "natural religion" that transcended denominational boundaries, and of a natural law that gave a universalistic justification to property rights and rule by the elite, lent themselves well to pleas for social order. Thus "even those who fought the Enlightenment in its political and social aspects were imbued with its philosophy" (Foster 1960, 125). In sum, then, as May's (1970, 1976) analyses have shown, certain aspects of Enlightenment thought—especially Lockeianism and later Scottish "Common Sense" philosophy—were co-opted into American culture on American terms. Less amenable forms, such as Hume's skepticism and Rousseau's radicalism, never gained a secure foothold in public discussion.

The Romantic ideology arose as a reaction to both Calvinist and Enlightenment rationalism. Ironically, changes within Calvinism itself, particularly the attenuation and eventual abandonment of the doctrine of predestination, made the Romantic rebellion possible. The emergent view that salvation is available to all served as a rationale for evangelism and benevolence, but it also opened the way to the characteristically Romantic perfectionism and individualism that the conservatives most feared (Thomas 1965, 658). Thus Romanticism sprang from the gaps in Calvinist theology and affirmed its kinship by its opposition. ˙

American Romantics were more directly opposed to Enlightenment thought than to Calvinism. The social implications of Romantic reformism lay in its rejection of gradualism—indeed, of governmental institutions entirely—in favor of millennial reform. Federalist thinkers such as John Adams and James Madison had conceived government as a Newtonian mechanism for reconciling and neutralizing individual passions and achieving gradual progress—a view that, as I have already argued, was compatible with conservative Calvinism and its tendencies toward oligarchy. The Romantics, by contrast, rejected rationalism in favor of spirit, politics in favor of education, and gradualism in favor of perfectionism (Thomas 1965, 659). As Parrington (1927, vol. 2, 382) wrote,

> In essence this new transcendental faith was a glorification of consciousness and will. It rested on the rediscovery of the soul that had been dethroned by the old rationalism; and it eventuated in the creation of a mystical egocentric universe wherein the children of God might luxuriate in their divinity. The Unitarians had pronounced human nature to be excellent; the transcendentalists pronounced it divine.

In social organizational terms, Romanticism assumed a posture of intellectual sectarianism counterposed to the orthodoxy of civil society. The movement showed three important qualities of a sect-type organization.[5] First, many prominent Romantics, such as Dorothea Dix and Samuel Gridley Howe, were taken from purely moral reform to humanitarianism through a conversion experience that led them to reject not only gradualist reform methods but also the entire world-

5. The evidence presented here is drawn from Thomas (1965, 662–665). The conclusion that the Romantic movement was essentially sectarian is my own, based on the sect-church distinctions drawn by Troeltsch (1960) and Weber (1978, 1204–1211).

view of liberalism. Thus they tended to reject institutionally approved ways of achieving social change in favor of total commitment to professional social reform. Second, Romantic leaders like Dix, Howe, and especially Bronson Alcott and radical abolitionist William Lloyd Garrison were charismatic "educator-prophets" (Thomas 1965, 663) who exercised power that derived from insight, persuasion, and decisive action rather than official roles. Finally, the movement's logical extension was ascetic withdrawal: "Education, seen as a way of life, meant the communitarian experiment as an educative model. Pushed to its limits, the perfectionist assault on institutions logically ended in the attempt to make new and better societies as examples for Americans to follow" (Thomas 1965, 665). This very sectarian quality determined the impact that the Romantics were to have on the refuge movement.

Social Bases of Jacksonian Reform

The early nineteenth-century religious benevolent societies provided a common vehicle for the aspirations of both reconstructed Calvinism and moribund Federalism. Both Puritans and patricians felt that only moral men were fit to govern: "In New England, the fit were Calvinists who supported the established church. Throughout New England, New York, and Pennsylvania, the fit were also Christian gentleman who alleged their right to control their brethren" (Griffin 1960, 10; see also Griffin 1957, 427).

The benevolent societies drew their leadership from prominent conservative clergy, merchants, and lawyers in the refuge cities of Boston, New York, and Philadelphia (Foster 1960, 132). There is some debate over the degree to which the benevolent movement can be considered an extension of Puritanism. Banner (1977, 305) has explicitly criticized this notion, pointing out that such associations as the American Sunday School Union and the American Bible Society, while dominated by Presbyterians, also included Methodists, Baptists, Quakers, and Episcopalians on their governing boards.

The crucial point, however, is not that the benevolent societies were made up solely of strict Calvinists, but that they served as a means of extending Calvinist ideology into a new and more cosmopolitan arena, thereby transforming its doctrine somewhat. Certainly, participating clergy had no need to alter their basic social conservatism; they were conspicuously unwilling to endorse such causes as abolitionism, female rights, working-class rights, elimination of capital punishment, and anything else that threatened to disrupt property rights and the social order (Lewis 1970, 86). At the same time, those leaders who were so anxious about the explosive and apparently disintegrative quality of American society in the early 1800s could not afford to be nostalgic in their social vision. Clergy and merchants alike were profiting from the expansion of congregations, the frontier, and the economy in general (Griffin 1960, 45). The horizons were limitless if growth could be properly managed.

Thus the purely religious and moral aspect of benevolent reform was strong mainly in rural areas. Urban benevolence "preferred a more utilitarian approach to the problem of instilling into the minds of the degenerate a proper regard for morality," an approach that resulted, for example, in exclusive eligibility requirements to restrict aid to the deserving poor (Heale 1968, 168). As benevolence gave way to more practical and specialized humanitarian movements of the Jacksonian period such as prison reform, conservative clergy remained prominent, but did not dominate (Rothman 1971, 76).

Unlike the Calvinist ethos, Enlightenment rationalism in the United States had no specific constituency or social location, and it never became manifest in a party, doctrine, or movement of its own. It functioned rather as a semitransparent cultural ambience that was "most successful not in attack but in permeating or being absorbed" (May 1970, 207). By the time of the Revolution, the works of moderates such as Locke had become standard in college libraries, and their ideas had become standard in middle-class minds outside the South (May 1970, 209–210; Lundberg and May 1976).

Despite evangelical conservatives' rantings against rationalism and godless deism, Calvinism as a whole was not the enemy of Enlightenment thought. Jonathan Edwards had used rationalist arguments to raise Puritan theology to a new and more comprehensive plane and even partially integrated the Lockeian *tabula rasa* into his own more rigidly Calvinist psychological system. The Puritan stronghold of New England had in general been the most receptive of all colonial areas to Lockeianism (May 1970, 207; Slater 1977, 142; see also Parrington 1927, vol. 1, 140–148). Enlightened American thinkers, Calvinists, and eventually the humanitarian reformers of the early 1800s all had a common enemy in enthusiastic revivalism. From an Enlightenment view enthusiasm was irrational; to the Calvinists it threatened schism; to the humanitarians revivals distracted attention from social problems in need of amelioration (May 1970, 207; Miller 1965, 20). Thus Enlightenment rationalism provided a common ground on which Puritans and humanitarians could meet and agree on an agenda of control.

Romanticism in America rose in the form of Transcendentalism among a new generation of New England intellectuals, from under the very thumb of Calvinist cultural orthodoxy (see Parrington 1927, vol. 2, 379–385). By mid century the movement was to flower into a distinctly American tradition of critical literature. In the late 1820s, however, Romanticism was inchoate, and even at their peak the Romantics lacked a firm political and social base because of their profound ambivalence, self-righteousness, and suspicion of supraindividual institutions. Like the Quakers up until the Revolution, they withdrew from movements for desired social ends rather than dilute their integrity in the struggle over means:

> Driven by their profound distaste for manipulation and chicanery, many of [the Transcendentalists] took on the role of a prophet standing aloof from elections, campaigns and party caucuses and dispensing wisdom . . . out of the vast private resources of the self. In this sense transcendentalism, like Christian perfectionism, represented a distinct break with the prevailing Jacksonian views of democratic leadership and the politics of compromise and adjustment. (Thomas 1965, 672)

Where Romantics did participate in more broadly based movements, such as the American Peace Society and the early Abolitionist movement, their intransigence often led to the fragmentation of the movements themselves (Thomas 1965, 660).

One area in which Romantic ideas did have a lasting impact was education. In the early nineteenth century the most influential Romantic education theorist was Johann Pestalozzi of Switzerland. Pestalozzi argued that teaching was a task of nurturing individual growth, not of coercing obedience or inculcating skills. Bronson Alcott of Massachusetts, the leading American spokesman for Romanticism, was especially influenced by Pestalozzi and published articles propagating his ideas in the late 1820s and 1830s (Slater 1977, 148–149). Through Alcott and his colleagues, Pestalozzian thought made a powerful and humane contribution to the movement for mass schooling in the United States. But it is important to note that the Transcendentalist view of education extended far beyond the schoolhouse. To them, education was more than a pedagogical method; it was the primary avenue of achieving social change. By acting as a guide on the child's voyage of self-discovery, the educator cultivates new men and thereby regenerates society (Thomas 1965, 664). Alcott, for example, thought of himself "as a Messiah, come to save the world through reforming education" (Strickland 1969, 7). This messianic impulse led other Romantics to play an important role in the creation of the refuges.

Calvinist, Enlightenment, and Romantic Views of Childhood

The colonial Puritans developed a paradoxical view of childhood that reflected a larger conflict in Calvinist theology between asceticism and moralism. On the one hand, Christians were encouraged to devalue worldly activity because it had no influence on their salvation. The doctrinal trinity of predestination, original sin, and purification by grace locked together in an "impressively tight" logical system (Slater 1977, 130) that affirmed the inscrutability and utter divinity of the redemptive process. On the other hand, the doctrine of the calling inspired the devout to invest their everyday behavior with transcendent moral significance: "The world exists to serve the glorification of God and for that purpose alone. The elected Christian is in the world only to increase this glory of God by fulfilling His commandments to the best of his ability," and those commandments included not only right conduct for the individual, but the construction of a Christian social order (Weber 1958, 108). Because the saved cannot be distinguished from the mass of sinners, the calling falls upon all members of the community as a collective responsibility. This paradox invites the Arminian heresy: if salvation is prior to action, why act morally? Weber argued that the characteristic solution to this paradox is psychological: moral behavior becomes a social display of received grace and an inner assurance of salvation to the individual. As we saw in Chapter 1, however, the Massachusetts Bay Puritans were forced to develop a more political solution: they created a legal regime in which official control over private behavior was justified in theological terms.

The issue of child rearing presents a special case of this paradox. If the child's salvation is independent of his or her conduct, what is the point of moral training? The Puritans' thought in this area developed in parallel to their more general social ethos. Moral training was initially justified only as a "support" for the child's eventual redemption, but over time it "implicitly became in Calvinist writings the real end of upbringing" (Slater 1977, 130). By finessing the theological dilemma in this way, the Puritans developed a practical approach to child rearing that was faithful to the parents' natural inclination to impart values to their children, as well as to the felt need to control the collective morality of the commonwealth. However, this implicit solution did not last long.

In a community that respected intellectual boldness less or that relied less on didactic means of social mobilization and control, the contradiction between theological doctrine and child-rearing practice might never have become explicit. In the postrevolutionary period, however, Calvinist clergy such as Timothy Dwight began more formal attempts to integrate the imperative of moral training with the doctrines of predestination and infant depravity. Dwight's most powerful justification for training virtuous children reflected the beleaguered status of New England Puritan culture in the new republic. Moral training, even though it could not assure the reception of grace by the individual, could achieve the safety and stability of society. "Put bluntly," this was an admission that "grace was too sporadic for society to rely upon it as a police force" (Slater 1977, 131).

Rationalizations of this sort eventually proved inadequate. In the late eighteenth century, orthodox Calvinist child-rearing advice became more ambivalent, finally in effect affirming the efficacy of environmental influences, especially parents, in molding the child's nature. Many Calvinist writers broadened Jonathan Edwards's previous partial acceptance of the *tabula rasa* metaphor and applied it to the moral as well as rational faculties. The marriage of Calvinist supernaturalism and Lockeian psychology was not a stable one. The orthodox view that innate depravity impelled the child toward sin waned; Calvinist theory at this point contradicted itself openly and became vulnerable to full-scale Enlightenment attack (Slater 1977, 138). By 1785, Unitarian writers had explicitly made the creation of a virtuous child—not salvation—the goal of child raising. More orthodox Calvinists had done this as well, but only implicitly and not without incurring fatal contradictions (Slater 1977, 143).

The infiltration of Lockeian psychological principles into child-rearing theory was aided by Locke's general intellectual and political acceptability. Because of this, the transition from Calvinist to Enlightenment thought is difficult to perceive. "As long as the Enlightenment outlook avoided extremes, the Orthodox as well as the Liberals could live with it and learn from it" (Slater 1977, 141). The difficulty of making empirical distinctions between the two approaches is increased by the fact that advocates of Enlightenment theories in the United States—mainly the Unitarians and Arminian liberals—were neither many nor prolific writers. Slater (1977, 141) identifies them by their lack of concern for the "primal trio" of "original sin, total depravity, and regeneration by grace" to which self-proclaimed Calvinists continued to cling.

Late eighteenth-century interpretations of Locke involved a straightforward, but incomplete, application of the idea of the *tabula rasa:* the child is born with entirely ductile faculties, which are shaped by purely environmental forces as the child grows. Divine grace was admitted into this system only as a means of reformation for those children who had been confirmed in sinfulness by the stresses and strains of life. In the nineteenth century, Unitarians finally banished the last lingering clouds of Calvinism by introducing the cheery notion that the child is born entirely morally neutral, if not inclined to the good, and by ignoring the agency of special grace altogether (Slater 1977, 142–143).

The position that asserted the absolute neutrality of the child's moral sense was difficult to maintain. Indeed, Locke himself qualified the pure *tabula rasa* idea by suggesting that most children were born with undesirable tendencies that could, however, be wiped out or balanced by education (Slater 1977, 145–146). American interpreters were inclined to credit the child with congenital tendencies toward good. This idea found significant support in the writings of the late Enlightenment Common Sense philosophers, whose general agenda was to establish a natural grounding for commonly held morality (May 1970, 1976). Applied to children, this implied the existence of very general predispositions, which to Enlightenment thinkers was less important than parental training in determining character. The goal of that training was to instill standards, to make the child virtuous by practice of the craft of parenthood. Thus a basic continuity with Locke was maintained. It remained for the Romantics to make a full commitment to the existence of an embryonic but complete moral repertoire in the child.

Calvinist thought, which had placed grace prior to moral behavior, had been reversed by the absorption of Enlightenment ideas in the specialized area of child rearing as it had in general social ethics. Both systems agreed on the necessity of an external agency—whether grace or education—for ultimate salvation. Romanticism turned this formulation on its head, denying both original sin and the primacy of external impressions: "The Romantic child possessed as part of his native endowment praiseworthy tendencies which had only to be developed to make him fit for heaven" (Slater 1977, 149).

Bronson Alcott, chief theoretician of Romantic education in America, was violently opposed to the Calvinist doctrine of infant depravity (Strickland 1969, 16–17). To Alcott, children were neither imps nor empty vessels to be disciplined and molded; they were "envoys from heaven with desirable native endowments which should be preserved and gently stimulated" (Slater 1977, 151). The full significance of the Romantic challenge lay not just in proposing a new version of childhood, but, more important, in altering the methodology of child rearing and with it the prescribed role of the parent. Child development was no longer the product of an inscrutable God or diverse outside institutions: "The Romantic conception [of child rearing] would seem to impose on parents a staggering obligation to protect the children from the world and at the same time to help the child realize his spiritual potential" (Strickland 1969, 12). The child had become a hothouse plant, and the parent a careful horticulturist.

Views of Deviance

The typology of deviance presented here does not fall into a convenient temporal scheme like the succession of child-rearing theories just discussed. Perhaps that is because, in contrast to the child-rearing literature, which was produced by a narrowly circumscribed group of clergy and religiously imbued intellectuals, the issue of deviant behavior was debated in both practical and theoretical terms by a wide variety of benevolent, humanitarian, and legal and prison reform groups. In any event, in the eighteenth century, the prison reform community, with which I will be primarily concerned, already contained a mixture of Enlightenment and humanitarian Christian approaches:

> One of these, representing the outlook of the Enlightenment, wanted above all else to make criminal law rational, to strip it of metaphysical

concepts and purge it of superstition. The second group, inspired to a large degree by religious conviction, saw the offender as a child of God who should be treated with compassion and love. Both points of view were influenced by the growth of toleration and humanitarianism in the eighteenth century, but they formed a somewhat unstable combination. (Lewis 1965, 16)

Neither of these views expresses the pure Calvinist view of deviance that operated in colonial New England. To the Puritans, crime was a manifestation of sin; it was "endemic to society" and could be neither prevented nor eliminated (Rothman 1971, 15). The Puritan magistrate's official goal was neither to reform nor to redeem the criminal—for salvation and redemption are God's alone to give—but rather to contain behavior that implicitly threatened the holy but tenuous social order.

After independence the benevolent societies reasserted the goal of containment and the efficacy of grace. In response to the sweeping social changes of the time—particularly the waning of Federalist influence—as well as to the manifest failure of legal reform and other rationalist methods of social control, the benevolents saw moral regeneration as the only check on crime and pauperism (Griffin 1957, 436–437). Likewise, despite their more hardheaded approach and more optimistic goals, the subsequent humanitarian societies such as the New York Society for the Prevention of Pauperism saw social problems as primarily caused by a lack of "correct moral principle" (Heale 1968, 166).

There was a gradual shift in the reformers' thinking at this time that is analogous to contemporary changes in views of childhood: just as a self-evident need for the moral training of children became an end in itself, so the felt need for social control and domination by a threatened elite invited a more practical approach to social reform. The key transitional concept on both fronts was environmental causation. If the child's spiritual fate is not predestined, then behavior is amenable to family discipline; if crime is not inherent in man, then it is a product of conditions that can be changed. Thus the Calvinist view of deviance accommodated itself to a modified Enlightenment environmentalism and in the bargain reasserted some of its most cherished principles: individualism, moralism, the importance of the family as the first line of social control, and an "emphasis on coercion rather than persuasion" in the control of deviant behavior (Heale 1968, 171–172).

The earliest and most direct Enlightenment influence on the area of crime was on the penal code reforms enacted in several northeastern states in the 1790s. The Enlightenment impact here was direct but not pure. Code reformers in Pennsylvania, with Quakers at the vanguard, sought first to replicate the mild colonial codes established by William Penn and later suppressed in favor of harsher English law. Second, however, the reformers were influenced by the thinking of Voltaire and Montesquieu and the classical criminological theories of Bentham and Beccaria. These Enlightenment views had seen some practical application in the work of English Quaker reformer Thomas Howard, and it was through his example that rational law and reformation became part of the agenda of such groups as the Philadelphia Society for Alleviating the Miseries of Public Prisons (Hawes 1971, 23).

Beccaria advocated humane punishments—usually confinement—graduated in severity to suit the crime. He assumed society's ability to rationally assess the degree of harm incurred by a given criminal act and the potential criminal's ability to weigh the relative costs and benefits of committing a crime. Penal law in this formulation became a system of contracts, complete with mutual remedies and the presumption of reasonableness (if not goodwill) on both sides—an arrangement wholly ideologically suited to an optimistic bourgeois society anxious to throw off the chains of the feudal past.[6]

At this early stage there was no expectation that penitentiaries would serve as places of rehabilitation (Rothman 1971, 62). There

---

6. On the relationship between classical criminology and liberalism, see Radzinowicz (1966, ch. 1); on contract law as an expression of laissez-faire individualism, see Durkheim (1933); on early American penal reform as an expression of antifeudal nationalism, see Rothman (1971, 59).

was no thought given, for example, to applying a Lockeian psychological model to the task of resocializing the criminal; no attempt was made to reach inside the criminal's mind and insert proper values. Rather, the criminal and the law-abiding citizen alike were implicitly assumed to operate on the same, fundamentally sound calculus—which, translated into spiritual terms, easiy becomes the Quaker "inner light." Criminals were not expected to change internally, but only to see their "true interest" (Heale 1968, 171). A rational and humane legal system would facilitate this process of change and act as a deterrent. The source of deviance was located not in the criminal, but in the legal system (Rothman 1971, 61).

By the 1820s, rational penal reform was generally perceived to have failed in curing crime. Humanitarian reformers of this period—including those responsible for the Auburn and Pennsylvania prisons and the houses of refuge—turned attention back toward the criminal in the attempt to identify the causes of crime. A basic continuity with Enlightenment thought was maintained, however, in that deviance was still not seen to be intrinsic to the individual. Its causes were rather environmental and developmental.

The elaboration of environmental and developmental concepts amounted in practice to a renewed emphasis on the family. This turn represented a rapprochement between Calvinist and Enlightenment theories and is probably a result of the increasing influence of Calvinist elites in humanitarian movements that had previously been the almost exclusive domain of the Quakers (Heale 1968, 171–172). More important, environmentalism suggested a methodology of control that allowed the Calvinist policy of containment to be turned outward.[7] In the hands of humanitarian societies, the new methodol-

7. Thus the adoption of environmentalism was an extension of the general post-revolutionary change in emphasis from pietism to moralism (see Griffin 1957, 424–425). In Erikson's (1966) terms it represents a new strategy of "boundary-maintenance": whereas the colonial Puritan community was attempting to define itself in the midst of a metaphorical (moral) and physical wilderness, Calvinists in the 1820s were facing the erosion of political and ideological boundaries in the form of encroachment by competing groups. Environmentalist reform offered a measure of control over a society that they could no longer directly dominate.

ogy legitimized efforts not only at didactic reform, but also at prevention. If the family is the cradle of crime, then the child is an embryonic criminal. The product of this line of thinking was a fully circular developmental etiology of deviance in which parental neglect was the "primary cause of deviant behavior" (Rothman 1971, 77). Neglected children become unruly, and unruly children turn into adult paupers and criminals who in turn neglect their children. Thus neglected, disobedient, and delinquent children, drunkards, paupers, and criminals became differentiated only by being at different stages on a common road. This etiological model eventually provided the operating ideology of the refuges.

The idea of a Romantic theory of deviance is a contradiction in terms. The moral relativism implied by the Transcendentalists' emphasis on perfection, individuality, spirit, and will, as well as their repugnance for coercive institutions, provides no foothold for a programmatic standard of deviant behavior, let alone an explanation or solution. Emerson's willingness to grant license to heroes appalled even the hero-worshiping Carlyle (Thomas 1965, 672). Reflecting on the futility of rationalistic efforts at social reform, Emerson (1876, 284–285) wrote:

> Obedience to . . . genius is the only liberating influence. We wish to escape from subjection and a sense of inferiority, and we make self-denying ordinances, we drink water, we eat grass, we refuse the laws, we go to jail: it is all in vain; only by obedience to his genius, only by the freest activity in the way constitutional to him, does an angel seem to arise before a man and lead him by the hand out of all the wards of the prison.

Emerson is speaking metaphorically here, of the prisons of the mind created by social institutions. But we may justly reverse the synecdoche to regard prisons as the exemplar of all social institutions and infer from it a transcendental condemnation of the penitentiary: prison discipline merely adds one form of corruption to another, change is growth, and a man's growth must proceed "in the way constitutional to him." But Emerson was writing theoretically, from the rather antiseptic remove of Transcendentalism. There were other, earlier Romantics who were not aloof from humanitarian movements and who thus had to develop in practice a response to bad behavior that they had not been provided in theory.

Educator Bronson Alcott will again serve as an example. Alcott's method was aimed toward "uncovering . . . goodness" rather than curbing bad behavior: "He sharply criticized his contemporaries for their fatal mistake of imposing partial and therefore false standards on their charges. Shades of the prison house obscured the child's search for perfection, and character was lost forever" (Thomas 1965, 664). In practice Alcott had to compromise this attitude and adopt a more pragmatic approach to moral education. He found it necessary to admit that children had basic, selfish "animal" drives, but saw those drives as a weakness, not a predisposition to sin. He insisted that the child also had higher faculties that needed only encouragement and cultivation to overcome the animal weaknesses and develop into spiritual excellence (Strickland 1969, 19–20).

On another point, however, Alcott's Romanticism betrays an internal contradiction and even a point of convergence with Calvinism. This had to do with the desired ends of education. Alcott felt that, in the raising of children, "gentle means must be used to promote ascetic ends" (Strickland 1969, 13). Despite his opposition to the prognoses of Calvinism, Alcott's ongoing experiments with his own children reveal that he did not differ materially with tradition about the *content* of moral behavior. Like most parents, he expected his daughters to be respectful, obedient, and dutiful; in addition he wanted them to be creative, intelligent, and self-motivated; and above all they must arrive at this exalted station naturally, through the cultivation of their innate spiritual gifts.

Alcott perceived that this approach tended to put children in a difficult double bind: to him the child was not a sturdy plant; she was rather a delicate specimen that required shelter from corruptive influences. Here Alcott forecast the communitarian tendencies of Transcendentalism and reached another point of convergence with moralistic Calvinism: "the family was a fortress from which worldly incursions would be vigorously repelled" (Strickland 1969, 14). By reasserting the family as both source and model of social control, Alcott adopted an important element of the Calvinist strategy of containment, with perhaps an even stronger taint of paranoia. The family, as the official operational analogy for the houses of refuge, was to provide the conceptual meeting ground on which divergent Calvinist, Enlightenment, and Romantic goals could be negotiated.

Although these interrelated ideological systems were all employed in reaction to a social order in flux, they were employed toward different ends by groups that are at least conceptually distinguishable. Calvinism was the faith of a threatened elite; Enlightenment rationality, the working agenda of an ideologically dominant middle class; and Romanticism, the protest of rootless intellectuals. Each group entertained ideal visions of social order, of childhood, and of deviant behavior that are in their pure form mutually exclusive.

What is equally remarkable as the observed differences, however, is the degree to which the three approaches overlapped. The most important example of this is the ability of the Calvinist impulse to become secularized and to adapt itself to the more broadly legitimate vocabulary of the Enlightenment. Similarly, the Romantics, prodigal sons of the Puritans, repaired to the family as the ideal of social order. In the early history of the refuges, identifiable groups of actors set the course of institutional development by attempting to work out the logic of these ideological perspectives.

The Dynamics of Refuge Reform

In the rest of this chapter, I show how contending groups involved in the foundation of the New York, Philadelphia, and Boston refuges strategically used Calvinist, Enlightenment, and Romantic ideologies. The analysis is presented as a comparison of institutional life histories. I examine the process by which the refuge idea first emerged, the

various needs that the institutions were expected to meet, the counter-
vailing philosophies that were brought to bear, and the conflicts that
ensued. I argue that this combination of groups and their motivating
ideologies contributed the most salient features of the American pattern of juvenile justice: a preventive model of control that focuses
particular attention on noncriminal forms of juvenile misbehavior, a
treatment regime that revolves around confining and classifying offenders, and a practical operating agenda characterized by coercion
and repression.

I discuss the development of the refuges in terms of three stages of
institution building: mobilization of support, organization of an internal regime, and eventual conflict over the means and goals of
refuge discipline. These stages describe not only the growth of the
institutions, but also the emergence of a rationalized ideology of
delinquency prevention. The mobilization stage includes the creation
of voluntary associations as sponsors of the refuge idea and the
formation of a stable cadre of movement leadership, as well as the
initial conceptualization of delinquency as a social problem. The
organization stage includes the formal founding of the institutions,
solicitation of political support, and staffing, as well as negotiation
over the form that the institutions would assume—in essence over
whose model of the family and deviance would prevail. The third
stage, conflict, describes the point at which tensions between alternative family ideals and between social control and rehabilitative paradigms became untenable and beyond which managerialism and control became the institutions' dominant tendencies.

Mobilizing Support

The creation of the voluntary associations that agitated for specialized juvenile institutions was just one aspect of the much broader shift
from religiously based benevolent reform to more secular humanitarian movements that occurred after the War of 1812. The shift from
benevolent reform to humanitarianism was not a radical departure.

Humanitarianism was in large part a reaction to the inefficiency of the scattergun approach taken by benevolent reformers to a variety of social problems, and as such it signified more a change of method and organization than a repudiation of traditional values and goals (Heale 1968, 163–165). Secular reformers of the 1820s sought, in effect, to reform the reform movement by creating a network of functionally specialized associations, each focused on a particular institutional solution to an identified social problem and all bound together by a shared conservative vision of social order. The best known example of this shift is the prison reforms that occurred in this period. The much publicized "Auburn system" of prison discipline was less a product of careful forethought about crime than a response to the evident failure of older penitentiaries, a hardened public attitude toward crime, and the resurgence of Calvinist over Quaker ideas about prison discipline. As Lewis (1965, 56) has written, the history of Auburn "reveals a determination to conserve established institutions, including the penitentiary, and not an impulse to create something new and different."

The history of the refuge movement shows a similar conservative dynamic. The founding of the first refuge in New York was the culmination of a series of developments within the Society for the Prevention of Pauperism: the society narrowed its focus from pauperism in general to delinquency and underwent a change in membership. To generalist humanitarians, many of whom were Quakers active in the discredited penal reforms of the 1790s, were added a cohort of ambitious, practical, secular reformers (Pickett 1969, 41; Lewis 1965, 78–80). These changes were formally recognized in 1823 when the Society for the Prevention of Pauperism dissolved itself and was reincarnated as the Society for the Reformation of Juvenile Delinquents. The first act of the new society was to call for a refuge in New York City. By literally re-forming itself, the society admitted the futility of curing poverty piecemeal and announced a more rational approach based on a more sophisticated etiology: "by attacking the problems of youth, they hoped to scotch pauperism at birth" (Pickett 1969, 49).

In Philadelphia the refuge idea was sponsored by the Society for Alleviating the Miseries of Public Prisons, "the first of the great prison reform societies" (Barnes 1927, 81). Founded by Quakers in 1787, the society continued primarily as a vehicle for Quaker ideas through 1830, despite the broadening of its membership base, and in general monopolized the field of prison reform in Pennsylvania (Barnes 1927, 84–85).

The Philadelphia society took up the refuge cause after many years of work devoted to revising the Pennsylvania penal code along Beccarian lines, building the Walnut Street Prison, and finally abandoning a rationalist approach to crime control in favor of the rehabilitative model established in the "Pennsylvania system" of solitary confinement at hard labor.[8] In 1823, the society appointed a committee to investigate the need for a separate juvenile institution, and in 1826, a memorial calling for the institution's establishment was addressed to the Pennsylvania legislature (Barnes 1927, 101–102). Thus both societies hit upon the idea after having failed with other institutional reforms. The New York group, after a series of disappointing efforts, settled on the refuge idea as a potential cure for pauperism; the Philadelphians approached it as a solution to the hitherto resistant problem of crime.

The impetus for the Boston House of Reformation came from government rather than a voluntary association, but its establishment reflects a similar desire to streamline and improve the existing system of almsgiving. The Massachusetts legislature, after a three-year investigation, recommended abandoning outdoor relief in favor of workhouses. The city of Boston carried out its own investigation and in 1823 built a workhouse for the able-bodied poor and a house of

---

8. The Auburn and Pennsylvania systems were pitted against each other in a fierce publicity war. Although their practical differences appear obscure from a twentieth-century perspective, Erikson (1966, 199–205) argues persuasively that the conflict between the two models of prison discipline was a manifestation of the larger and much older conflict between Calvinist and Quaker social control ideologies. For a prescient contemporary comparison of the two systems, see Beaumont and Tocqueville (1964).

correction for adults convicted of minor crimes. In 1826, spurred on by the example of New York, the city council recommended that one wing of the House of Correction be reserved as an institution for juveniles. The act authorizing Boston to establish the House of Reformation—the only one of the three refuges established under fully public auspices—was passed by the Massachusetts legislature in 1826 (Hawes 1971, 51).

The reform group most associated with the Boston refuge is the Boston Prison Discipline Society. The society's concern with the refuge, however, appears to have been tangential to its main concern, advocating the Auburn prison system. The Prison Discipline Society was narrowly based and rigidly focused; it was "mainly the mouthpiece for the thoughts of one man," its founder, Louis Dwight, "and was intellectually straightjacketed by its leader's continued control and stubborn resistance to change" (Lewis 1965, 220). Dwight is reported to have been an enthusiastic promoter of the refuge idea in Massachusetts and elsewhere (Pickett 1969, 87). But the society's reports show no evidence of active involvement in the Boston refuge (Prison Discipline Society 1972), and the society had no legally sanctioned formal role in refuge management.

Just as the concern of the humanitarian societies evolved from quite general reform programs to the more specific problem of delinquency, so individuals turned to refuge reform as the culmination of careers in more broadly focused benevolent and humanitarian efforts. They were as a group prosperous, Christian, and public spirited. The New York group tended to be of Federalist, and later Whig, persuasion; they were repelled by the French Revolution and found it reincarnated in Jacksonian democracy (Mennel 1973, 6–7). They saw their reform work in Calvinist terms, as a calling: "Basking in the grace of their munificent Maker, the managers served as stewards of the earthly vineyard. One of their chief works was to minister to the less fortunate than themselves. The Refuge constituted such a ministry" (Pickett 1969, 115–116).

Two New York Quakers, Thomas Eddy and John Griscom, provided most of the early energy and direction behind the first refuge (Pickett 1969, 23–24). Eddy's career in particular recapitulated the evolution of Jacksonian reform. He was a retired insurance magnate who had developed valuable political connections through his sideline investment in the Erie Canal project. He devoted most of his time to prison reform, but he was also a member of the Humane Society and the Society for the Prevention of Pauperism, an organizer of the Free School Society, an abolitionist, and a proponent of institutional treatment for the insane (Ekirch 1943, 378, 389–390). Eddy gathered forces to revise New York's penal code in 1796 and sought to implement Beccaria's and Howard's ideas as superintendent of Newgate prison through a regime emphasizing humane treatment, spare diet, and labor. He resigned from Newgate, partly for political reasons and partly because his superiors insisted on contracting inmates' labor and increasing disciplinary severity. He became pessimistic about Newgate's future, but not about institutions as such. He managed to have some of his ideas incorporated into the compromise that became the Auburn system (Ekirch 1943, 379–381, 384; Hawes 1971, 24–25; Lewis 1965, 34–35). By the 1820s, he saw in the refuges an extension of his hitherto unrealized ideas on rehabilitation and prevention (Ekirch 1943, 388). His primary role in the movement was as an "educator and dispenser of information" (Pickett 1969, 46)—in short, a lobbyist.

Griscom was a fellow Quaker, also a friend and neighbor of Eddy (Hawes 1971, 29). He was a younger man, however, and an educator, and his contribution was not from the field of prison reform, but from philanthropy in general, and particularly education. He was a founder of the Society for the Prevention of Pauperism, and it was on his suggestion that the SPP was reorganized as the Society for the Reformation of Juvenile Delinquents. Griscom was a student of European educational methods; he tended to favor the more organizationally sound Lancasterian system over Pestalozzi's highly personalistic style. By maintaining personal contacts with educators and intellectuals both domestically and throughout Europe, he was the ideal pipeline for information and ideas in the area of reform (Pickett 1969, 27, 34).

Another New York refuge patron was Mayor Stephen Allen, a self-made capitalist, Tammany politician, and Auburn proponent with a merciless attitude toward adult criminals (Pickett 1969, 50; Lewis 1965, 82). The group included John Pintard, vice-president of the American Bible Society, "lifelong Federalist," and rabid anti-Jacksonian (Griffin 1957, 429); General Matthew Clarkson, chair of the first meeting of the Society for the Prevention of Pauperism, Federalist, vice-president of the American Bible Society (Pierce 1869, 38), and prison commissioner; Divie Bethune, American Bible Society and Sunday School Union member (Griffin 1957, 29) and "benevolent merchant" (Pierce 1869, 38); Mayor DeWitt Clinton, Republican presidential nominee with Federalist supporters, American Bible Society member, business partner of Thomas Eddy, and advocate of public education; and Mayor Cadwallader C. Colden, supporter of Clinton, Federalist, and abolitionist.[9]

The Philadelphia refuge reformers were an equally august and conservative group. Quaker Roberts Vaux delivered the address before the Society for Alleviating the Miseries of Public Prisons that led to their resolution in favor of a refuge. He, like Eddy, was a retired businessman who devoted all his time to benevolence. Four of the refuge managers were prominent in the American Sunday School Union; another, John Sargeant, was a leading Philadelphia lawyer, congressman, and advocate of the United States Bank; and William Tilghman was a loyalist during the Revolution, later a judge. In Boston two mayors enthusiastically supported the House of Reformation (Mennel 1973, 5). Louis Dwight of the Prison Discipline Society was a conservative Congregationalist with grandiose dreams of order. He was attracted to the Auburn program as "a system which produced the tightest form of order and literally compelled

9. The facts presented here, unless cited otherwise, are from entries in the *Dictionary of American Biography* or from Mennel (1973, 4–5).

men to be abstemious and industrious" and advocated its extension into factories, schools, and homes (Lewis 1965, 82–83).

Thus the refuge movement consisted of a combination of old and new men: Quakers and Congregationalists, patricians and capitalists, benevolents and pragmatists.[10] They did not come together with a fully drawn plan of what the refuges were to become, and they had no model of rehabilitation. At the outset their intention was only to end the commingling of adults and wayward, runaway, and homeless children in jails and almshouses (Teeters 1960, 166). They were not at this stage much concerned with juvenile criminals (Mennel 1973, 9). In New York by the time the Society for the Reformation of Juvenile Delinquents got around to the issue, calls for the separation of juvenile and adult offenders had already been made by two mayors, the Common Council, the grand jury, and the chaplain of the almshouse (Hawes 1971, 33–34). In 1823, the district attorney reported to the Society for the Prevention of Pauperism that over four hundred fifty persons under twenty-five were in Bridewell and Newgate Prison. Many were between nine and sixteen; of these all were vagrants—"none had been charged with a specific offense" (Hawes 1971, 37). In March of that year, a report of one of the society's committees demanded the construction of a "House of Refuge" for juvenile criminals released from prison that would serve as a "school of moral rehabilitation," presumably from the influences of prison life, "as well as a training center in mechanical skills" (Pickett 1969, 44). Lewis (1965, 47) suggests that legislation establishing the refuge was an expedient attempt to ease population pressures at the tottering Newgate facility.

In Philadelphia also the refuge idea first gained salience mainly as an alternative to more severe sanctions. The Society for Alleviating the Miseries of Public Prisons launched investigations that resulted in resolutions for two kinds of institutions: the first a home for

---

10. Somehow the refuges were not part of the controversy between the Philadelphia and Auburn systems. "Being on good terms with both belligerent camps, the refuge reformers kept their lines of communication open" (Pickett 1969, 87).

vagrant juveniles as an alternative to prison and the second an institution for juvenile criminals who had been discharged from prison (Hawes 1971, 54; Pickett 1969, 98). The former resolution contained no positive plan for rehabilitation, but rather demanded

> that a suitable place be provided by the Guardians of the Poor [for vagrant and homeless minors who are now placed in common prisons], which place is provided to be made sufficiently strong for their safe keeping, until suitable places can be obtained for binding them out apprentices, at such distance from the city as will, in all probability, break off all connections with their former associates. (quoted in Teeters 1960, 168)

The refuge movement up to this point lacked a persuasive, comprehensive, affirmative ideology, and its appeals for new institutions were unsuccessful. The public was out of patience with the idea that institutionalization per se could reform criminals; therefore the refuge had to be identified as something more than just a prison for children. The missing element was the concept of prevention. The official history of the New York refuge recalls this juncture:

> Thus far the Society had simply modified the offensive name of the place of confinement for young offenders, from a prison, with all its offensive and disgraceful associations, to a House of Refuge; it was still to be a refuge to those that had been in prison, or a separate place of confinement for young criminals. Individuals, indeed, had suggested the preventive work to be performed, as in the instance of Mr. Eddy. The next and final stage was to entirely divest the Refuge of its penitentiary associations, and to permit magistrates to send into its sheltering and nurturing folds the vagrant and perilled children of the streets—thus, in a degree, anticipating the corrupting influences of early evil associations. (Pierce 1869, 53–54)

To Pierce both the child and the refuge were stigmatized by being associated with prisons. The divestiture by the refuge of its "penitentiary associations" required the legal authority to take charge of a child's person before a criminal act had been committed. The divestiture process was begun by John Griscom in the meeting that inaugurated the Society for the Reformation of Juvenile Delinquents. His message in support of the refuge had two main points. First, he suggested that reformation must replace revenge as the goal of incarceration and suggested that the old penitentiaries—for example, Newgate, Eddy's stillborn child—had failed not because they were too lenient, but because their program of classification and separation had not been fully implemented. Second, he declared it the responsibility of civil officials to act *in loco parentis,* to prevent the corruption of the social order by assuming familial authority and intervening to root out the sources of temptation, pauperism, and crime (Pickett 1969, 47–48).

Griscom's statement had several important ideological and political implications. First, he presented the refuge as an institution that would meet the needs of two groups of reformers—those who wanted to remove vagrant children from almshouses and those upset about juvenile crime. Second, he revived the discredited Quaker-Beccarian reform agenda and offered the refuge clientele to frustrated reformers as a new and more promising field of endeavor. Finally, he gave a philosophical justification, based on the idea of prevention, for civil intervention unrestrained by common law into the lives of children.[11] In brief, the idea of prevention, focused on the not-yet criminal child, forged a conceptual link between deprivation and criminality and a political link between benevolent reformers and crusaders against crime.

The new ideology was a success, not only in New York but in Philadelphia as well. In place of the previous plans for bifurcated custodial institutions for vagrants and postprison delinquents, an 1826 resolution of the Society for Alleviating the Miseries of Public

11. The crucial importance of this extraordinary authority to the identity of the refuges is further attested to by Pierce's (1869, 34) summary of Mayor Cadwallader Colden's testimonial: "European institutions had been constructed for young criminals, but no one had secured the power from the state of withdrawing, from the custody of weak or criminal parents, children who were vagabonds in the streets and in peril of a criminal life, although no overt act had been committed. The mayor well remarks, 'Deprived of this power, the institution would lose much of its influence.' "

Prisons called for the establishment of a single house of refuge for both vagrant and criminal children. The resolution is notable, when compared with the resolution of 1824, for its emphasis on rehabilitation and prevention:

> This meeting, being duly impressed with the importance of the employment of means not only for the prevention of vice, but for rescuing those especially in their tender years, who have, through the influence of various temptations, committed offenses, whereby they have become objects of legal correction by confinement in prisons, where association with accomplished and hardened offenders too often confirms their depraved dispositions and enlarges their knowledge of crime; and, whereas, experience has shown that much benefit has resulted to individuals and to society from establishments devoted to the safe keeping and moral improvement of juvenile offenders.
>
> Therefore, resolved: That it is expedient and necessary to organize in or near the city of Philadelphia, an institution to be called "The House of Refuge for Juvenile Offenders." (quoted in Teeters 1960, 169)

The refuge reformers thus had an effective ideology that would see the project off to a successful start. The ideological foundation was of the sort that the previous typology would predict: a combination of moralistic sentiment and Enlightenment environmentalism, appropriated to serve an essentially conservative reform position. When all was said and done, the preventive program borne in the minds of the refuge sponsors could be boiled down to one simple term: control. Recall that Griscom, chief ideologue of the movement, disapproved of Pestalozzian methods of education (Hawes 1971, 32); he and most of the community adhered to a simplified version of Lockeianism and expected the plastic child to be reformed by expert guidance and a regime of "knowledge, religion, and work" (Pickett 1969, 108).

The reformers of the Society for the Reformation of Juvenile Delinquents and of the Society for Alleviating the Miseries of Public Prisons were given active management positions under the laws establishing the New York and Philadelphia refuges, and their priorities were generally shared by the board that managed the Boston

House of Reformation. They all brought to their positions the conviction that discipline and respect for authority were of supreme
importance both for the child and for society itself; they felt that the
child could suffer from a lack of discipline, but never from too much
(Rothman 1971, 216–221). At the same time they idealized the
family and sought to replicate it within the institution. The refuge
was designed in part to teach the family to be a citadel against vice;
its severity was "a rebuke and an example to the lax family. The
problem was that parents were too lenient, not that the refuge . . .
[was] too strict" (Rothman 1971, 236). At last, through the legislation establishing the institutions, refuge managers had the power of
the family as well.

Organizing an Institutional System

The statutes that established the houses of refuge gave institutional managers unprecedented power to take custody of a wide
range of problem youths, commit them without a trial, and maintain
surveillance over them until they became adults. The laws did not,
however, contain any provision for funding. Even in the case of the
Boston House of Reformation, which was run by the city council,
the enabling law merely authorized, but did not require, the maintenance of a refuge. The reformers' ambitions went beyond their private means, however, and the refuges became a political issue as the
managers sought a secure source of public support.

The managers were in an ambivalent position in their attempts to
establish the institutions' legitimacy. Of necessity they had to differ-
entiate the refuges from both schools and prisons:

> On the one hand, [the managers] longed to boast of the institution's
> originality so that it would attract world-wide philanthropic interest; on
> the other, they were afraid of antagonizing a local constituency into
> thinking that the facility would coddle confirmed juvenile lawbreakers.
> (Schlossman 1974, 124)

These somewhat antithetical goals may be thought of as ordered tasks that the organizations had to fulfill even to begin functioning: first, finances had to be arranged, land acquired, and buildings built; second, an internal regime had to be established that would faithfully embody the reformative ideology. Because the long-range goal included not just public support for the first refuges but their adoption throughout the country, the two tasks were interdependent: political legitimacy required a demonstration of extraordinary rehabilitative success, and, conversely, rehabilitative success required funding that depended on political legitimacy.

The New York refuge's struggle for support is the most interesting of the three cases. Its history shows the absolute indispensability of the sponsorship and political acumen of the patrician managers of the Society for the Reformation of Juvenile Delinquents. Pickett (1969, ch. 3) recounts their efforts in detail; here it will suffice to touch only on those points that will help define the institution's political position.

The New York refuge managers devoted nearly as much effort to lobbying in the first few years as they did to actually supervising the institution (Pickett 1969, 124). In this endeavor the younger, more politically ambitious members were more valuable than the old-time reformers. Their first success, resulting from a deal made by Mayor Allen and Congressman Colden, was a land swap between federal and city governments that resulted in a net donation to the society and the sale of some unused armory buildings that would house the refuge. However, a further attempt to get the state legislature to underwrite the refuge on an ongoing basis was not successful (Pickett 1969, 53–54; Hawes 1971, 39–40).

Instead, the reformers ingeniously drew on their ideology to gain access to special sources of support. Delinquency and pauperism, they reasoned, are caused by vice; therefore why not let vice support the refuges? They sought and received shares of amusement taxes on theaters and circuses (Hawes 1971, 40), liquor taxes, and poor relief and educational funds (Pickett 1969, 120, 134). Because immigration, especially of Irish paupers, was believed to be a cause of delinquency, a portion of the immigrant head tax was committed to the refuge (Mennel 1973, 15). Thus the managers had achieved a double victory: they "could continue to entertain a theory of moral development focused upon external elements such as liquor and plays and receive substantial revenues from them as well" (Pickett 1969, 120).

The first regular support came in the more settled political climate of 1825. Once again through the efforts of Colden, who was now a state senator, a bill that guaranteed the refuge a minimum level of operating expenses was passed (Pickett 1969, 62–63). The refuge had made the transition from a private to a publicly supported institution.

The opening of the Philadelphia refuge was delayed largely because of the difficulty of getting funds. Reformers there hesitated to seek public support partly because the expensive Eastern Penitentiary was still under construction. How support was gained is not entirely clear. Some impetus was added by a group of "militant Quaker women" (Pickett 1969, 99) from the Society of Women Friends (Teeters 1960, 168) who offered their support for the refuge. A public meeting was held, and a resolution in favor of the refuge was passed. The original plan was to house the refuge in a cell set aside for imprisoned debtors next to the Walnut Street jail. Both refuge board members and jail inspectors agreed that this was an unsatisfactory plan, and the inspectors offered their aid in securing funds from the legislature. Whatever the decisive factor—perhaps the authorities were emboldened by the previous example of New York—a lump sum from the state and an annual stipend from the Philadelphia city commissioners were eventually secured (Pickett 1969, 169–171).

The most important consequence of this quest for public funding, especially in the case of the New York refuge, is that it demanded an emphasis on control and internal security equal to that placed on the institutions' reformatory capabilities (Schlossman 1974, 125–126). One result of this was that the managers' plans for indenturing promising inmates to outside employers, which they touted as the key to the whole reformative process, received less attention than recurrent efforts to make the institutions escape-proof. It also confirmed the managers in their predisposition to institute a severe internal regime (Pickett 1969, 124–127).

There is no need to detail here the refuge programs that the managers set up.[12] It will suffice to observe that in formal structure all three refuges were similar: they were to be characterized by labor, discipline, moral education, classification of inmates, routine, and plain food. It is more important to describe the men who were hired to run the institutions day-to-day, for it was in their choice of personnel that the refuge managers brought the latent conflict over the institutions' identities out into the open.

The salient facts are simple. The first superintendents of all three refuges were professional educators, all were students of European educational reform, and all were at least nominal Pestalozzians. It was through their agency that Romantic child-rearing ideas found their way inside the refuge walls (McKelvey 1936, 14–15; Teeters 1960, 166; Mennel 1973, 24–27). Of the three the most establishmentarian and least subversive was probably Joseph Curtis, superintendent of the New York refuge. He was a convert to Quakerism, like the managers he was affiliated with most of the philanthropic organizations in New York City, and he was a student of Beccaria as well as Pestalozzi. He took his post with every intention of treating his charges kindly. Perhaps he was too much of a middle roader to make a consistent attempt to implement his principles; in any event, soon after he assumed his position, he encountered a series of problems with recalcitrant boys, from vandalism to escapes. When corporal punishment had no impact, some measures of self-government were introduced through which the inmates would hear each others' cases and mete out punishment. But on the whole, Curtis's administration was characterized by radical oscillations between appeals to

12. Accounts of life inside the refuges are presented in Hawes (1971, 47–55), Pickett (1969, ch. 4, 5), Rothman (1971, 223–236), and Mennel (1973, 18–25).

the inmates' better natures and increasingly severe punishment (Pickett 1969, 68).

The first superintendent of the Philadelphia refuge left after only a month for unknown reasons. He was succeeded by Dr. John Keagy, who was both an educator and a physician. Keagy was a friend of Bronson Alcott and corresponded with him on Pestalozzian methods. He, like Curtis, found it necessary from time to time to apply severe punishments, but he does not appear to have felt Curtis's inner turmoil: "While he espoused the Pestalozzi school of educational philosophy, he found it easy to concur with the Board in advocating the use of the 'cat' as a disciplinary persuader" (Teeters 1960, 172).

The most interesting of the refuge superintendents, and the most true to the Romantic type, was E. M. P. Wells of the Boston House of Reformation. He was different from Curtis and Keagy in that he had a more comprehensive and less ambivalent vision of humane reformation. In his eyes the refuge was a potential utopian society. Wells instituted measures of inmate self-government at the outset, but not out of desperation, as Curtis had done (Pickett 1969, 89–91). He established the most elaborate classification system of all the refuges; it was unique in having positive steps, where extra privileges were awarded, as well as the customary levels of negative sanctions. Wells's most radical move was to limit corporal punishment for each inmate to an initial two-week probationary period (Hawes 1971, 53). So remarkable was Wells's program, and so apparently successful, that Beaumont and Tocqueville (1964, 148–149) singled it out for special praise. With great insight, however, they also found its flaw: it was not transferable; it depended too much on Wells's personal gifts. As they predicted, it would be succeeded by a more mundane, but managerially sound, system.

The role of Curtis, Keagy, and Wells must not be misunderstood. They were not subversives in the refuge world; they were not Thoreaus, nor Byrons, nor even Alcotts. They were all in varying degrees committed to the idea of institutional humanitarian reform. Even

Wells, the most consistently visionary of the three, would be considered a tough disciplinarian today; his ideal of the refuge as a small utopia is at least formally compatible with the managers' aim of replicating the family's social control functions. Yet they were chosen by the managers to embody the rehabilitative side of the refuges' proposed functions, and what they brought to the institutions was an emphasis that reflected that aspect: "they were humane men, more interested in developing each child's individual capacities and talents through programs emphasizing self-government and education than in compelling children to follow an inflexible workshop routine" (Mennel 1973, 25). The conflict that ensued in each case between superintendents and managers exemplified the structural contradictions of the institutions themselves.

Conflict

In their attempts to work out an approximation of a Pestalozzian approach to reformatory education, the three superintendents ran head-on into the more fundamental and compelling demands of the managers that the refuges be exemplars of order. Each superintendent was forced to leave—Curtis and Keagy after about a year, and Wells after eight years. A review of the precipitating events and results of their departures is the last stage of this discussion.

The first factor contributing to Curtis's dismissal was, ironically, the managers' success in wresting support for the refuge from the New York legislature. This success had two long-range effects. First, it freed the managers to turn their attention from lobbying to the institution itself; second, it increased the refuge's visibility. The managers, expecting the long string of visitors that were soon to arrive, began to insist that the refuge's internal functioning be brought into line with public pronouncements (Pickett 1969, 81).

The ostensible cause of the ensuing power struggle between Curtis and the managers was the escapes that had plagued the refuge almost since it opened. Curtis responded to the escapes with typical ambivalence. On the one hand, he instituted more severe punishments within the institution; on the other hand, he maintained his policy of not punishing escapees who returned voluntarily. After a series of skirmishes throughout the spring of 1826, Curtis refused the managers' demand that he punish an escapee, and they forced him to resign. To Curtis the issue was not just escapes, but control over running the institution and determining its policies in the long run. He felt that he had tried to institute a humane system of reformation but had been thwarted by the managers' insistence on punishment and labor; he maintained that an educational institution could not be run like a prison or factory (Pickett 1969, 73–75, 82–83; Mennel 1973, 25; Teeters 1960, 66). Pierce's history of the refuge presents a delicate summary of Curtis's difficulties from a management perspective:

> While [he was] inimitable in his power to win the affections of the young, and overflowing with paternal goodness toward the sad, misguided youths sent to his institution, others might excel him in managing the multifarious details of such an establishment, and even in the administration of discipline. (Pierce 1869, 77)

Unfortunately, little is known about John Keagy's departure from the Philadelphia refuge. Teeters's history mentions, first, that he served only a year (Teeters 1960, 172), but does not mention why he left. Second, it is noted that in his early years the refuge had problems of order, including "escapes, incipient riots," and "at least three fires . . . set by the children" (Teeters 1960, 183). The escapes alone may have cost Keagy his job, even though he had none of Curtis's scruples about punishing inmates. It is also possible that he realized at the very beginning that the refuge was not a practical place in which to employ Pestalozzian ideals. Unlike the other refuges, the Philadelphia institution occupied a new, specially designed building that could not be mistaken for anything other than a prison. Both the Boston and New York buildings lacked workshop facilities at first, which gave Wells and Curtis early leeway to set up their own systems

(Mennel 1973, 25). Perhaps Keagy was simply presented with a *fait accompli*.

It is an interesting question why Wells, who was the most consistently idealistic of all the superintendents, should have lasted so much longer than Curtis and Keagy. Several answers may be suggested. First, the refuge in Boston was directed by a committee appointed by the Common Council rather than a voluntary association. It is conceivable that these public officials lacked the ideological fervor and will that propelled the New York and Philadelphia groups and were thus less able to mobilize an attack on Wells. Second, because Boston already enjoyed a wealth of various kinds of child-care institutions, the refuge was intended mainly for juveniles convicted of criminal offenses, even though it was not restricted to them by law. It does not necessarily follow, however, that this would incline the overseers to be tolerant of Wells's methods. A third factor, and probably of somewhat greater importance, is that Wells and his methods were enthusiastically supported by Louis Dwight, the guiding influence of the Prison Discipline Society. That the dour, conservative Dwight would approve of Wells's positive discipline is somewhat of an anomaly, but it is worthy of note that Dwight prophetically urged Wells to be more diligent in his surveillance of the inmates (Pickett 1969, 92). In the end, however, the consistency of Wells's formal administration probably accounted for his longevity, regardless of its content. Even from the directors' social control perspective, it seems to have worked (Pickett 1969, 89).

When the end came for Wells, however, it came as a decisive political rebuke not only of the public face of the refuge, but of the most cherished and fundamental aspects of his educational methods. Most of the directors viewed Wells favorably, but one of them attacked him, saying he knew no more about running an institution than "your horse." On this director's prompting, the Common Council began an investigation through which years of simmering antagonisms rose to the surface (Mennel 1973, 25–26). Officially, the investigators' report criticized Wells for stressing academic and recreational education at the expense of labor. They maintained that this had produced boys with an excess of spirit and a lack of obedience and docility. But beneath this official conclusion lay two more practical complaints. First, an educational regime did not pay for itself as a workhouse program would. Second, Wells himself was too much the typical Romantic reformer: he was self-righteous and scornful of the politicians' attempts to tamper with his experimental utopia. He resigned in protest and devoted himself to private reform schools and the antislavery movement (Pickett 1969, 92–93).

Wells's departure signified the end of the Romantic influence in the refuge movement and accelerated the shift in emphasis from humane treatment to coercion:

> Pestalozzi's heritage to American children—the reduction of physical punishment in common schools—left little impression on the houses of refuge and later reform schools. . . . In the romantic tradition, Curtis and Wells believed that the essence of juvenile reformation lay in the cultivation of a child's essentially good qualities and sentiments. Refuge managers, on the other hand, saw children as blank tablets upon whom parents and acquaintances had already made enough unfavorable impressions to lead the children into the institution. What these youths needed, the managers argued, was an inflexible routine built around the workshop and the schoolroom, impressing them with the importance of personal cleanliness, sobriety, frugality, and industry. Punishment would be the invariable result of rule violations. In this scheme, pious and orderly conduct by an individual child signified the success of reformatory methods; good behavior meant everything, noble thoughts little. (Mennel 1973, 26–27)

The changes made by the institutions' managers at this juncture signify the triumph of organizational rationality and of the compromise Calvinist-Enlightenment ideology. In Boston a number of new and presumably more amenable directors were appointed; they straightaway assured the Common Council that they had "no disposition to convert the House of Reformation into a boarding-school, to be supported at the expense of the city. They do not forget that its inmates are offenders against the good order of society, and are sent there for restraint and punishment not less than for reformation and instruction" (quoted in Mennel 1973, 26). After a period of reflection following Curtis's resignation, the New York managers appointed as superintendent Nathaniel Hart—a "tough-minded administrator and a thorough disciplinarian" (Pickett 1969, 84).

This outcome was not a simple triumph of cruelty over kindness or of repression over freedom. We fall prey to Wells's own delusion if we mistake his paternalistic benevolence for liberalism. Rather, it was a triumph of system over charisma[13] and a triumph also of the Calvinist family ideal. The managers wanted an orderly institution that maintained its own legitimacy and paid its own bills. Curtis and Wells were actors in the dialectical routinization of treatment into a regime of administration and custody.

The new superintendent in New York was said to be "of an organizing mind" (Pierce 1869, 122); hence he was ideal. Hart established a code of regulations, assigned duties to officers, and set up a timetable and formal code of discipline. His system was efficient, severe, and totally transferable. Hart's successor subsequently assumed routine administration with hardly a ripple. "Far less talented personally than Wells, Hart and his successors subordinated imagination to system and got consistent results" (Pickett 1969, 92). In time, control over the institutions passed from the original tight-knit group of private citizens to absentee correctional officials and state bureaucrats (Pickett 1969, 182). The institutionalization of the houses of refuge, and of a pattern of legal domination over children, had been achieved.

---

13. "Altogether too much of a human being, Curtis' inconsistent loving and thrashing of his children had made the more orderly souls of the society restive. They wanted system and Curtis seemed wholly unsystematic" (Pickett 1969, 85). "Not that the Boston house of refuge does not appear to be admirably conducted, and superior to both the others, but its success seems to us less the effect of the system itself, than that of the distinguished man who puts it into practice" (Beaumont and Tocqueville 1964, 148).

Conclusion

Applying the typology of reform impulses previously developed to the histories of the early houses of refuge brings out three salient points. First, Calvinist-inspired, conservative reform organizations in the 1820s sought to establish institutions through which they could reestablish a controlling grasp on the social order. The refuges, initially proposed only as an alternative placement to prisons and almshouses, represented a rationalization and specification of that control impulse. Second, adaptation of Enlightenment notions of environmentalism and prevention provided an affirmative and broadly legitimate rationale for the extension of social control mechanisms beyond the bounds traditionally permitted by law. The installation of Romantically inspired educators to supervise the institutions added credibility to their claims of moral education. All concerned were united for a time in the desire to establish an exemplary model of child raising, but the specific content of that model was a source of disagreement. Third, the underlying conflicts of method emerged when it became clear that the managers' desires for security, consistency, and political legitimacy were not compatible with the superintendents' relatively idealistic approach to administration. The superintendents, lacking both an inclination to compromise and a political base from which to negotiate, were forced to retreat.

A cautionary note must be attached to this interpretation. I do not mean to suggest that ideas made refuge history. On the contrary, a major point of the chapter has been that Calvinist theories of child rearing had to be adapted and compromised by their proponents before they could provide the dominant philosophy of refuge management. Refuge development was not the result of the inexorable development of an idea; rather, it emerged from the interaction of groups that, from their strategically different positions, perceived the problem of juvenile deviance differently and acted on the logic of their perceptions. The dynamic nature of the larger society brought them together briefly, and the conflicts of that society drove them apart. Specifically, Calvinism alone did not create the refuges, but Calvinist-inspired interests, threatened and abetted by Locke and Pestalozzi. The refuges did not develop as they did in spite of Wells and Curtis, but in large part because of them.

3

The Diffusion of
Moral Institutions

Subsequent juvenile justice reformers disclaimed the refuges like a disreputable ancestor. Nonetheless, throughout the nineteenth century the basic reform ideology remained much the same as it had been in the 1820s. Reformers sought to convince the nation that the family was the cradle of crime, that the child was a capable and worthy object of rehabilitation, and that early intervention was the key to preventing more serious deviance. And despite occasional changes in organization and architecture, the goal of juvenile institutions remained the same—to achieve a more perfect imitation of the family and eliminate all connotations of the prison (see Hart 1910, 14–19). Most important to this study, reformers in this period sought and achieved legislative sanction to pursue the goals of prevention and rehabilitation. Building on the model established by the refuges, the later reformatories and industrial schools thoroughly changed the legal status of children through-out the United States by the end of the nineteenth century.

In this chapter I explore the process by which the states adopted those legal changes that imposed formal distinctions between children and adults under the law: child criminals were differentiated from adult criminals, both by definition and treatment, and a differentiated institutional system was established and elaborated for their maintenance. Some states adopted these innovations more eagerly than others, but eventually all converged on a remarkably consistent pattern of reforms. Thus it will be possible to describe the reform process in comparative terms, using quantitative indicators, and to develop multivariate models of adoption rates across states.

The analysis presented here reflects critically upon an evolutionary systems model of legal change. Such a model offers two general predictions: first, that law will tend increasingly to be characterized by formally rational rules designed to constrain official discretion in the treatment of offenders and, second, that the structural differentiation of the institutional system will proceed farthest and fastest in states with relatively more complex socioeconomic structures. I addressed the first of these predictions in Chapter 2, where I showed that the intended effect of refuge legislation was to *increase* official discretion. The charter, structure, and procedures of the refuges did not arise from the general expansion of the rule of law or from the technically rational application of a valid theory of deviance. Rather, they were the outcomes of ideological conflict and political negotiation among competing groups within the refuge movement itself. The second prediction remains to be tested.

The analysis complicates the basic evolutionist account in three ways. First, I offer an argument about the sequence of reform. Using graphic data-analytic techniques, I show that the creation of a reformatory was a necessary precondition for the legal redefinition of juvenile deviance in each state. This means, in broad terms, that the legal concept of delinquency does not exist apart from a policy of reformatory treatment; I argue that, indeed, delinquency was invented to justify the incarceration of children. Second, through the use of multivariate dynamic models of the adoption of reformatory legislation, I show that the reformatory was a politically contingent phenomenon, not a straightforward product of systemic imperatives. Indicators of socioeconomic modernization provide a foundation for the analysis, and models are elaborated to explore institutional factors as well. Finally, I estimate more comprehensive models in which the interrelationships of social-structural factors, reformatory diffusion, and changes in children's legal status are summarized in formal terms.

Institutions and Legal Innovation

From about 1850 to the end of the century, state legislatures throughout most of the United States enacted a package of three fairly specific legal reforms aimed at children. Taken together, these reforms faithfully embodied the ideology of the refuge reformers by identifying new categories of deviance applicable to children and by sanctioning increased official control over their behavior. The first and most straightforward of these was the designation of specialized penal institutions for juveniles. The second was the extension of legal jurisdiction over noncriminal juvenile deviants, and the third was the explicit denial of due process rights to children as a prerequisite for incarceration. In this section I first describe the specific language of these enactments; then I explore their temporal interrelationships. I argue not only that the reformatory provided an ideological center of gravity for the other innovations, but—based on evidence about the sequence of reform enactments—that it served as a necessary cause for them as well.

The Legal Implications of the Reformatory

The first innovation of interest here is legislative authorization for the commitment of children in institutions separate from adults.

Usually, this meant simply that the state built a reform school, but not in all cases. In New York, Pennsylvania, and Massachusetts, for example, state legislatures initially gave only an official charter to houses of refuge founded by local voluntary associations, with no initial financial involvement (see, e.g., 1824 New York *Laws,* ch. 126). In Wyoming local agencies were authorized to send delinquents to reformatories in other states (1884 Wyoming *Laws,* ch. 53). These enactments all implied at least some outlay of public funds—the houses of refuge received most of their operating expenses from their respective states or cities (Pickett 1969; Mennel 1973), and the Wyoming law authorized the reimbursement of states receiving delinquents. In all cases, however, the important point is not expenditures of funds, but the creation of a policy of separate treatment for children.

The second innovation is the extension of official jurisdiction over children not accused of criminal acts. This includes both "incorrigible" or "beyond control" juveniles (i.e., status offenders) and neglected (or abused or abandoned) children. The distinction between the two types of offenders was salient, though often troublesome, to reformers because it implied differing levels of moral learning and culpability. Thus although the statutory language tends to be fuzzy, I have coded the two areas of jurisdiction separately by distinguishing between two types of moral attributions: where a statute authorizes commitment of a child for behavior that is not criminal for adults and no attribution of parental responsibility is expressly stated, incorrigibility jurisdiction is coded; where commitment is authorized for reasons mentioned in the statute that are attributable to parents, neglect jurisdiction is coded. An example is offered by an 1835 amendment to the Pennsylvania law that originally chartered the Philadelphia House of Refuge. The act first authorizes commitment of any child who "by reason of incorrigible or vicious conduct . . . has rendered his or her control beyond the power" of parents or guardians. Second, commitment is recommended also for children whose "incorrigible and vicious conduct" is due to the "moral deprav-

ity or otherwise of the parent" or whose parent is "incapable or
unwilling to exercise the proper care and discipline" over the child
(1835 Pennsylvania *Laws*, ch. 92, §1). For the purposes of this
study, the former is considered to be incorrigibility and the latter
neglect.

The final important innovation occurred when states permitted
commitment of juveniles after only summary or informal hearings.
Here the decisive issue is whether the statute distinguishes clearly
between the procedural standards applicable to adults and those available to children. In some cases this is quite clear: in Connecticut, for
example, parents could "indenture" their children to the state reform
school without any formal legal proceedings whatever (1859 Connecticut *Laws*, ch. 79, §1). In other cases terms that usually connote civil
rather than criminal procedures are used. In Illinois after 1863, when
a child was arrested, parents were issued an order to "appear . . . and
show cause" why the child should not be committed (1863 Illinois
Private Laws, ch. 14, §8). A Delaware law authorized commitment
on "complaint and due proof" of delinquency, incorrigibility, or
neglect (1883 Delaware *Laws*, ch. 495, §5).[1]

It is not my point to suggest that these finely worded distinctions
signify sweeping practical changes in the conduct of juvenile hearings. Historical accounts show clearly that in many jurisdictions children, like adult vagrants and misdemeanants, were treated summarily
in lower courts even before legislation of this sort was passed. What
is important here is that these laws transformed routine discretion
into formal policy. By institutionalizing a procedural distinction between adults and children, they laid a foundation for future legisla-

---

1. A "show cause order" is one issued as part of an injunction in a civil case; it
notifies the defendant of an opportunity to give reasons why the injunction should not
be carried out. It implies a reversal of the burden of proof from that normally required
for a criminal case, whether felony or misdemeanor. "Due proof" implies a standard of
evidence inferior to proof "beyond a reasonable doubt," likewise standard in criminal
cases. See *Black's Law Dictionary* under headings "show cause order," "due proof," and
"standards of proof."

tion (such as the juvenile court) and set parameters for subsequent case law.[2]

In the following discussion I use graphic data-analytic techniques to explore the temporal relationships between the adoption of reformatory institutions and the legal innovations just described. I am concerned with two issues: First, how tightly associated are the two kinds of events over time and across states? Second, in what order did these reforms occur? The data show that the reformatory is not only closely bound to other changes in the legal status of children, but in fact served as the precondition for the wholesale redefinition of juvenile deviance.

The Dynamics of Innovation

Figure 1 is a residual display that shows the relationship between the establishment of reformatories and the passage of incorrigibility legislation in all fifty states. The horizontal axis is time in years, and the vertical axis is the number of states with reformatories. States are placed from bottom to top in the order in which they adopted reformatory legislation. The year of adoption is indicated by the small circles (a line connecting these circles would form a cumulative frequency polygon), and the passage of incorrigibility legislation is indicated by the short vertical bars. Horizontal lines connecting the circles and bars represent temporal lags between the passage of reformatory and incorrigibility laws; where the bars intersect the circles,

2. It is conceivable, for example, that the watershed *ex parte Crouse* case of 1839 (4 Whart. 9) would not have been decided as it was without the previously discussed 1835 Pennsylvania law. *Crouse* introduced the doctrine of *parens patriae* into American jurisprudence and officially declared the Philadelphia House of Refuge to be a school rather than a prison, hence not subject to procedural constraints. This decision was probably made easier by the statute, which not only prescribed summary hearings but also formally recognized a class of juvenile deviants diagnostically distinct from adult criminals.

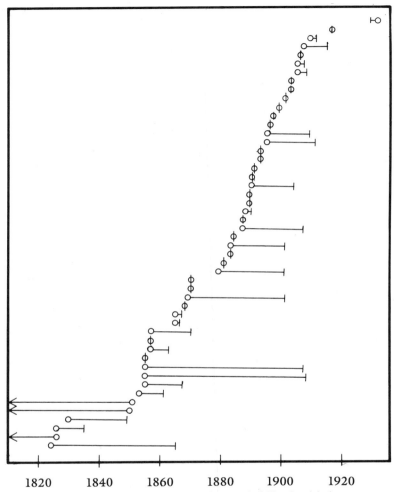

Figure 1. Residual Plot: Institution and Incorrigibility Legislation

the two reforms were simultaneous. Lines terminating in arrows indicate lags that exceed the scale of the diagram.

The first point to be made about Figure 1 is that the two reforms appear closely associated in time. The simple correlation between the timing of reformatories and incorrigibility laws across all states is .60. This figure is spuriously low, however, because it includes the three New England states that enacted "stubborn child" laws in the seventeenth century (see Chapter 1) and maintained them into the early national period (these cases appear toward the bottom of the figure, with arrows to the left).[3] Although these laws are in some sense prototypical incorrigibility statutes, for the purpose of this analysis they are deviant cases. When they are removed from the sample, the correlation becomes .84. But the sequencing of these reforms is more important than their statistical association. Note that the three New England states are the only ones to expand jurisdiction to include incorrigible children before establishing a specialized juvenile institution. In about half of the states the two enactments were simultaneous, and in the rest the institution preceded the jurisdictional change. The mean lag time from institution to jurisdiction when the New England states are removed is 7.0 years, with a standard deviation of 12.9 years. The reformatory institution appears, then, as a necessary and almost sufficient condition for the extension of jurisdiction over incorrigible juveniles.

Figure 2 shows the relative timing of institutions and neglect statutes. The simple correlation between the two reforms is .83 for all states. Only two states created neglect jurisdiction before establishing reformatories; in the rest either the enactments were simultaneous or neglect jurisdiction followed the institution. Again, the institution appears as a necessary condition for the expansion of jurisdiction; however, the relationship is not as close as that shown in Figure 1. Here the mean lag time is 12.7 years, nearly twice that for

3. Rhode Island eliminated its stubborn child law in a colonial code revision. I have been unable to locate the exact date, but there was no such law in the first collection of state statutes.

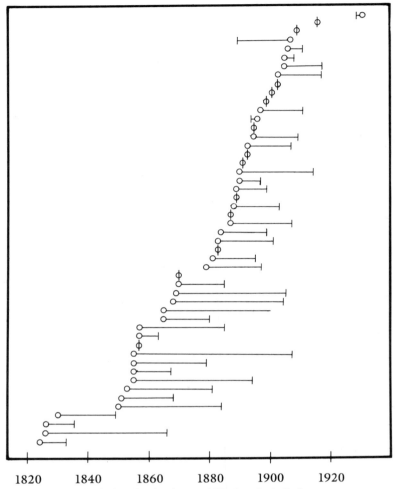

Figure 2. Residual Plot: Institution and Neglect Jurisdiction

incorrigibility, and the lag standard deviation is 15.2 years. This suggests that neglected children were not considered as central to the mission of the reformatories as were incorrigibles.[4]

Finally, the functional relationship of institutions to informal commitments, shown in Figure 3, again appears to be that of a necessary but not sufficient condition. The timing of the reforms correlates at .79, and the mean lag is 9.2 years. Here the relationship appears to be looser than in either of the other two models; indeed, the lag standard deviation is 16.8 years. Also, there are a few more conspicuous deviant cases: two states made no provision for informal commitments until after 1940.

Examination of these lag models to this point supports the most fundamental issue of this analysis: in almost all cases legal innovations were preceded by institutional differentiation. Beyond this, however, two more important observations can be made. First, the residuals in Figures 1–3 are not evenly distributed over time. The later a state authorized separate reformatory commitments, the more likely it is to have made the associated jurisdictional and procedural changes either simultaneously or very shortly thereafter. This pattern appears with less clarity for neglect jurisdiction but is nonetheless discernible. Thus these figures provide graphic portrayals of combined processes of organizational diffusion and institutionalization: as more states adopted reformatory discipline, collateral legal changes appeared as constitutive components of the institution. As the reformatory organization became accepted as the normative means of response to juvenile deviance, its power to redefine that deviance grew accordingly.

Another observation can be made by examining the end points of

4. Dependent and neglected children have always been somewhat of a problem clientele for the juvenile justice system. They appear as victims rather than perpetrators of criminal acts; nonetheless, in the ideology of the refuge reformers and the later child savers, they were proto-delinquents in need of reformative treatment. In many cities in the nineteenth century, charitable organizations sought to care for neglected and orphaned children in competition with the refuges (Mennel 1973, 13). More recently some states have exempted neglect cases from the treatment accorded less sympathetic varieties of juvenile deviants, often creating a special code section for child protection proceedings (see, e.g., 1976 California *Statutes,* ch. 1068).

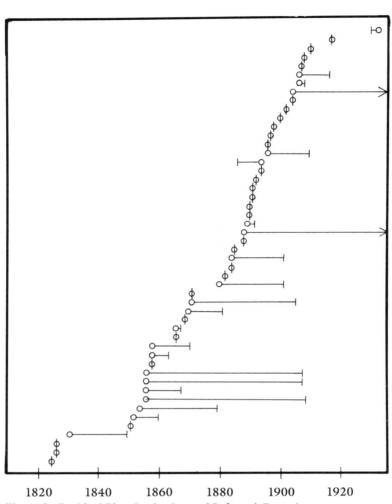

Figure 3. Residual Plot: Institution and Informal Commitment

the lag lines in Figures 1–3. In a substantial number of cases where incorrigibility, neglect, or informal commitment provisions were not made at the same time that institutions were established, they were made instead some time shortly after 1900. (Again this is most obvious in Figures 1 and 3; the lag for neglect is distributed in a more nearly random fashion.) This was the period in which the juvenile court movement was spreading most rapidly among the states. The first such court was established in Illinois in 1899; twenty-five states had juvenile courts of some sort by 1908, and courts had spread to thirty-five states by 1911.[5] It appears, then, that some states maintained a more frankly legalistic and penal ideology of juvenile crime, despite their adoption of reformatories. For these resistant states the juvenile court movement provided the occasion to update the machinery of therapeutic justice.

These findings indicate that the reformatory was a crucial interven-ing variable in redefining children's legal status in the nineteenth century. But is this a real or spurious relationship? One might argue, for example, that the reformatory did not cause the legal changes with which it is associated and suggest instead that both phenomena are by-products of some more general social process through which the status of children was defined. Three types of evidence have been offered in support of the causal ordering proposed here. First, the extension of jurisdiction over noncriminal juveniles and provisions for informal commitment show clear ideological continuity with the goals of institutional reformers. Sources reviewed in Chapter 2 show that reformers sought to increase the impact of their preventive ef-forts by intervening as early as possible in the child's delinquent career and by minimizing the legal obstacles to control. Second, statutory changes that expanded the legal liability of children and decreased their procedural rights show a close temporal association with the establishment of reformatories across all states. In almost all cases reformatories either preceded or were established simulta-

5. These counts are from data collected for this study. See Chapter 5.

neously with the extension of jurisdiction and informal commitments. The third type of evidence is legislative intent. Legislators, like reformers, apparently viewed these legal changes as aspects of the institutional reform agenda. In almost every case where the reformatory preceded a given legal change, the legal change was enacted as an amendment to a previous statute establishing the reformatory.[6] In cases where the two innovations occurred in the same year, provisions for expanded jurisdiction and informal commitment were included as parts of statutes establishing reformatories, in sections defining the authority of institutional officials. Taken together, these findings suggest that reformatory institutions, as they spread among the states, redefined children's legal status. The question that arises now is what factors drove the diffusion of the reformatory.

The Process of Diffusion

Diffusion processes, like many phenomena of sociological interest, unfold over time in complex ways: in a sample of political units such as nations, states, or cities, some will adopt a reform before others, and some may never adopt it at all. Over a given historical period, exogenous factors may change in unexpected ways that alter underlying causal relationships and shift the course of the diffusion process. Diffusion studies using cross-sectional research designs—such as regression models in which rank ordering or time to adoption is the dependent variable, and independent variables are keyed to a single baseline date—must by necessity ignore or assume away much of this complexity. In this analysis information on the timing of state reform legislation is treated as explicitly dynamic event-history data. Like regression techniques, event-history methods permit the estimation

6. The few exceptions are among those states in which jurisdictional and procedural changes occurred between 1900 and 1920. In these cases juvenile court and reformatory laws tended to overlap in time, and procedural reforms were enacted as part of court legislation. Even so, it is fair to say that the reformatory was causally prior because (as I discuss in Chapters 4 and 5) the juvenile court was in large part an extension of the nineteenth-century reformatory program.

of multivariate models. The advantages of dynamic models over static models are that they rely on more realistic assumptions and make the most thorough use of available information.

A more detailed discussion of the methods used here is presented in Appendix A. For now it will be useful to highlight two points that will be important in interpreting the models. The first concerns the dependent variable: event-histories record the nature and timing of qualitative changes that occur in the sample—in this case the enactment of reformatory legislation. The dependent variable is the rate of change in the probability of adopting a reform. This rate is not observed directly, but rather calculated across all states and over every year in the sample. A second and related point is that dynamic techniques yield estimates of variation not only across cases, but also over time. Thus it will be possible to look for accelerative and decelerative trends in adoption rates and to explore whether these trends are more pronounced in some states than in others. Beyond these major caveats, models may be read in a fashion very similar to multiple regression models. Parameters are presented in such a form that values over 1.0 indicate a positive association and parameters below 1.0, a negative association. Statistical tests are straightforward: F-tests apply to partial relationships, and X^2 is used to evaluate nested models and the overall significance of single models.

Each analysis is limited to a specified time period. In this chapter I restrict my focus to the diffusion of reformatory legislation between 1850 and 1910. This restricted scope allows me to take advantage of a broad selection of independent variables measured consistently over time while still capturing almost all of the diffusion process. The four states that established houses of refuge between 1824 and 1830 are included in the sample, but the only information that appears in the analysis is that they had already made the relevant transition before 1850.[7] In effect this choice of dates partitions the dynamics of

7. In more technical terms their score on the reformatory variable is 2 for every year. The four states treated in this way are New York, Pennsylvania, and Massachusetts, plus Maryland, where a refuge law was passed in 1830, but no institution was built until the 1850s.

extreme early innovation from the more general diffusion process; this seems acceptable on both substantive and methodological grounds.

A potentially more serious limitation is that the sample for this analysis includes only those thirty-one states that were admitted to the Union by 1850. This is because there are not enough data on independent variables for the other fifteen admitted by 1910. Strictly speaking, therefore, inferences must be limited to the original thirty-one cases. If this omission creates any bias, however, that bias runs against the institutional argument offered here, not in its favor. The data show that late-admitted states—which were generally western and relatively rural—were quite receptive to reformatories and tended to found institutions very shortly before or after being admitted to statehood. The temporal association between statehood and passage of reformatory laws, moreover, appears to grow closer over time. More impressionistic evidence from collections of yearly session laws shows that in many cases reformatories were part of larger institution-building programs that included prisons, schools for the deaf and feeble minded, and universities. This suggests that late in the century, as the reformatory spread among established states, it came to be taken for granted in frontier legislatures as a natural part of the institutional complement of statehood. Thus I would speculate that in such states the reformatory served a more purely legitimating function, and was rather less tied to instrumental need, than in the older and more developed states that will concern us for the rest of this chapter.

The South as a Control Variable

Southern states frequently appear as difficult exceptions to generalizations about social change in America, and so too here. Although in general reformatories did not diffuse among the states along regional lines—a point I address in more detail later in this chapter— southern states displayed a conspicuous, systematic deviation from the norm, lagging an average of twenty-five years behind other states in enacting reformatory legislation. On the surface this fact fits well with functionalist imagery: the South was slow to adopt formal strategies of control because of its poor agricultural economy and caste-bound social structure. The true story, however, is more complex and situation specific. Significant evidence shows that the slow pace of reformatory building in the South had less to do with incremental socioeconomic development than with the direct disruptive effects of the Civil War and Reconstruction politics.

The Civil War affected reformatory development through its impact on the southern penal system and on the political system that emerged after the war. Before the war the South was not isolated from advanced penological thinking or conspicuously backward in its institution-building program. Edward Livingston, former New York politician, prison reformer, and sponsor of the New York House of Refuge, moved to Louisiana and influenced penal thinking there; Frances Liebert, translator of Beaumont and Tocqueville, agitated for reform in South Carolina (McKelvey 1935, 153). In Mississippi an Auburn-style prison was built in 1840 (Foreman and Tatum 1938, 256). All the southern states except Florida and the Carolinas had penitentiaries by the 1860s, mostly based on the Auburn plan, and their conditions were not notably different or more primitive than those in northern prisons (Green 1949, 114–115).

This is not to say that southern prison conditions were good. On the contrary, it is to suggest that no prison, northern or southern, placed as much emphasis on humane treatment and rehabilitation as on a decent return on the state's investment through the exploitation of convict labor (Green 1949, 115). The war did not change these priorities, but it eliminated one means of achieving them: it destroyed the prisons. During Reconstruction a system of leasing convicts to private entrepreneurs took the place of the penitentiary, and the endurance of the leasing system until the end of the nineteenth century directly resulted in the failure of the reform school to penetrate the South.

The leasing system arose as the logical response to a number of conditions: the absence of prison facilities, the need for cheap labor, the abundance of unemployed black freedmen, the rapaciousness of contractors, and the corruption of Bourbon Democratic legislators. It persisted because it was a good deal for the contractors, for the states, and for the legislators who were associates of the contractors, and because most of the lessees were black (Carleton 1967, 6–7; Green 1949, 115–116; Floyd 1946, 28). Leasing was the closest thing available to the reestablishment of slavery—only this time under a contractual rather than paternalistic system of administration (McKelvey 1935, 154).

The leasing system came under fire from the Populist movement of the 1880s and the 1890s (Taylor 1942, 274–275; Woodward 1951, 257). It was not abolished, however, until the rise of the more urbane Progressives around the turn of the century. Members of prison reform associations and newly created state boards of charities and corrections, Progressive politicians, and various other members of the New South elite called for the abolition of the leasing system. Significantly, they promoted juvenile reform schools as part of general prison reform packages (Green 1949, 121; Carleton 1967, 23; Floyd 1946, 29; Holmes 1965, 229; Zimmerman 1949, 174–177, and 1951, 476–481; Bailey 1969, ch. 1).

There are two important points to draw from this discussion. First, the issue of reformatories became salient in the South only when organized pressure began to mount against leasing, and comprehensive proposals were offered for reform.[8] Second, despite the clearly greater brutality of the southern system, convict leasing should be seen as a variant or approximation of the administrative

8. This is not to say that juvenile institutions were established as leasing was abolished; the correlation between the two is far from perfect. In most states leasing was phased out gradually, often giving way to the only slightly less oppressive prison farms and chain gangs. At the same time juvenile convicts were often exempted from lease gangs, along with some women and the sick. My contention is that as the leasing system weakened and the states were urged to regain their control over convicts, the egregious plight of child convicts suggested a likely place to begin.

model of the penitentiary, not as a sign of its rejection. Leasing differed from the prison mainly in the amount of administrative control the state exercised over the labor and welfare of prisoners (see the typology in Cable 1969); it resulted from the weakness of centralized state authority and the destruction of an institutional resource base and was only indirectly related to socioeconomic modernization. Because the lease system as a political strategy had an independent effect on the spread of reform schools in the South, the effects of modernization variables on the rate of reformatory adoption will be spuriously high and should be controlled. The solution adopted here is to create a dummy variable (LEASE), which identifies those twelve states in which convict leasing was dominant (i.e., the eleven states of the Confederacy and Kentucky—see Cable 1969; McKelvey 1935, 169). The following analysis will explore not only the simple effects of modernization variables on the adoption of reformatories, but also their partial effects controlling for LEASE.

Bivariate Relationships

One goal of this analysis is to explore the predictive power and coherence of a systems approach to legal change applied to reformatory legislation. The first task, then, is to specify a model that faithfully represents the functional logic of the systems argument. Following Turner's (1980) conceptual schema, I have selected indicators of three central components of societal complexity: economic growth, educational expansion, and political development.[9]

9. The fourth factor in Turner's model—religious secularization—is not examined here or in the quantitative analyses to follow for two reasons. First, I assume that all states were equally constrained to frame reforms in a secular language, even when they were clearly informed by religious ideas. Second, neither the reformatory nor the juvenile court were themselves purely secular strategies of social control. Although, as Rothman (1971) points out, clergymen did not dominate the refuge movement (see Chapter 2), "private sectarian interests" played an important role in the growth of child welfare in the nineteenth century, and that role was sanctioned by the juvenile court (Fox 1970). The United States may represent a special case in which formal law does not replace, but rather extends, the religious agenda. Turner's hypothesis is clearly inappropriate for explaining change within such a context.

Wherever available data permit, I use multiple indicators to distinguish among various kinds of substantive effects. Economic development, for example, implies both high productive capacity and density of exchange relationships. These factors are represented respectively by indicators of the per capita value of manufactured products and the percentage of the state's population living in urban areas. As Stinchcombe (1965, 151–152) has argued, wealth sets an upper limit on the capacity for institution building, and urbanization increases societal competence for mobilizing resources and constructing rational solutions to social problems. On a more concrete level, manufacturing not only created wealth to build reformatories; it also created dependent populations of underemployed workers, widows, and orphans—all important resources for reformers. Urbanization can be expected to influence demand by fostering cosmopolitan networks of reform groups and increasing the perception of vice and crime.

Educational development similarly has more than one meaning. In the first place, education may increase the aggregate capacity for institution building through its effect on individuals: a more learned population has a greater capacity for absorbing and communicating new ideas and for adopting more formal and impersonal instrumental roles (Stinchcombe 1965, 150–151). The most appropriate indicator of this aspect of education is simply the literacy rate among the adult population. At the same time, education is a complex *institution* that represents a collective commitment to the formal socialization of children. Thus expansion of the educational establishment could offer an encouraging precedent for accepting reformatories, independent of individual-level differences in learning. An indicator of the percentage of the population attending school will be used to test this hypothesis.

Political development is an equally complex notion, but a severe lack of good data on state government structure prevents the use of multiple indicators. I have chosen to focus on the *formalization* of political authority, as measured by the number of state and federal officers per ten thousand population. This variable is intended as a rough measure of the degree to which administrative functions had been transferred from informal groups and local government to more centralized agencies; the obvious hypothesis is that states with more formalized administrative structures overall would be more receptive to formal strategies of social control. The aggregation of state and federal officers is unfortunate because it confounds two levels of authority, but published census records do not permit them to be distinguished. Effects of this variable will thus be interpreted with caution.

Some aspects of the evolutionary systems model are also compatible with a more critical functional approach. Most conspicuously, manufacturing output could be interpreted not only as an indicator of available resources, but also as a measure of capitalist expansion, elite power, and the need for stable means to intimidate the industrial working class. In interpreting the results of the analysis, therefore, it will be important to observe not only the effects of individual variables, but also the patterns shown by different relationships. Beyond this, however, I have chosen to include one factor that appears as a central component of many critical analyses of social control: immigration. Several writers have suggested that late nineteenth- and early twentieth-century moral reforms in general, and juvenile justice reforms in particular, were driven in part by nativist attempts to subdue immigrant populations (e.g., Platt 1969; Rothman 1971; Hawes 1971; Mennel 1973). If this is the case, states with higher percentages of foreign-born residents should have been more eager than others to adopt the reformatory.

In support of the institutional argument offered here, I examine three types of effects. First, it will again be important to take critical note of the patterns of associations shown by the variables. Where models yield weak or contradictory results on a series of indicators, it may be more illuminating to discard abstract systems arguments in favor of more substantive, historically specific interpretations. Second, the temporal dynamics of reform will be of interest: if reform is driven by institutionalization processes, rates of statutory change should increase over time in response to the growing legitimacy of the reform without regard to exogenous factors. I describe methods for discerning such "bandwagon effects" in the next section. Third, we may hypothesize that diffusion effects occur most powerfully among states that consider themselves similar and therefore form something like a reference group. Classic studies of state legislative innovation by Walker (1969) and Gray (1973), as well as research on municipal reform by Knoke (1982), have discovered patterns of regional influence, with states tending to follow the lead of their nearest neighbors. I test this "spatial diffusion" hypothesis using dummy variables that group the states into eight census regions.

Bivariate effects on the adoption rate of reformatories, and effects controlling for the dummy variable LEASE, are shown in Table 1. Three points may be made by way of summarizing the findings. First, societal complexity and immigration variables show few strong and significant simple effects. Interestingly, both education variables are significantly related to adoption rates, as is percentage foreign born. All other relationships are in the expected direction, except for the effect of political formalization, which is negative but insignificant. Second, when the control variable LEASE is added, most of the significant bivariate relationships appear to be spurious: the effects of literacy and immigration drop below significance; manufacturing and political formalization change the direction of their effects. Third, the simple effects of regional variables appear strong in the first instance, lending support to a regional diffusion model: North Central and New England states were the most rapid adopters, southern states were the slowest, and all others were distributed in between. However, all significant regional relationships disappear when LEASE is controlled. This suggests that all apparent regional patterns are more efficiently explained as deviations from the behavior of states with leasing systems.

To sum up, examination of bivariate relationships does not yield a coherent, theoretically interpretable picture of the determinants of

Table 1.   Effects of Independent Variables on Rates of Institutional
            Diffusion: Bivariate and Controlling for LEASE

	Simple	Partial[a]
Societal Complexity:		
Value manufactured products (hundreds)	2.13	.64
Percent urban	1.01	.98
Percent attending school	1.08**	1.06*
Percent literate	1.21*	1.11
Government officers per 10,000 population	.73	1.15
Immigration:		
Percent foreign born	1.05*	1.00
Regions:		
New England	5.76**	2.88
North Atlantic	1.27	.52
North Central	5.79**	2.98
Midwest	1.10	.43
South	.35*	.89
South Central	.63	1.13
Pacific	.76	.31

*p < .05
**p < .01
[a]Parameters for the control variable LEASE (not shown) range from .40 to .24,
in all cases (except with region dummy South) significant at p < .05.

reformatory adoption rates. Only educational development, as measured by rates of school attendance, shows an effect that overrides
North-South differences. Legal evolution, immigration, and regional
diffusion models are not supported. It remains to be seen whether
multivariate analysis will reveal more interesting interrelationships.

A Multivariate Model of Institutional Development

I estimated multivariate models of reformatory adoption rates in
three steps. First, I entered three variables into the equation as specifications of the legal evolution model, along with the dummy variable
LEASE, based on the more promising findings from the bivariate
analysis: per capita value of manufactured products, school atten-

dance rates, and ratios of state-federal government officers. I left these variables in as controls throughout the analysis. Second, I tested the resulting relationships for time dependence by dividing each effect into two time periods. I chose the year 1880 as the dividing line after some preliminary testing because it yielded the most interesting results and also because it is the midpoint of the observation period and near the median adoption date for the cases analyzed here. Third, I entered each of the remaining measures from Table 1 into the equation and tested for both time-independent and time-dependent effects. Likelihood ratios provided a test of significance for all additions to the model.

Table 2 presents the results of this process in summary form. Model I presents results from step 1: it is a single-period equation that includes the three legal evolution variables and LEASE. Models IIa and IIb show the results of time-dependence tests carried out in the second step of the analysis. Model IIa is a time-dependent equation in which only the constants, and not the effects of the measures, are allowed to vary. It estimates the degree to which changes in transition rates from one period to the other can be considered a direct function of time, or perhaps of unobserved variables. The time-independent constant (not shown) is constrained to equal 1 in order to achieve identification (Tuma et al. 1979, 834); the period-specific constants and their levels of significance are read as (multiplicative) deviations from that value. Likelihood ratio tests show that model IIa is a significant improvement over model I (p ≤ .001), which means that transition rates were indeed higher in the period 1880–1910 (a = .054) than they were in 1850–1880 (a = .007). In model IIb the substantive effect of school attendance has been allowed to vary between time periods. This equation is again a significant improvement over the single-period equation in model I (p ≤ .001), but it does not improve significantly over time-dependent model IIa (.05 ≤ p ≤ .10). Models IIa and IIb are both illustrative; neither is clearly superior to the other. The modeling process stopped at the second step: no other

Table 2. Multivariate Effects on Rates of Establishing Juvenile Reformatories

		Value Manufac- tured Products	Percent Attending School	State- Federal Government Officers	LEASE	Constants[a]	X^2
I		1.54	1.07**	1.44	.46	.015***	14.63**
IIa	1850	1.36	1.10***	1.65	.19***	.007***	31.17***
	1880					.054***	
IIb	1850	1.00	1.13***	1.46	.14***	.004***	34.70***
	1880		.87			2.163	

**p < .01
***p < .001
[a]In models with time periods, time-independent constants are constrained to equal 1.

time-dependent parameters or additional variables offered a significantly improved fit to the data.

What do these findings tell us? At the most fundamental level the results from Table 2 are consistent with those drawn from the previous bivariate analysis: no single theoretical model receives clear support. More specifically, manufacturing output is shown to have no effect whatever, and political formalization shows a consistently insignificant—though positive—relationship to adoption rates. Substantive causal effects seem to come entirely from the positive influence of school attendance and the negative influence of convict leasing.

More detailed and provocative interpretations of the dynamics of the reform process can be made based on time-dependence tests. In model IIa the significant increase in adoption rates after 1880 suggests that the reformatory movement gathered momentum over time. This institutional momentum probably resulted from the efforts of national professional reform groups to establish the reformatory as a legitimate and necessary institution. Unfortunately, no data that would allow this interpretation to be directly tested exist. This conclusion is qualified but not mitigated by model IIb, which suggests that changing rates of adoption were in part due to the changing effect of educational development. From 1850 to 1880, a 1 percent increase in school attendance is associated with a 13 percent increase in adoption rates, and after 1880, school attendance shows no significant effect. Substantively this shows that the effect of educational development was strongest early on and dwindled steadily as the diffusion process continued. In parallel tests other variables in the model showed the same erosion of effects over time, though not at significant levels. Further, as the effects of independent variables eroded, gathering institutional momentum increased the pace at which states established reformatories. Finally, and very important, increased specification of time-dependence terms in the equations strengthens the negative effects of LEASE and thereby sharpens the hypothesized contrast between southern and nonsouthern states.

The conclusions to be drawn from this analysis can be stated briefly. Legal means of institutionalizing juveniles apart from adults were adopted earliest by states that had already made significant commitments to the publicly supervised socialization of children. As reformatories became more common, they also appear to have become more legitimate. The momentum of the movement itself soon outran the prior influence of education. These effects hold across all states, but on average southern states lagged in establishing reformatories because of the destructive effects of the Civil War and the corrupt penal system that ensued. Thus behind institutionalized changes in the legal status of children one finds not just modernization or economic development in the abstract sense, but a series of semiautonomous institutions.

An Institutional Model of Legal Change

I have suggested that the legal status of children in the nineteenth century was the product of a two-step causal process. The establishment of formal deviant categories of incorrigibility and neglect and provisions for informal commitments were predicated on the existence of specialized reformatory institutions for children. Reformatory diffusion rates, in turn, depended on a combination of political and institutional factors. The analysis has worked its way backward along this causal chain; it is possible now to turn about and estimate these relationships quantitatively.

One obvious way to do this would be to estimate a causal model in which the four variables in Table 2 are exogenous, reformatory adoption rates are intervening, and adoption rates for incorrigibility, neglect, and informal commitment legislation are endogenous. Unfortunately, techniques to develop such a model using event-history data do not exist. A good second-best choice is to code reformatory adoption as a dummy variable with values of zero in years before reformatory legislation was passed and with values of one thereafter and to add this into a model containing manufacturing, education, political formalization, and LEASE indicators as predictors of legal change. If reformatory diffusion is truly an efficient cause of these associated legal changes, one would expect its effects to outweigh those of the other exogenous variables and to increase the predictive power of the model as a whole. Based on previously presented graphic evidence, I further hypothesize that the relation between reformatories and the other legal changes will prove to be time dependent. However, peculiarities in the data may obscure the effects of the reformatory variable. Recall that in many states these legal changes were enacted simultaneously with the adoption of reformatories. In these states the reformatory was not temporally prior to the other changes even though it was—in terms of ideological focus and legislative intent—an effective cause. Thus the parameters of the models will likely underestimate the effects of reformatory diffusion.[10]

Resulting models are shown in Table 3. Although far from powerful, they support the plausibility of the causal argument just outlined. The pattern of exogenous effects is similar to that in Table 2. But, as anticipated, most associations are statistically insignificant. Most important, the reformatory dummy variable shows consistently strong effects in the period 1850–1880, and parameters are statistically significant in two of the equations. Although likelihood-ratio tests show that the reformatory measure does not make a significant independent contribution to any of the models, standardized parameter estimates (not printed in the table) show that it is the most powerful joint predictor in all three equations. Thus it appears to affect the models in two ways. To a limited degree it behaves as we would expect of an intervening variable, by absorbing much of the direct effects of the exogenous factors. Beyond this, however, it increases multicollinearity in the models and reduces their overall efficiency.

10. In fact, event-history models will *reverse* causal ordering in these cases. Where transitions are coded as occurring at the same time as changes in independent variables, available software assumes—for otherwise quite sensible reasons—that transitions occur instantaneously before the point of change. The only way to override this assumption is to impose on the data artificial values that force changes to be read in the "proper" sequence. I have chosen to leave the data in their natural state.

Table 3. Multivariate Effects on Rates of Legal Innovation

		Value Manufactured Products	Percent Attending School	State-Federal Government Officers	LEASE	Reformatory Diffusion	Constants[a]	X^2
Incorrigibility	1850	1.50	1.12*	.91	.33	4.32**	.001***	29.29***
	1880		.95			1.30	.226	
Neglect	1850	1.75	1.06	.77	.53	4.52	.001***	31.65***
	1880		.98			1.46	.092	
Informal commitments	1850	.68	1.02	.54	.15*	3.43*	.012***	25.19***
	1880		.91			.42	1.569	

*p < .05
**p < .01
***p < .001
[a]Time-independent constants constrained to equal 1.

The most interesting result shown in Table 3 is the relative decline in the effect of the reformatory variable after 1880. This appears to run counter to the hypothesis of an increasingly tight relationship among reform innovations over time, but in fact it confirms it. As graphic evidence presented earlier showed, the suggested tendency toward simultaneous enactments increased over the course of the diffusion process. This means that states that began the process of reform early on did so piecemeal, by first chartering a reformatory and only subsequently adopting related jurisdictional and procedural reforms. To late-adopting states these innovations appeared as a single, highly rationalized reform package that could be enacted all at once. By recording such wholesale enactments literally, these data yield estimates that are statistically accurate but substantively misleading: as the growing legitimacy of the reformatory accelerated the redefinition of juvenile deviance, its apparent statistical effect on that redefinition process declined.

Conclusion

In this chapter I have taken the first step in exploring the ability of evolutionary models to explain the early development of the juvenile justice system in the United States. Subsequent chapters carry this analysis further. I suggested that evolutionary theories do not provide a complete explanation either for the rate at which change in juvenile law occurred among the states or the form in which that change took place. I tested models that emphasized the priority of institutional development, the potential independence of various aspects of societal complexity, and the dynamic influence of legitimizing social movements.

The most significant finding of this analysis is that the reform school served as the vehicle and prerequisite for the formal, legal creation of delinquency as a deviant role for children. The institution not only required application of the delinquent label to juveniles who would under any circumstances have been considered criminal, but also implied inclusion of misbehaving and mistreated children and exempted them from the rule of law. The precedent for such extraordinary discretionary power was set by the reformers of the 1820s only with great effort, but the precedent became the norm as reformatories developed nationwide. Long after the refuges' familistic ideology had lost its public appeal, the subsequent reform schools maintained their familistic authority.

The second major finding is in regard to the rate at which reformatories were established among the states. The lack of systematic structural effects from manufacturing growth, urbanization, political formalization, or immigration suggests that the reformatory is not efficiently explained either as a functional outcome of modernization or as a simple instrument of class control and industrial discipline. Analysis revealed no general and abstract effect of modernization, but a direct and concrete effect of educational development. In this case the best predictor of the phenomenon is past behavior: the states most prone to establish separate institutions for deviant children were those in which general purpose institutions for children were already most entrenched. A broad explanation for these reforms lies not in the abstract realm of functional need, but in the ideologically rooted demands of groups committed to nation building (Meyer et al. 1979). Further, I showed that the Civil War and its aftermath had the specific effect of limiting the penetration of reformatories into the South. Finally, the diffusion of reformatories appears to have been accelerated by an internal momentum that I have suggested represents the growing legitimacy of the institution over time.

In another sense the analysis to this point has not refuted the systems argument, but has rather begun to respecify it. A major point of Turner's (1980) argument is that different aspects of societal complexity may be expected to have differential effects on legal change. In this case educational development encouraged legal change independent of economic or political factors. It has furthermore been possible to suggest the form of that effect. Educational expansion encouraged innovation at the institutional level rather than through the individual effects of schooling, and then only in the early stages of the diffusion process. Schools appear to have offered a model of institution building that allowed the idea of the reformatory to take root, but once established it spread on the strength of its own legitimacy. As I show in the next three chapters, the impact of modernization is similarly complex at later stages of the development of juvenile law.

4

Ceremonial Justice

The juvenile court was the next major step, after the establishment of the reformatory, in the legal differentiation of children and adults. This chapter and the next are concerned with the process by which the juvenile court became the dominant institutional model for judging and sanctioning delinquents. Current literature presents contradictory pictures of the origins of the court, its initial impact, and its continuing significance. On the one hand, it is portrayed as an important legal innovation that broadened the legal liability of children, institutionalized the rehabilitative ideal in the treatment of delinquency, and set an agenda for delinquency control policy that remains dominant. On the other hand, it is pictured as merely an extension and formalization of the ideology of prevention and the discretionary methods of child regulation pioneered in the nineteenth century.

It is ironic that proponents as well as critics of the juvenile court have offered both interpretations at various times. Court reformers themselves were at pains to demonstrate the innovativeness of the new institution. Judge Julian Mack (1908, 372), for example, portrayed the court as a revolutionary improvement over the old reformatory system and as the first real attempt to provide diagnosis and training to delinquents. More recently, Platt (1969, 3) has held that juvenile court reformers founded the modern enterprise of delinquency control and invented the concept of delinquency itself. To Rothman (1980, 205), these reformers "revolutionized social policy toward the delinquent."

Yet some of these same writers raise doubt about how revolutionary the new court really was. While reformers emphasized the court's distinctiveness, they also sought to demonstrate its continuity with Anglo-American common law (e.g., Lou 1927, ch. 1; Mack 1916). Recent revisionist analyses have suggested that the ideology of the child savers was just a more professionalized version of the ideology of prevention that sustained the reformatories throughout the previous century and that the first juvenile court in Chicago was an unintended consequence of attempts to reform the private child-care system in Illinois (Platt 1969, ch. 2, 3; Fox 1970). Supporters and critics seem to agree that the juvenile court was an important substantive reform; they differ primarily over the interests the reform was intended to serve and its effects.

This chapter offers an interpretation of the movement's history that crosscuts both traditional accounts of the juvenile court and more recent revisionist analyses. My argument is that the juvenile court was not an important substantive innovation, but was primarily a ceremonial institution through which the ideology of the broader charity organization movement was enacted and within which the routine practices of child saving established in the nineteenth century could be continued in a more legitimate form. This thesis provides a foundation for the quantitative analysis presented in Chapter 5.

The writings of critics and proponents show that the juvenile court offered no innovations in theories of delinquency prevention. Nor, as I show in Chapter 5, did the juvenile court represent a distinctive technology through which traditional theories could be put into practice. I argue instead that the juvenile court was distinctive in terms of its institutional character and administrative ideology and that it was readily accepted because it was an exemplar of the least controversial and most broadly legitimate aspects of a general Progressive reform agenda and, more specifically, of the movement for charity organization. The juvenile court was notable not for its goals or technology, but for the derivative ideology upon which its authority rested.

Juvenile justice reformers had long sought to protect children from the stigma and punitive sanctions applied to adult criminals; the juvenile court was in part a means to further that end. But as an institution the court incorporated two historically distinct sets of constitutive rules, one deriving from the legal profession and the other from the emergent social welfare profession. It signified the decoupling of juvenile justice functions from the criminal courts, to the mutual benefit of the court system and reformers. The court allowed the legal system to appear responsive to demands for a more humane system of justice without really altering its routine decision-making practices and allowed juvenile justice agencies to maintain their ideology and discretionary authority. Research by Hagan and his colleagues on the origins of the juvenile court and federal probation movements (Hagan and Leon 1977; Hagan 1979) and on the impact of local probation services (Hagan et al. 1979) has emphasized the symbolic functions of these reforms. All "had more to do with the making of legal myths than with the restructuring of the way decisions are actually made. . . . The source of this change was more ideological than material, resulting in ritualized court practices characterized more by ceremony than substance" (Hagan et al. 1979, 507).

Such developments were the essence of Progressivism. By the turn of the century, the demise of an agrarian society and an awakening urban-industrial consciousness had provoked a new concern for the maintenance of social order. Although concern for order was not new in American history, a characteristic feature of Progressive movements was their tendency to see social control not as a moral or political problem, but primarily as an administrative problem. Progressives sought to depoliticize the growing demands for the protections of a welfare state by promoting reforms that emphasized administrative efficiency and professional expertise rather than substantive changes in the allocation of rights and economic resources. This tendency stands out in a variety of studies, regardless of the motives ascribed to Progressive reformers and whatever the goals of specific movements. Whether the transformations of the period are seen to result from the status anxieties of déclassé elites (Hofstadter 1955; Gusfield 1963), the structural inadequacies of capitalist institutions (Wiebe 1967; Chandler 1977), or the ambitions of professional groups in law and social welfare (Platt 1969; Rothman 1980), in municipal government (Schiesl 1977), or in education (Tyack and Hansot 1982), the common thread that bound them together was the search for new strategies of administrative control.

The juvenile court, and the charity organization movement of which it was a part, are exemplars of the Progressive obsession with administrative rationality. In this chapter I describe the emergent characteristics of the juvenile court as solutions to four generic administrative problems that concerned Progressive reformers. One such problem was goal setting: how could the traditional values of native elites be made binding on society as a whole? The solution was to link those values with the norm of efficiency and to articulate a dual set of goals that distinguished conceptually between substantive ends and administrative means. The second problem was to maintain effective boundaries on citizenship, participation, and decision making. The solution here was nonpartisanship, which meant in its broadest sense separating politics from administration and in a more practical sense weakening immigrant-based patronage systems. The third problem was one of structure: how should authority be distributed? The constitutional fragmentation of power among federal, state, and local governments discouraged the formation of hierarchical bureaucracies, but the principles of federalism suggested an alternative model in which broad policy decisions were centralized and decoupled from local implementation. Finally, there was the problem of technology: how would the work of industry, charity, and government be done? The characteristic answer was professionalization, which signified a diagnostic, problem-solving approach to decision making and a commitment to decision rules legitimated by occupational status. Professional expertise was never well integrated into the juvenile court; in charity organization it was emergent at best. The point is not that routine work changed dramatically, but that it was given an aura of legitimacy that was impervious to justice claims based on formalistic standards.

I detail these ideological solutions further in the following section, first for Progressive reform generally and then more specifically for the charity organization and juvenile court movements. The data used in this chapter are drawn mainly from those sources that contain the most information on reform ideology and organizing strategies at the peak of the Progressive period. These include articles, reports, and meeting notes published in the *Proceedings of the National Conference of Charities and Correction* (cited as *PNCCC*). The NCCC was an umbrella reform association that was a prime sponsor of juvenile court reform and eventually became the main organization of the emergent social welfare profession. Other materials are drawn from *Charities* magazine, the influential review published by the New York Charity Organization Society.

The Ideological Principles of Urban Reform

Philanthropic responsibility was institutionalized as an aspect of the American civic culture long before the Progressives came upon the scene. They did not contribute the motivation to do good or even distinctively new means for doing good. Rather, their contribution lay in the notion that philanthropy, social services, and government in general had to be administered according to sound business principles that would ensure maximum efficiency. Thus the first characteristic of the Progressive urban reform ideology is the dual goals of "efficiency and uplift."[1]

The "uplift" side of the equation was not problematic. In the most general sense Progressivism sought to institute a form of Protestant civic morality that had been dominant since the colonial era. Nor was there any doubt about who needed to be uplifted. Just as in the Jacksonian institutional reforms, it was the immigrant groups, who concentrated in the cities, wallowed in poverty, and strained available resources, who were perceived as most in need of ministration. In contrast to the Jacksonian period, however, immigrants in the 1890s were not entirely without resources and organization of their own. They were able to achieve some measure of political influence through party bosses and their urban political machines, and the specter of patronage democracy animated reformers as much as the more fundamental problems of poverty and urban decay. Thus municipal reform was underlaid by a strong component of class-based politics. The reformers themselves tended to be middle-class men and women "who interpreted democracy in terms of property rights and assumed that government should be in the hands of well-educated and 'respectable' people" (Schiesl 1977, 2).

The Progressive reformers were not, however, simple racists or elitists. In this they differed from their Know-Nothing and Mugwump forebears, who had sought to exclude the immigrant from public affairs entirely. The Progressives offered a "structuralist" critique of urban society (Schiesl 1977), which suggested that only a

---

1. The phrase "efficiency and uplift" is taken from Haber's (1964) history of Taylorism. It is used here with the conviction that scientific management, insofar as it sought to suffuse rational production methods with moral significance, was a special case of a more general Progressive trend. The fundamental bimodality of Progressivism is echoed in the titles of other institutional analyses of the period—for example, Rothman's (1980) "conscience and convenience," Schiesl's (1977) "politics of efficiency," and Tyack and Hansot's (1982) "managers of virtue."

general overhauling of the machinery of public life would free the immigrant from the illegitimate and subversive power of the bosses. They proposed a government run by "principles and abstract laws" that would be able to "moralize the lives of individuals" (Hofstadter 1955, 9). The immigrants clung to the political machines because they resembled the particularistic, hierarchical, and kinship-oriented societies they had left and because they offered material security in the form of direct patronage. The reformers were convinced that an efficient "good government" could eliminate corruption *and* expand the boundaries of democracy to include the immigrant.

Thus for the Progressives, no matter what the focus of any specific reform, the main issue was one of administration rather than content. Specific goals, whether involving civil service or child labor or education, had been articulated by earlier reformers and were made part of a general agenda of structural reform in the cities: "Now the panacea of the patrician had given way to the administrative tool of the expert, with efficiency rather than moral purity its objective" (Wiebe 1967, 171). Through coordinated effort the reformers attempted in one thrust both to destroy the power of the spoils system and to replace it with a permanent, efficient bureaucracy in city government.

The second principle of Progressive urban reform, and the most crucial step in achieving a rational and efficient city administration, was nonpartisanship. Nonpartisanship was, in turn, exemplified by the drive for civil service reform. Civil service was the keystone of the urban reform agenda in part because it satisfied a variety of interests. The older gentry were attracted to it because it offered a means to eliminate machine control over civic appointments. Structuralist reformers saw it as a step toward comprehensive bureaucratic management and as a weapon in the fight against monopolies and big business. Where cities had once welcomed corporations, they now viewed them as a form of alien economic domination and a source of corruption that, in turn, supported the spoils system (Schiesl 1977, 36; Patton 1940, 49).

Pleas for civil service reform were aimed primarily at a middle-class audience and had little appeal for the urban working class that depended on patronage for jobs and social services. Critics suggested that a merit system of employment would create an elite class of professional bureaucrats, and proponents responded in turn that civil service exemplified democracy by guaranteeing access to public employment regardless of "blood right" or party affiliation (Schiesl 1977, 29). Reformers claimed they were trying to "make government accessible to the superior disinterestedness of the average citizen" (Hofstadter 1955, 257). In fact a "recurrent ambiguity" toward urban politics underlay attempts at reform: on the one hand, reformers sincerely believed that civil service would modernize democracy and would not exclude qualified members of the lower classes. On the other hand, the reform impulse rested upon the implicit assumption that "most urban dwellers were incapable of governing themselves" (Schiesl 1977, 40).

Intentions aside, it is clear in retrospect that nonpartisan reforms, by applying "universalistic" standards of merit that sprang mainly from middle-class notions of efficiency, did increase the power and participation of upper-income groups in city government (Schiesl 1977, 190). As Walker (1977) has shown, this trend is nowhere more apparent than in the area of police reform. Control over the police was crucial to the political machines because they provided a wealth of patronage jobs and the ability selectively to enforce or subvert the law. Various urban reform groups and the National Prison Association began to support the separation of the police from politics through civil service reform in the 1870s, though their plans were not widely accepted until the 1890s. Where civil service laws were introduced and enforced, they increased the percentage of policemen who were native-born Americans: "The meritocratic standards of professionalism inevitably discriminated against the lower class and helped to break the power of the blue-collar-dominated political machines" (Walker 1977, 45).

The third characteristic of the urban Progressive ideology was the imagery of rational administration structured in a federated fashion. Federation here means, quite simply, the centralization of responsibility for the formulation and dissemination of general policies and the fragmentation of authority for implementation. In city governments, federating tendencies were expressed in the drive for home rule— that is, giving the cities power to do business on their own behalf, free of state or other exogenous influences—fixing responsibility of city officials, increasing the power of mayors in relation to partisan city councils, and rationalizing the finance process of urban government.[2] The significant point is that these efforts were not exclusively local ones, but were coordinated by networks of reform elites, often armed with copies of standardized "model" legislation (Patton 1940). Reform movements tended to centralize their own policy-making activities as local groups dedicated to specific issues made informal alliances that in turn grew into networks and eventually into national-level federated associations dedicated to social reform.[3] This strategy was a repudiation of strict hierarchy, but it permitted the growth of communication networks of unusually broad scope and flexibility, allowed local reformers to draw ideological sustenance from a cosmopolitan audience, and fostered a shift from piecemeal change to comprehensive adminstrative reform. One model for this shift may have come from education, where local school systems were increasingly linked by professionally administered state boards (Tyack and Hansot 1982). But another model surely came from major changes already under way in the economy—toward the formation of national business alliances (Wiebe 1967, 173–174) and toward the differentiation of industrial empires into semiautonomous region- or product-based republics (Chandler, 1977).

2. For example, these and other specific measures were called for in the model city charter published in 1897 by the National Municipal League (Patton 1940, 34).

3. These groups are too numerous to permit a representative listing of examples. Hofstadter (1955) and Skowronek (1982) discuss many of the most influential national-level reform organizations, and Schiesl (1977) surveys those groups that were most active in the area of municipal reform and traces many of their interconnections. Patton's (1940) short book gives many examples of relations between local- and national-level organizing efforts.

But the ideology of federation was more than just an organizing strategy. It betrayed a profound shift in reformers' attitudes toward the role of the state. Jacksonian reform ideology had emphasized voluntaristic philanthropy as a source of moral uplift for both giver and receiver and as a source of general civic betterment. Late nineteenth-century Mugwumps attempted only to replace bad individuals in government with good ones. For structuralist Progressives the power of trusts and monopolies and the perversion of the political process by private interests led to a reevaluation of the state as a potentially benevolent source of universalistic authority. The Progressives were, as Hofstadter (1955, 231) writes, "haunted by the specter of a private power far greater than the public power of the state," but they did not seek to replace the moralism of earlier reforms with coercion. Rather, they insisted on the need for rational administrative techniques, usually exercised by specialized boards, agencies, and commissions, which were "disinterested" and therefore implicitly moral. Their strategy was to centralize governmental authority and place it squarely behind local efforts to moralize the lives of individual participants.

The significance of this strategy cannot be overemphasized, particularly as it influenced emergent theories of law, social welfare, and the treatment of children. Progressivism reasserted colonial Puritan attitudes toward civil authority: whatever the spiritual condition of the individual, participation in a rule-bound and benevolent system of public authority was an inherently moralizing experience because it was aimed toward the good of the commonwealth rather than the good of the individual. Jacksonian reformers steered away from the imagery of commonwealth, adopted a sectarian vocabulary, and claimed to do good directly and voluntarily with only minimal reliance on the official government. This approach was more compatible with the political trends of the mid nineteenth century, when laissez-faire economics and the metaphors of contract law set the tone for the domestic role of the state. But by the 1880s, faith in the efficiency of the market as a regulator of social life had waned. Progressives turned again to the state—and more particularly to positive law—for means of social control, but they offered a secular rationale for state expansion. They could no longer claim that the state was moral because it was Christian; rather, they contended that government would be moral if it could be made rational. The state was revered not because it was the biblical commonwealth, but because it could potentially provide the transcendent authority and methodical rules that such a commonwealth would offer.

The fourth component of the Progressive reform ideology was idealization of expertise and the tendency toward professionalization. The emphasis on the necessity for expert leadership was a somewhat divisive issue for reformers. As discussed previously, many Progressives were sincerely attempting to broaden the base of civic participation, albeit in terms of predefined standards of efficiency and merit. In these terms, nonpartisanship meant standardization, not restriction, of government employment; these reformers also favored such measures as the direct primary, which would put the nomination process in the hands of voters rather than party regulars. Ultimately, these radical neopopulist reforms were deemphasized by the dominant Progressives in favor of "responsible leadership" by professional groups such as lawyers and businessmen. Thus Hofstadter (1955, 264) suggests that the Progressive faith in expert judgment was an aspect of the class politics that underlay Progressivism in general: "The historical root of this point of view lay in the longstanding Mugwump concern with good government and in the implicit Mugwump belief in elite leadership." Whatever its sources, "government by experts" became a key plank in the platforms of municipal reformers (Patton 1940, 34).

The effect of this ideology was revolutionary, but not democratic. The demand for expertise invited professionals into government service, and the civil service system guaranteed them tenure and the ability to survive transient partisan administrations. Schiesl (1977, 191) writes that Progressive reforms did not remove politics from government, but rather altered the form in which power was exercised by introducing expert administrative agencies with ties to business and civic groups: "the machine bureaucracy, popularly based, was . . . replaced by career agencies, professionally organized." These agencies could, in turn, establish relationships with groups in the private sector:

> In redirecting the goals of municipal efficiency from changing governing personalities to the establishment of better administrative methods, the structuralists made it easier for various "functional" organizations representing all occupational classes to gain greater access to government without the intervention of the machine and with the assurance that their goals would be more readily achieved. (Schiesl 1977, 192)

In summary, although structuralist Progressivism contributed little in the way of new social reform goals, the form in which Progressives sought to achieve and institutionalize those goals left an indelible imprint on twentieth-century American democracy. They had some success in limiting the power of the immigrant lower classes as expressed through machine politics, but in many cases the reform ideology was co-opted by the bosses who could with little effort assume the mantle of "Progressive" reform themselves. The reformers' major accomplishment was not to alter the allocation of power within American society, but to change the way it was exercised in two decisive ways. First, the Progressives laid the foundation for the modern welfare state by suggesting that government should formally assume responsibility for the material welfare of its citizens, and that that responsibility should be exercised in a rational fashion by expert administrators. Second, by attacking party politics and institutionalizing professional, nonpartisan input into policy formation, the Progressives introduced an organizational form of democracy that placed unprecedented emphasis on the bureaucracy and provided ingress to a range of formally constituted collectivities with legitimate claims to represent recognized occupational or status groups. As the following discussion demonstrates, the reformers' emphasis on form over content, and on organization over substance, had a decisive impact on the structure, and perhaps even the political success, of the juvenile court movement.

The Ideology of Charity and Juvenile Court Reform

In the remainder of this chapter, I discuss the charity organization movement as a special case of structural Progressivism and the juvenile court movement as a special case of charity organization. All three levels of reform activity were characterized by an isomorphic set of ideological principles, and all were bound together in important ways by the substantive issue of child welfare (Wiebe 1967, 169). By placing the juvenile court in the wider context of the charity organization movement, I argue that child welfare policies were decisively informed by the institutional politics of Progressivism.

Dual Goals in Charities and Juvenile Justice

The charity organization movement, which rose to prominence in the 1880s, was the direct descendant of the American tradition of individualized philanthropy and the forebear of the modern social welfare system and of the social welfare profession itself.[4] It spread as a "missionary movement" (*PNCCC* 1897, 142) that sought to bring order to the old, unsystematic practice of indiscriminate almsgiving and to extend the scope of services provided.

Charity organization replicated the goals of "efficiency and uplift" by applying scientific methods to an old set of humanitarian ideals. Reformers sought to be "secular, rational, and empirical as opposed to sectarian, sentimental, and dogmatic" (Leiby 1978, 91). The "science of charity" (deForest 1904, 17) was thus distinguished from mere almsgiving by its emphasis on method. The dual goals of the movement, as well as its attempts to distinguish itself from earlier forms of charity, are well expressed in this lyric credo: "The progressive charity organization society is trying to prove that modern charity is gentle as well as wise; that it can forgive and love as well as guide. It is substituting for the frugal motto: 'Not alms but a friend,'

4. For a comprehensive history of the charity organization movement, see Leiby (1978).

a more humane one: 'Organized charity is organized love' " (*Charities* 1904, 327).[5]

"Scientific charity" and "organized love" in this context meant rigorous investigation of individual charity applicants and careful accounting of expenditures and outcomes. The results of these procedures, the reformers maintained, would be twofold. On the one hand, the giver would be saved the expense of duplicated effort and the waste of funds on the "undeserving poor," and, on the other, the recipient would be guaranteed the kind of aid that would do the most good. "Scientific charity is Christian impulse reduced to natural rule," one advocate wrote. "It asks that men shall be investigated, that the giver shall take a little pains with his investments" (Smart 1905, 952).

In the field of child welfare, the juvenile court was seized upon as a means of focusing and maximizing resources. One reason for this was the growing disenchantment with juvenile reformatories as means of dealing with delinquent and dependent children. Conflict between supporters and opponents of institutional care for children grew within the National Conference of Charities and Correction, until a truce was declared in an 1899 report of the Committee on Dependent and Neglected Children. Their consensus was that homes should be preserved as a preventive effort wherever possible and that institutions should be used only for "children who are prevented by circumstances from being placed in homes" (Mulry 1899, 167). This report did not lay the issue to rest entirely, however; delegates' remarks betray a deep ambivalence about whether reformatories were positive steps in the evolution of child saving (e.g., Wentworth 1901, 248) or fundamentally cruel follies (e.g., Mack 1906, 126).[6]

The juvenile court was the most conspicuous response to this

5. By invoking the phrase "Not alms, but a friend," the writer is mocking the ideology of the "friendly visitor," who was distinguished from the modern caseworker not only by her amateur status, but also by her condescending preference for moral rather than material aid.

6. Hastings Hart (1906, 93) provides some evidence that the detente of 1899 was promoted by a convergence of interest among the partisans. He notes that the placing-out societies, the chief critics and competitors of the institutions, had begun establishing temporary homes of their own. As they became institutional proprietors, they "were no longer in a position to indulge in indiscriminate criticism of institutions."

general disenchantment with institutions. In the first place, it was claimed to be more efficient. Ben Lindsey of Denver estimated that his court saved the state of Colorado $88,000 in eighteen months by reducing institutional commitments (Lindsey 1903a, 213). This favorable cost-benefits ratio was made possible by its effectiveness in preventing crime and keeping the child in the home: "The juvenile court and probation system will keep him there if it is proper and possible. . . . Its purpose is, of course, to prevent crime before crime is committed" (Lindsey 1903a, 209). Of course, the idea of prevention did not originate with the juvenile court, but with the refuges; the new court promised only to institutionalize the same goal in a more cost-efficient manner.[7] Nonetheless, the court's ideology was so powerful that it eclipsed the memory of its predecessors. In 1908, Judge Julian Mack characterized reformatories primarily as agencies of punishment and lauded the juvenile court as the first organized system for rehabilitating deviant juveniles (Mack 1908, 372).

It was proposed that while the juvenile court was saving money, it would also increase the impact of charity efforts on behalf of children. One way in which it was expected to do this was by broadening the scope of the legal system. The child who had been treated with leniency in adult courts and freed to "gratify his anti-social impulses with impunity" (Henderson 1904, 364) could now be adjudicated in a setting of indisputable benevolence. More important, perhaps, the juvenile court would provide the legal means to reach beyond the child to the real cause of the problem—the parents. Children, it was suggested, were often placed in reform schools unreasonably because of parental sloth (*PNCCC* 1904, 574). The 1903 Denver juvenile court law contained a widely copied provision holding parents responsible for their children's misbehavior, which was expected ultimately to reduce institutional commitments (Lindsey 1905, 153–155).

The issue of parental responsibility is an important one because it

7. The purported economies of the juvenile court were perceived by reformers as a potent political weapon. "Proof that the probation system, even with paid probation officers, yields an immediate cash saving for the taxpayers . . . will win over any legislature. A few might hold out for old-fashioned severity of punishment for adult criminals, but not for children" (Almy 1905, 337).

illustrates the similarity of thinking in charity organization and juvenile court circles. In both areas, scientific investigation would prevent inefficient expenditure of scarce resources. The capabilities of the juvenile court in this regard, and the characteristically ambiguous Progressive attitude toward the urban poor, is revealed in an anecdote related by a Pennsylvania probation officer in 1904:

> A small boy of ten was brought by his father to a magistrate in Pittsburgh with the request that the boy be sent to the Pennsylvania reform school in Morganza. The boy was sent home with his father. The next week the child was brought again, this time before the juvenile court, the father saying he had stolen fifty cents. I was asked to investigate the matter. The father did not know I was a probation officer and when I asked him why he wanted his boy to go to Morganza he said, "My friend tella me, 'you send your boy Morganza, they give him shoe, give him stocking, give him coat with brassa button, give him books in a head, costa me nothing;' I send my boy Morganza." I found a good home for the boy and the father was compelled to pay two dollars a week for his board. (*PNCCC* 1904, 573–574)

Nonpartisanship in Charity and the Juvenile Court

Charity organizers appropriated the drive for civil service reform as a part of their own reform agenda for two reasons. They argued, first, that nonpartisan administration would provide the autonomy and administrative consistency required to carry out the institutional reforms they envisioned and, second, that it would cleanse the institutions of the taint of the spoils system in the public mind. The ideal institution was one in which "politics and religion are absolutely an unknown entity [*sic*] . . . from top to bottom" (*PNCCC* 1899, 234).

As in other Progressive enterprises, modern business methods were idealized as the model of successful management: "After all, we must come back to the one known modern method, which forces public business to be transacted according to business principles. There should be no hamper on the power of removal. Discipline and efficiency demand that." Nor should appointments be made politically: "The only known method of preventing this is the eligible list, made up after competitive tests open to all, from which list the topmost, without regard to any kind of a pull, is entitled to the first trial" (*PNCCC* 1899, 241; see also Garrett 1900, 36).

Civil service is conceived here primarily as a means of promoting expertise and eliminating incompetent employees, not as a means of guaranteeing employee tenure. Ideally, administrators were to be appointed by nonpartisan commissions. Civil service requirements for lower-level employees were seen as aggressive means of ridding institutions of "the 'hospital tramp,' or institutional rounder. These people have been the bane of the service and the perpetrators of the institutional abuses which so completely shook public confidence in the institutional methods in the past" (Moulton 1910, 315).

Nonpartisanship influenced the juvenile court as well in terms of both ideology and structure. For example, Ben Lindsey, the crusading Denver judge, often told bathetic tales that offered a child's-eye view of the adult world and implicitly set the innocence of children and the children's court in opposition to the corruption of the cities. In this case, the question of a child arrested for penny-ante gambling provided a springboard for a brief parable:

> "Judge, if So and So . . . can stuff the ballot box, why can't the kids play for money?"
> This was the query of a newsboy who associated with a gang of crap shooters within a stone's throw of a gambling house protected by the police department. . . . A petty imitation of their elders made criminals of the boys, and the same crime on a larger scale made protected and even prominent citizens of the men. (Lindsey 1905, 157)

Although Lindsey's every word (and there were many of them) smacks strongly of self-promotion, and despite the fact that he was somewhat of a maverick even within the juvenile court movement, his comments illustrate the general harmony of purpose that existed among juvenile court reformers, child welfare advocates, and charity workers within the Progressive movement. His lampoons of the police aligned the juvenile court with those who were opposed to corruption and inefficiency in government (see, e.g., Lindsey 1903a, 218–219).

But juvenile court reformers sought as well to make nonpartisanship a principle of court organization. A Utah judge opined in 1905, "I think we have in Utah one of the best laws. I think it is the first State which has a law completely out of politics. We have a Juvenile Court commission . . . and they appoint the Judge. I should not have had one vote if it came in politics, because I had lived in the city but one week" (*PNCCC* 1905, 484). In Chicago, juvenile probation work was assigned to private citizens in order to keep party hacks out of those positions (Leiby 1978, 147). Florence Kelley pleaded before the NCCC that juvenile court appointments should be made through the civil service in order to protect officials from reprisals by disgruntled parents, saloon keepers, and others who profited by juvenile waywardness (*PNCCC* 1904, 575). Hastings Hart agreed with Kelley that independence from politics was a criterion that separated the effective juvenile court from the ineffective one. According to Hart, the usefulness of the juvenile court

> depends chiefly upon the character and spirit of the Judge and the efficiency of the probation officers. To preserve these essentials, it is necessary to free the Judge and the probation officers from the vicissitudes of partisan politics. . . .
>
> Where the Court has been left to be simply an agent of perfunctory officialism, with probation officers selected under the old spoils system, as a reward for partisan services rendered, it will invariably be found that the Juvenile Court law is held in contempt both by the judges and the officers of the Court and by the intelligent members of the community who observe its operations. (Hart 1906, 90, 91)

Perhaps because judges were so inextricably involved in politics, however, most of the emphasis in the campaign for a nonpartisan juvenile court was placed on the probation officer. Homer Folks, chair of the New York State Probation Commission and secretary of the State Charities and Aid Association, proposed at one point that probation officers should be regulated and supervised by an "independent committee." Under questioning, Folks made it plain that he meant the committee—and therefore the probation officer—should be independent not only of partisan politics, but also of the judge's

influence (*PNCCC* 1906, 578).[8] As I show later, emphasis on probation work here is indicative of a trend: as the ideology of a bureaucratized juvenile court became solidified, the expert contribution of the
probation officer became more salient, and the judge's merely legal
expertise became more peripheral to the reformers' concerns.

Federation as a Structural Principle

As the term "charity organization" itself implies, a major advantage claimed by the new scientific philanthropy was the ability to
coordinate relations between donor and recipient in order to achieve
maximum efficiency. When the first Charity Organization Society
was formed in New York in 1882, the goal was to centralize administration within a single metropolitan area. By the turn of the century,
the NCCC was agitating for centralized charity boards at the state
level, and before the first decade of the twentieth century had passed,
the U.S. Children's Bureau had been established to coordinate child
welfare efforts nationally. Thus within a very short period of time,
the strategy of federation allowed charity organization to become a
national issue.

At the local level, coordinated administration promised to yield
efficiency first by ameliorating competition for funds among individual charities. Mary Richmond, a pioneering advocate of professional
social work, suggested that public esteem was increased and all charities benefited when charities presented a united front: "It does not
follow that, as the work of one charity becomes better and more
favorably known, the subscriptions to others will fall off. . . . To put
the question on the lowest possible plane, it *pays* charities to be co-
operative" (Richmond 1901a, 311; emphasis in original). Furthermore, by banding together, charities could eliminate fraud in the
form of "charity fakirs," confidence men who formed bogus charity

---

8. Folks's proposal probably had another aim, besides assuring that probation
work not fall into partisan hands. Like Judge Mack of Chicago, Folks sought to
institutionalize a professional probation service that would not be overshadowed by
charismatic judges like Lindsey of Denver.

organizations and solicited funds for their own "base and selfish ends" (*Charities* 1904, 944). By fostering efficiency, centralization in turn increased the benefits that could be provided to the recipient. In the well-organized city, there would be a standard means of classification, registration, diagnosis, and treatment; duplication of effort would be eliminated. Richmond's advice to charity workers in this regard is typical: "If an applicant who is unknown to you comes to your door asking help, it seems to me that the first thing you owe to him and to your city is to see that you don't get in the way of others who are in all probability trying to help him, to see that you do not undo their good work" (Richmond 1901b, 327).

The issue of state supervision of charities seems to have presented a thornier problem than that of local coordination. The issues and appeals were similar, albeit cast on a larger scale. First, charity organization offered benefits to institutions. State supervision was presented as a means of rationalizing individual philanthropic duty: "None able to contribute can shirk, because all such bear as taxpayers the burdens of the state. And, at the same time, all are relieved of individual care and responsibility, when the state takes all care and responsibility upon itself" (Platt 1908, 20). Nonpartisan charity boards could, in addition to rationalizing funding and service delivery, act as a buffer between partisan legislators and institutions (Butler 1908, 43).

Second, state supervision would benefit the recipients of charitable aid. One commentator complained that, in the absence of clear legal authority, child welfare workers were forced to use extreme means to protect endangered children: "I can recall an instance . . . when a case of the serious ill-treatment and neglect of a child became so acute, and legal barriers so insurmountable, that one of the good ladies of the society cut the 'Gordian Knot' by planning and executing a very neat case of kidnapping" (Griffin 1909, 56). Only if caseworkers were officially chartered as agents of the state, he argued, could such rescues be made routinely. At the same time, the state had a responsibility to those already under institutional care that could be exercised only through the legal authority for inspection and supervision (Barrett 1908, 31). Some advocates of state supervision felt that even institutions receiving no public funds should be inspected, if only because "the State should be in a position to know at least annually the nature and extent of the dependency within its borders, and to make certain that the helpless and friendless, and particularly the young, are receiving proper care and attention" (Hebberd 1907, 21).

Serious conflict arose over the issue of public supervision of private charity organizations. Most private charities were run by sectarian religious groups, and the majority of sectarian charities were Catholic. For obvious reasons, the private charities sought to maintain their independence, while charity organizers tended to see state supervision as a means to standardize service delivery and prevent institutional abuse. The literature reviewed for this study reflects mainly the opinions of the advocates of supervision, but the depth of the conflict can be gauged by the ferocity of their rhetoric. In one NCCC annual meeting, private charitable institutions were referred to as "wild-cat private charities" (*PNCCC* 1903, 33). Although the private charities claimed as their *forte* the ability to provide more personalized and humane service than the bureaucratized public agencies, Rev. A. W. Clark of Omaha questioned this distinction: "In spite of all this talk about personal touch and personal sympathy, my observations have led me to believe that in the work of private societies there is a good deal of officialism and lack of personal sympathy and self-sacrifice" (quoted in *Charities* 1904, 581). Another writer suggested that the private institutions' resistance to state supervision was motivated by more sinister goals than the desire for autonomy:

> For a private charity, receiving public money, to object to state supervision is almost *prima facie* evidence of the fact that there is something wrong in its methods which would not commend itself to enlightened public sentiment and might result in having its revenues reduced or cut off, if the knowledge of its methods became public. (Barrett 1908, 30)

The long-run solution to this conflict was in keeping with the federalist model: a place was made for private agencies in the child welfare system, subject to professionally informed state regulatory and licensure laws. But debate continued within the NCCC over how much authority state supervisory agencies should exercise. On one side were advocates of the board of control model—according to which the state would directly administer charitable institutions—and on the other, advocates of boards of supervision, which had only advisory power. The major issue was whether a centralized body could really direct the day-to-day affairs of a remote institution. Some consensus emerged that boards in large states should be concerned with business matters, and professionals should run the institutions directly; in smaller states, some more direct control might be feasible (*PNCCC* 1907, 45–51). Thus the official NCCC position was a compromise that balanced the priorities of centralization and professional autonomy. State legislative response to NCCC advocacy was uneven. By 1911, twenty states and the District of Columbia were reported as having only supervisory boards of charities and corrections; two states had supervision by a single commissioner of charities; sixteen states, mostly southern, had no provision whatever for supervision of institutions; and only nine states reported centralized boards that directly controlled institutions (*PNCCC* 1911, 10–11).

The ideal of federation was an important part of the ideology of the juvenile court as well. The court's very existence as a specialized legal tribunal for children, and the doctrine of *parens patriae* upon which its authority rested, signified a special relationship between the child and the state. On the one hand, this relationship implied a responsibility for the state to assure the child's welfare, if necessary, "for the protection of society, and for the welfare of the child himself, to place him in an environment and under a training specially adapted to secure his reformation and to prepare him for honest and intelligent citizenship" (Wentworth 1901, 253). Through the juvenile court, the state need not resort to institutional confinement, but could prevent serious deviance by teaching the child "that the state occupies the same position as its parent, and is his friend and protector, and the government is for his own welfare" (*PNCCC* 1902, 424–425). On the other hand, by contributing to the welfare of children, the juvenile court created benefits that ultimately accrued back to the state. In the words of Julian Mack, "in determining what is best for the future of the child the Court determines what is best for the future of the State" (*PNCCC* 1905, 481).

But the juvenile court was not just intended to serve the public in the long run. As a local outpost of the state, its value also lay in the present, in its ability to coordinate a variety of child welfare services. In one NCCC session devoted to various aspects of child saving, a speaker suggested that the juvenile court should be the hub of all charity activities: "There is not a thing on this program that does not concern the juvenile court. . . . We want to know what to do with all the children in order to cure them of their troubles, and make them good citizens. . . . In large cities juvenile courts are little more than clearing houses to get together the boy or girl that needs help and the agencies that will do the most good" (*PNCCC* 1908, 385–386).

The juvenile court was welcomed as an agency that could give legal teeth to the efforts of charity workers, who often felt themselves hampered by a lack of authority to intervene in families. Armed with a court order, the previously mentioned charity worker would have found it unnecessary to carry out her "neat case of kidnapping." The court gave institutions "the legal status and powers they have most stood in need of" (Hurd 1905, 328). At the same time, the court could compel cooperation by child-saving agencies. Hastings Hart recommended, for example, that any decision to remove a child from the home must involve the juvenile court because of the court's ability to coordinate the efforts of a variety of agencies (Hart 1909, 44–45). Indiana had passed a law to that effect that permitted children to be supported at public expense only after adjudication in the juvenile court (*PNCCC* 1907, 541).

In summary, charity organizers and juvenile court advocates derived mutual benefits from the strategy of federation. To the charity agencies the juvenile court appeared as a means of rationalizing client flow and as a source of legal authority. The court, by assuming a leadership role among local charities, could distance itself from the punitive imagery of the criminal court and add some substance to its claim to offer therapeutic services.

Professionalization of Social Work and Probation

Full realization of the ideal of scientific charity required expert personnel to carry out the duties of charity administration. The increasing emphasis on expertise, in turn, is directly related to the rise of social welfare as a profession. Professionalization in charity societies increased significantly toward the end of the nineteenth century, and by the 1890s, "the day had passed when any one was considered capable of readjusting the family affairs of others" (Watson 1922, 333). By 1906, charity organizers were comparing themselves favorably to other established professions and were seeking to enforce similar standards of training and ethics: "The quack, the unprofessional doctor, is no greater menace to the community than the unprofessional, paid charity-worker, and the sooner we cease to tolerate the latter, the better it will be for the community" (Pear 1906, 106).

Mary Richmond was the most vociferous advocate of professionalization. Richmond made explicit the link between professionalization and rational administration. The scientific charity worker's role was not to hand out doles, but to be familiar with available resources and agencies and to provide to the applicant aid that would cause the least dependence—"to develop, by cooperation, all possibilities of help within and without the family" (Richmond 1901a, 306–307).

The ideology of expertise in charity work had two components that were implicitly contradictory and that betrayed a typically Progressive ambivalence toward the urban poor. On the one hand, because the scientific charity worker sought to be rational and empirical in her approach to family problem solving, she eschewed the moral judgments and sentimentalism that had characterized earlier forms of charity:

> We need not assume, or seek to prove or disprove, the moral delinquencies of our poor. We may wisely confine ourselves to the attempt to aid in the solution of their economic problems, and may leave to the church in the exercise of its spiritual function, to moral philosophers and to ethical teachers, all questions of motives, and personal merits and moral virtues, and teleological relations. I think we may throw overboard once and for all the idea that the poor are our moral inferiors. (Devine 1903, 541)

But on the other hand, the "scientific" criteria by which aid was offered consistently revealed implicit moral judgments: the home is superior to the institution; sobriety is better than drunkenness; and a job is more helpful than a dole. The Progressive charity worker, like the Progressive political reformer, could not quite believe that the poor were capable of making decisions regarding their own welfare. The writer just quoted argues in another context that only the expert judgment of the professional can save the poor from their own folly: "To give without knowledge is not only unwise: it is wicked. It is administering an opiate without a diagnosis, to quiet pain, instead of ascertaining the nature of the disease in order that it may be cured" (Devine 1901, 323).

The charities literature of the period is unanimous in its support of the professionalization of social work: professional status appeared as an unalloyed good and as a well-precedented means of promoting the prestige and influence of the charitable enterprise. In the juvenile court movement, however, there was some debate over the type of expertise required and who should exercise it. The overt conflict was short-lived, but it had important long-run consequences. It resulted in a routinized division of labor within the court organization and the ultimate exaltation of the probation officer as the embodiment of professional expertise.

The conflict revolved around the personal style of Judge Ben Lindsey of Denver. Lindsey was more than just another judge; he was the best known of all the evangelists for the juvenile court cause. His personality was "warm and erratic," his style was anti-intellectual and antibureaucratic, and he continually praised the importance of the "personal touch" in dealing with wayward youth (Mennel 1973, 137–139). What galled his contemporaries most was not his conduct within his own courtroom, but the fact that he publicly emphasized the importance of the juvenile court judge at the expense of the probation officer. "Especially in the very large cities," he conceded at one point, "the important part of [juvenile court] work must fall to probation officers. The best results, however, under the new system, will depend largely upon the personal, active, earnest work of those who are called upon to administer the law" (Lindsey 1903b, 403)— that is, the judges.

Lindsey advocated a court characterized by charisma, personal insight, and khadi-like judgment. His most outspoken opponent, Judge Julian Mack of Chicago, was concerned with establishing a court system that was professional, bureaucratic, and as distinct as possible from adult criminal courts. Mack recognized that the judge and probation officer had separate spheres of competence, and in explicit contrast to Lindsey's charismatic system, he recommended that "the two lines of work ought to be clearly separated in the law," that probation officers be appointed according to civil service criteria, and that they be supervised by an official probation commission (Mack 1906, 124–125). As previously mentioned, Probation Commissioner Homer Folks also advocated executive organization of probation and a rationalized division of labor between judges and probation officers. Judges are not prepared to assume ongoing supervision of juveniles, Folks maintained; they are trained to think "case by case, eliminating all other considerations and the facts in that one individual case, then to pass on to another, and to another and another." In contrast, effective oversight of children by probation officers requires consistent organization and administration (Folks 1906, 121).

The role of the probation officer was crucial to the ideology of the juvenile court for two reasons. First, probation was offered as the humane alternative to institutionalization for juveniles (Hurley

1907, 227); as such, it was the major factor that distinguished the juvenile court from other courts. According to a statement made by Judge Tuthill at the first session of the Chicago juvenile court, "The probation feature in my judgement is the keystone which supports the arch of the juvenile law" (quoted in Hurley 1907, 225). Through the probation officer, the court was given the means to intervene and correct the juvenile's wayward tendencies: "The voice of pity and compassion must reach him in his home, and reach his parents also in his home. Down to the very depths of that home it must go" (Heuisler 1903, 400). "The probation officer is the right arm of the court. . . . It is through this officer that the court exercises the parental care of the state" (Hurd 1905, 327).

Second, the probation officer's role provided the link between the methodologies of organized charity and juvenile justice. The probation officer, like the trained charity worker, was to be a professional, trained in the methods of investigation, diagnosis, and treatment.[9] The goal of the probation investigation is to reconstruct the conditions that led the juvenile into waywardness:

> The investigation of the family conditions must be complete and thorough. No point is too small to be noticed and sometimes a casual sentence leads to a knowledge of the true inwardness of things. . . . The investigation should cover the whole field of family relations, not only to its own members but to the outside world, the school, the church, the workshop, the street. (Ramsey 1906, 134)

In short, the contemporary view was that "a juvenile court without a thorough probation system is both unscientific and unhumanitarian" (Rogers 1904, 378). And just as the demand for expertise in charity work eventuated in the volunteer being displaced by the trained professional, so demands were heard that probation work

9. And like that of the charity worker, the role of the probation officer was that of professional mother. Charles R. Henderson of the University of Chicago recalled, "An old proverb ran thus: God could not be everywhere, so he made mothers. The judge cannot be everywhere, so he must have made probation officers" (Henderson 1904, 367).

should be a paid, career occupation (Rogers 1904, 373; Henderson 1904, 368–369).

Conclusion

The emergent division of labor between judge and probation officer in the early stages of the juvenile court movement signified more than any other single phenomenon that the court's true goal was not a new technology of rehabilitation, but a comprehensive administrative apparatus that coordinated and formalized routine practices of the past. The salient feature of this apparatus was the distinction between judicial-legal and administrative-expert functions. The new court offered nothing in the way of procedural innovations—in fact, one of its much-touted features was the absence of formal procedure; and as Chapter 3 showed, procedural guarantees had been dispensed with in most states through legislation establishing reformatories.

Nor was there any change in the strategy for attacking delinquency. "Prevention" continued to be the ideal, as it had been since the refuges, and "predelinquents" (incorrigibles or noncriminal offenders) continued to be the focus of the preventive effort. If anything, the juvenile court movement merely helped promulgate the myth of prevention and placed it more conspicuously on the agendas of reformers of every stripe. Police Chief August Vollmer, for example, urged police to assume responsibilities for crime prevention by aggressive surveillance of wayward children: "Inasmuch as we have had pointed out to us by scientific studies and our own observations that the majority of our professional crooks were troublesome children long before they became criminals, it behooves the policeman to concentrate his attention upon the problem child during the predelinquent period" (Vollmer 1923, 281).

Finally, despite all the rhetoric about "scientific" investigation, the new science of psychiatry, and the like, the theories of delinquency causation espoused by juvenile court reformers remained remarkably unsophisticated and largely unchanged from those that had prevailed for a hundred years. In addition to the usual causes—poverty, drunkenness, and a generally poor home life—otherwise reasonable people occasionally offered hypotheses that now seem remarkably naive. An Indianapolis judge asked rhetorically, "How is the great increase in the number of delinquent children in all our large cities to be accounted for?" His answer was that "by far the worst thing to be met with in the cases of boys charged with delinquencies is the *cigarette habit*. . . . We have found that when a boy is guilty of a grievous offense he is generally found to be a user of cigarettes" (Stubbs 1904, 356; emphasis in original). No less an authority than Judge Mack of Chicago offered his own, somewhat more complex, etiology: "One of the great causes of delinquency is truancy. Adenoid growths lead indirectly to truancy. They lead to the penitentiary" (Mack 1908, 380).

The major accomplishment of the juvenile court was administrative, in that it provided a legally sanctioned arena within which diagnostic investigations could be conducted and therapeutic treatment initiated. To at least one radical in the child welfare field, it would ideally be possible to dispense entirely with the trappings of the courtroom and make the state directly responsible for the "moral, physical, and economic education and training of its children" through the agency not only of probation officers, but of teachers and other public servants (Jewell 1910, 152). But for reasons I have already discussed, the juvenile court as a legal institution was a crucial part of the child-saving enterprise. The court lent the power and prestige of the state to the charity organizers, and in return it received the legitimacy and discretion that accrued from association with "scientific" philanthropy.

What is the significance of these findings for the apparent success of the juvenile court movement? If the court was not a revolutionary achievement in child welfare, why was it touted as such? And most important, what is the relationship between the origins of the juvenile court as an administrative phenomenon and the character of the contemporary juvenile justice system? The general theme of this chapter has been that the juvenile court embodied characteristic ideological features of the national Progressive movement and in particular that it ceremonially enacted the goals and administrative principles of the charity organization movement that preceded it. The precise nature of the relationship between the charity organization and juvenile court movements is, however, unclear. One possibility is that the juvenile court was a part of a national charity agenda, with the diffusion of the former depending on the influence of the latter. The alternative possibility is that the juvenile court was politically, if not ideologically, independent of the broader charity movement and that its diffusion was propelled by some unique impetus. I test these competing hypotheses in the next chapter.

Whether or not there is any causal relationship between the juvenile court and charity reform, they clearly shared a partnership of some kind that left a strong imprint on the subsequent development of American juvenile justice. As some contemporary observers noted, their partnership was an inherently precarious one because it involved a coordination of effort by two institutions with disparate historical origins and potentially incompatible normative systems. The drive to "socialize" justice—the attempt both to individualize the application of law and to make law an instrument of public policy—is an enterprise fraught with conflict that threatens the integrity of both participating institutions.

George Herbert Mead explored this point in a 1918 essay titled "The Psychology of Punitive Justice." In this essay Mead begins with the assumption that, in its pure form, criminal justice is a collective form of retribution. By rendering judgment on a criminal who has done them no personal harm, members of the collectivity not only exact vengeance due the injured party, but symbolically protect the well-being of society as a whole. Based on this assumption, Mead suggests further that such social reforms as the juvenile court repress and redirect group hostility toward an abstract, symbolic, "criminal" condition. But, he cautions, the fundamental motive of hostility is never eliminated entirely; hence the drive to do good is constantly in danger of degenerating to a more primal form.

Mead argues that the socialization of justice has as its most fundamental requirement a transformation of method to permit the consideration of evidence that would not be relevant under a more punitive model of law and that this requirement in turn necessitates a relaxation of procedures and the invasion of expert judgment. This transformation is shown most clearly in the contrast of criminal and juvenile proceedings:

> The adult criminal court is not undertaking to readjust a broken-down social situation, but to determine by the application of fixed rules whether the man is a member of society in good and regular standing or is an outcast. In accordance with these fixed rules what does not come under the legal definition not only does not naturally appear but is actually excluded. Thus there exists a field of facts bearing upon the social problems that come into our courts and governmental administrative bureaus, facts which cannot be brought into direct use in solving these problems. It is with this material that the social scientist and the voluntary social worker and his organizations are occupied. In the juvenile court we have a striking instance of this material *forcing its way into the institution of the court itself* and compelling such a change in method that the material can be actually used. (Mead 1918, 595–596; emphasis added)

Note the choice of language: Mead sees the material "forcing its way" into the court and "compelling" changes in method. As this imagery suggests, the logic of diagnosis and treatment cannot be taken up and dropped at will; its normative integrity—upheld by professional ambition—demands that it be worked out and rationalized. The much-complained-of weaknesses of the juvenile court—its arbitrariness, abusive discretion, and vulnerability to vague pseudo-professional opinion—are typically explained as results of a failure of will or lack of resources, as problems of underdevelopment rather than as structurally induced outcomes. Mead's analysis is important because he sees the juvenile court not simply as a regrettably vague and even slipshod organization, but as an institution that is vague *because* it is inherently conflictual. On the one hand, there is the inviolability of the child and, on the other hand, the punitive tendencies of the law. In one mind, there is the desire to redeem; in another, the hostility that motivates judgment. And behind each attitude lies a set of interests and institutional forms that are only precariously balanced. To Mead the juvenile court was of "particular interest" in this regard

> because the court is the objective form of the attitude of hostility on the part of the community toward the one who transgresses its laws and customs, and it is of further interest because it throws into relief the two types of emotional attitudes which answer to two types of social organization. Over against the emotional solidarity of the group opposing the enemy we find the interests which spring up around the effort to meet and solve a social problem. These interests are at first in opposition to each other. The interest in the individual delinquent opposes the interest in property and the social order dependent upon it. (Mead 1918, 596–597)

The precariousness of the juvenile court, and of the social welfare system in general, arises from the difficulty involved in mobilizing collective hostility toward an objectified, but nonetheless abstract, "problem." The simplest outcome, and the one that the juvenile court fell heir to early on, is the tendency to fall to the lowest common denominator, to express hostility in its punitive form rather than its problem-solving form. If this were the only difficulty, the result would be straightforward: the juvenile court today would resemble the criminal court. But this is not the case. The juvenile court of today is in many ways an elaboration of the juvenile court as it was founded in 1899. The reason lies in the deeper problem identified by Mead: the conflict within socialized justice is not just a conflict of attitudes or goals, but of social-organizational forms. Moreover, as this chapter has been at pains to demonstrate, the organizational forms of charity and law are not only in conflict; they are interdependent in the context of the juvenile court.

Thus it is possible to say at the same time that the juvenile court was not revolutionary and that it has enduring importance in the history of law and child welfare. Juvenile court legislation crossed no legal frontiers; its contribution was rather ceremonial and administrative. The delinquent, alleged to be the subject of therapeutic intervention, in fact became an object bent to the conflicting needs of an ambivalent institution.

5

The Diffusion of
Ceremonial Justice

The discussion of the juvenile court to this point has outlined the close ideological affinity between the juvenile court movement and the more broadly based movement for reform in charity organization. I have suggested that the ideological thrust of the two movements was ceremonial in nature in that it emphasized formal, administrative innovation rather than new theories of causation or treatment practices for the problems of children and the poor. I extend the argument in this chapter by closely examining legislative data drawn from juvenile court statutes. By shifting the discussion from ideology to policy, I can define the juvenile court as a legal entity, describe its implications for the treatment of children, and explore the causal determinants of juvenile court reform among the states.

Although the interpretation of reform as a ceremonial activity suggests that the juvenile court was a spurious *legal* development, it does not imply that the court was an unimportant *social* phenomenon. As I show, the juvenile court was a significant step in the rationalization of a model of discretionary control over children. It represented an officially sanctioned linkage between the substantive concerns of social welfare and the formal, procedural orientation of the law. In that sense it was an extension of the ideals of the refuge movement. At the same time the juvenile court set a new high-water mark for the principles of socialized jurisprudence. Previous reformers had devoted most of their attention to perfecting methods of institutional treatment and tended to regard the court process as a troublesome formality they had to observe before they rescued a child from his or her home. Juvenile court reformers sought instead to make adjudication the indispensable first step in an extended process of diagnosis and rehabilitation.

The Legal Implications of the Juvenile Court

Although the reformatory institution was a relatively straightforward extension of the idea that children and adults should be institutionalized separately, the juvenile court was an ambiguous phenomenon: as defined in state laws, juvenile courts had no particular structural or procedural characteristics. And although the reformatory had clear implications for the legal status of children that followed from the philosophical assumptions of the refuge reformers, the relationship of the juvenile court to the legal innovations associated with it was complex and interactive. In this section I first describe the juvenile court as it was realized in state statutes, not only to portray its inherent ambiguity but also to develop an operational definition of the juvenile court to be employed later in the analysis. Then I describe the kinds of changes in the treatment of juvenile offenders that followed in the wake of the juvenile court.

The Ambiguity of the Juvenile Court Idea

Contemporary reformers seem to have shared no common vision about how the juvenile court should be organized. They all seemed to agree that it was *not* an adult criminal court, just as earlier reformers and several appellate courts had agreed that reformatories were not prisons. There was also general agreement that juvenile courts should be created by state statute, as was the first juvenile court in Chicago (1899 Illinois *Laws,* pp. 131–137), although this was by no means a prerequisite.

Indeed, the tendency to create juvenile courts by local fiat appears to have been common. For example, Ben Lindsey was fond of claiming that he had established the first juvenile court on the basis of a Colorado compulsory school-attendance law. Before a juvenile court law was passed in Indiana, reformers noted approvingly that an Indianapolis police court judge held children's trials privately and informally in a room not used for adult trials (*PNCCC* 1902, 46; for a full account, see Collins 1932). By 1903, informal juvenile courts had also been set up in Baltimore and New Orleans (*Charities* 1903, 56, 58). In at least one case, an informal court was set up as an example to prod legislators into action. Following a meeting of the NCCC in Atlanta, the City Federation of Women's Clubs sponsored an informal court in that city that could be "pointed to by those who were primarily concerned in pushing through the juvenile court project as evidence of its ready success" (*Charities* 1904–1905, 85). In Massachusetts, by contrast, child welfare legislation was so well developed that legislators took a rather indifferent attitude toward the new court. In 1905, they defeated a bill that would have required one municipal court judge in Boston to hear all children's cases, "largely . . . because it was not radical enough to seem worthwhile." The municipal court itself subsequently assigned separate rooms for children's trials, and the Boston Civic League began a statewide campaign to achieve compliance with an 1874 law requiring separate trials for children (*PNCCC* 1905, 57).

Juvenile courts were eventually established by statute in all fifty states, but they varied greatly in the geographic scope of their enabling legislation and in the place assigned to them in the state court administrative systems. It was common for legislatures to create courts only in the one or two largest cities or counties in the state. This was the case in Illinois, for example, where section 3 of the 1899 juvenile court law authorized courts in "counties having over 500,000 population" (i.e., Chicago). In Ohio, courts in Cuyahoga County (Cleveland) were given juvenile court jurisdiction (1902 Ohio *Laws*, ch. 785, §1), and juvenile courts were established in Oregon counties with more than one hundred thousand population (1905 Oregon *Laws*, ch. 80, §3). In California, all superior courts, justice's courts, and police courts in all counties were empowered to act as juvenile courts (1903 California *Statutes*, ch. 43, §2).

The contemporary reform literature did not prescribe any particular organizational form for the juvenile court, but a few modes of court organization were dominant. In his survey of courts, Lou (1927) identified three general types. The first and most common was the designated court, where a judge serving in the regular court system (whether of civil or criminal jurisdiction, and at whatever level) was assigned to hear juvenile cases.[1] The second type was the separate court, an administratively distinct court with unique jurisdiction and status equal to those of other courts in the system. The third type was the coordinated court, which had jurisdiction over family matters such as divorce and adoption as well as delinquency. To these may be added a fourth type of court, midway in status between designated and separate courts, which I have labeled divisional courts. This label means that state legislation established juvenile courts as "divisions" or "branches" of other courts. Divisional courts were often empowered to make their own budgets and rules, but were obviously inferior to courts of general jurisdiction.

---

1. In the words of the Illinois act, "the judges of the circuit court shall . . . designate one of their number whose duty it shall be to hear all cases coming under this act. . . . The court may, for convenience, be called the 'Juvenile Court.' " This "convenience" formula was copied verbatim into the juvenile court acts of many other states.

The trend in early juvenile court legislation was clearly toward designated courts, the least differentiated of the four organizational forms. Forty states established their first juvenile courts as designated courts, four as divisional courts, five as separate courts, and one as a coordinated court. Over the eighty-year period covered by these data, there has been a weak trend among the states toward increased formalization and autonomy, but this does not mean that juvenile courts in general have grown in practical stature or power. The data show no clear relationships between court organization and jurisdiction, procedural autonomy, or budgetary power.[2] That is, inferior as well as superior courts could have "exclusive, original" jurisdiction over juvenile matters; level of court organization has no apparent relationship to whether judges served full time on the juvenile bench or were mainly concerned with other matters; and right of appeal seems to vary independently of court type. Furthermore, states often established more specialized courts without abolishing less specialized ones, and two states established less formalized courts after more formalized courts already existed.

Differences in organizational form apparently meant very little to reformers. Their writings—especially those during the early part of the movement, before serious criticisms of the juvenile court began to be heard—offer so few prescriptions in this regard that it is doubtful the reformers gave much thought at all to what the court should look like as a legal entity. At least one commentator felt that the juvenile court should not become a separate court, lest it be corrupted by its authority; rather, it should function as a part of the chancery court. Juvenile jurisdiction "should be given to a court having common law chancery powers—not a criminal court. It is not desirable that a new court be created, even if the constitution will allow of it. A court of general jurisdiction is preferable, has better judges, and is not likely to fall into police court ways" (Hurd 1905, 327).

2. No systematic, quantitative data were collected on the prerogatives of each court. These observations are based on notes taken while recording legislative histories.

Decisions about court organization appear to have been made pragmatically and situationally and are not explainable by any generalized drive for increased legal authority and prestige. Reformers seem to have preferred to take the path of least resistance, establishing courts by the simplest legislative route and deriving authority from their tenuous association with courts of general jurisdiction. In Georgia, for example, a separate juvenile court was established not out of any desire to improve court functioning, but because of an adverse decision by the Georgia Supreme Court. The original Georgia juvenile court act (1908 Georgia *Laws*, p. 1107) empowered each county to establish juvenile courts "as branches of the superior courts" on the concurrent recommendation of two grand juries. This law was declared unconstitutional in *Law et ux.* v. *McCord* (85 SE 1025 [1915]) on the grounds that it violated the constitutional requirement of uniformity of jurisdiction (in that a superior court acting as a juvenile court would differ in its "powers, proceedings, and practices" from a superior court in a county lacking a juvenile court). In legislative session that same year, the Georgia legislature reestablished the juvenile court as a separate court in counties of over sixty thousand inhabitants (1915 Georgia *Laws*, p. 36, §1).[3]

Just as the juvenile court was poorly defined in law, so it was unevenly realized in practice. Ben Lindsey noted that the 1899 Illinois juvenile court law was "much neglected" outside Chicago and observed that some large cities had made no moves at all to establish juvenile courts (Lindsey 1905, 160). So amorphous was the juvenile court concept that reformers seemed willing and able to call any special provisions for children's hearings a juvenile court law. For example, in 1903, a Louisiana delegate to the NCCC announced the recent passage of a juvenile court law in her state (*PNCCC* 1903, 54). The only delinquency-related bill passed by the Louisiana legisla-

---

3. As the Georgia case suggests, some state constitutions forbade legislatures from establishing new courts. Constitutional provisions do not explain the distribution of organizational forms, however, because designated courts were the norm even in states where no such prohibition existed.

ture in the preceding session never actually mentioned the juvenile court (1902 Louisiana *Acts*, no. 136). Sections 2 and 3 of the bill required separate detention and trials for minors, standard elements of other states' juvenile court acts, but section 1 required the appointment of counsel for all accused juveniles after a preliminary hearing, a blatant violation of the spirit of the juvenile court (indeed, of juvenile justice throughout the nineteenth century). This situation was not corrected until a 1908 bill removed the requirement of counsel and allowed the court to consider evidence that would be inadmissible in adult court. Another delegate announced in 1904 that Minnesota had passed a juvenile court act (*PNCCC* 1904, 64). The law in question (1903 Minnesota *Laws*, ch. 387) again never mentioned the juvenile court but did require separate detention and trials for minors in Minneapolis–St. Paul. It is interesting to note that in the subsequent statewide juvenile court law (1905 *Laws*, ch. 285) the detention restriction was repealed, perhaps in deference to officials in rural areas.

A contemporary commentator acknowledged great differences among the states in their conceptions of juvenile courts:

> Precisely what is meant by a juvenile court there is difficulty in determining. The inference that it signifies a special court or judge to try all kinds of children's cases is, with respect to most states, erroneous. There are certain states that have the separate features of a juvenile court law and yet lay no claim to one, and *vice versa*. (Bates 1905, 333)

As late as 1914, a committee of the National Probation Association made a similar criticism that the court's work was hampered by its inconsistent development (Flexner and Baldwin 1914, viii).

In sum, states were vague and unsystematic in their statutory definitions of juvenile courts, and actual court organization varied from statutory prescriptions. These features of the juvenile court movement are consistent with the notion that it was concerned more with legal symbolism than with legal behavior. The reformers' aim was to protect children from the law, not to bring more law to bear on them. They had little inclination to specify what the court should look like as a legal institution. Thus they emphasized the personal and professional qualities of court personnel and largely ignored the formal properties of court decision making.

Although the juvenile court did not have a distinct legal structure, it implied a set of broad but nonetheless empirically distinct legal rules for the treatment of children. I describe those rules in detail in the next section. But in order to relate these innovations empirically to the foundation of the court, we must first settle upon some operational definition of the juvenile court. How are we to know it when we see it if reformers and legislators themselves could not define it consistently? The strategy I have adopted here is to rely on the words of the statutes themselves: for the purposes of the discussion to follow, states had juvenile courts when they declared they had juvenile courts, by name, in the language of a statute.[4]

The Legal Correlates of Juvenile Court Legislation

There are five legal innovations that reformers supported as part of their juvenile court program and that legislators tended to accept as such: (1) the explicit labeling and definition of delinquency as an offense category, (2) the labeling and definition of dependency and neglect, (3) the requirement of separate preadjudicatory detention for juveniles and adults, (4) the requirement of a separate trial and/or "docket and record" for juveniles, and (5) the establishment of a specialized juvenile probation service. In the following discussion I describe these innovations in more detail. I again use residual plots,

4. This definition includes, for example, legislation such as the Illinois act quoted in note 1 in which a circuit court session hearing children's cases is "for convenience" called a juvenile court. It also includes any act that, in the body of the law, declares as its purpose the establishment of juvenile courts. It excludes the titles of acts when those titles are not specified in the statute. In a few cases, laws that never mentioned the juvenile court were given the short title "juvenile court act" in collections of session laws and code revisions. These titles are created by editors and do not have the force of law. Finally, the term "children's court," as used, for example, in New York, is considered synonymous with "juvenile court."

like those in Chapter 3, to explore the temporal relationships between these reforms and the establishment of juvenile courts. The
analysis will show that the meaning of these reforms is more ambiguous, and their pattern of diffusion more complex, than was the case
with reformatory legislation.

JURISDICTION, LABELING, AND DEFINITION. One subtle but
notable feature of juvenile court legislation was the tendency to specify formal definitions for delinquent and neglected (or dependent,
abused, or abandoned) children. In earlier legislation the word "delinquent" was used as a catchall term, at times overlapping with dependency and at times indistinguishable from it. The relative specificity
of juvenile court legislation is exemplified in the Oregon juvenile
court law:

> The words "delinquent child" shall include any child under the age of
> sixteen . . . years who violates any law of this State or any city or village
> ordinance, or who is incorrigible, or who is a persistent truant from
> school, or who associates with criminals or reputed criminals, or vicious
> or immoral persons, or who is growing up in idleness or crime, or who
> frequents, visits, or is found in any disorderly house, bawdy house or
> house of ill-fame, or any house or place where fornication is enacted, or in
> any saloon, bar-room or drinking shop or place, or any place where
> spiritous liquors are sold at retail, exchanged, or given away, or who
> patronizes, frequents, visits, or is found in any gaming house, or in any
> place where any gaming device is or shall be operated. (1905 Oregon
> Laws, ch. 80, §1)

The "dependent child" is defined in the same section at similar
length; the salient distinction is that dependency is defined as a result
of parental misconduct. It is worth noting that, despite its apparent
detail, the statute maintains its catchall quality by subsuming incorrigibility under delinquency. This was a general tendency: Massachusetts defined incorrigibles separately from delinquents in 1906 and
Rhode Island in 1915, but no other state did so until 1957. Interestingly, the original Illinois juvenile court act did not mention incorri-

gibility (or any of its accepted euphemisms) at all; rather, it defined a delinquent child simply as "any child under the age of 16 years who violates any law of this State or any city or village ordinance" (1899 Illinois *Laws*, p. 131, §1). California defined delinquency in the same fashion but initially subsumed incorrigibility under dependency and neglect (1903 California *Statutes*, ch. 43, §1). Thus different states began with different classificatory schemes, but through subsequent amendments a remarkable degree of consistency was achieved in a short period of time. Above all, it is important to observe that these definitions imply no changes in the population of offenders considered liable for state intervention—juvenile court statutes were more exhaustive but no less inclusive than the reformatory laws of the previous century. Their major effect was to offer formal, if fuzzy, distinctions between types of children who were already subject to the law.

Residual plots in Figures 4 and 5 display the temporal relationships between the definition of delinquency and neglect and the establishment of juvenile courts. As before, circles indicate the passage of a juvenile court law, vertical bars indicate the definition of delinquency and neglect, and horizontal lines denote either a positive or negative time lag between court and offense definition. The figures show that forty states defined delinquency as part of their juvenile court acts, and twenty-nine states wrote in definitions of neglect.

Why was the definition of offense types such a common phenomenon, and why was it so tied to the new court? One obvious reason was the reformers' desire to formalize a set of offense classifications for children that did not carry the stigma of an adult criminal charge. Thus the very creation of the delinquency label symbolized the contradictory nature of the juvenile court: on the one hand, the label conformed with the legal expectation of a specified charge and signified that the court's clientele consisted of real, identifiable types of children on whose behalf appropriate action would be taken. On the other, the labels were so vague and all-encompassing that they placed no practical limits on the court's decision-making latitude.

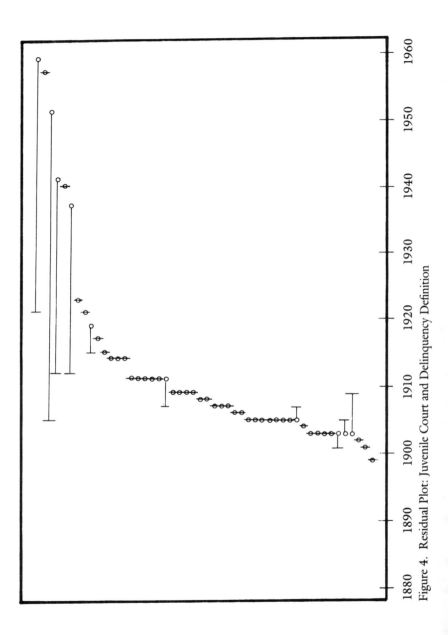

Figure 4. Residual Plot: Juvenile Court and Delinquency Definition

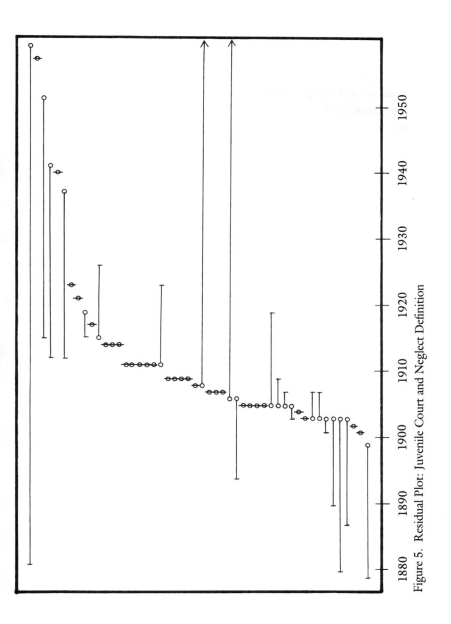

Figure 5. Residual Plot: Juvenile Court and Neglect Definition

One reformer suggested that formal categories provided a means for rationalizing and controlling the participation of treatment agencies:

> It is found much more convenient . . . in dealing with cases affecting children to embody in definite statutory form the definition of delinquency and dependency, and to provide many details by statute, the working out of which without the statute would depend upon the cooperation of various officials, which might not be so easily obtained, and which would be largely voluntary. (Kelley 1904, 43)

ᶜ Thus the proposed reason for labeling delinquents and dependents was to distinguish them for treatment purposes. This distinction was a direct echo of earlier reformers' desires to distinguish between "criminal" and "delinquent" offenders, amplified by the recognition that the delinquent label had acquired a stigma of its own. A committee for the National Probation Association, for example, felt that neglected children did not belong in the juvenile court at all (Flexner and Baldwin 1914, x). But this new taxonomy was purely symbolic because there were almost no provisions that the two groups of offenders should receive different treatment. For example, significant numbers of states did not begin to prohibit the placement of neglected juveniles in reformatories for delinquents until the 1960s.[5]

This matter was a source of early conflict among reformers, with managers of private institutions, in particular, resisting binding classifications. At the NCCC meetings in 1902, James Allison of the Cincinnati House of Refuge proposed that the two types of offenders should be classified differently at the outset and not put in the same institutions because the stigma of incarceration was unfair to dependent children. George Robinson of the New York Catholic

5. Of course, even such rules are rendered meaningless by eclectic and vaguely worded offense categories. In many statutes, such as the Oregon law quoted previously, the definitions of delinquency and neglect were so broad and imprecise that the majority of children brought before the court could have been charged with either condition, depending on the whims of the judge and probation officer.

Protectory disagreed, making the familiar claim that the source of all juvenile deviance was in the family and that the institution was the proper place for classification and treatment distinctions to be made:

> The distinction which may properly be made between the destitute and delinquent and the destitute and homeless is based on the individual character of the children. The separation into classes as indicated can be done only by the teachers of the reformatory. They are all amenable to the same kind of attention and instruction. (*PNCCC* 1902, 442)

The issue of classification was another front in the ongoing struggle between private charities and advocates of state supervision. Robinson, as a representative of a private child-saving agency, sought to defend the discretion and prestige of his institution against state encroachments. To do so, he reasserted the basic credo established by the refuge reformers in the 1820s, and his position became official NCCC policy. At the organization's 1906 meetings, separate committees on delinquent children, dependent children, and the juvenile court were combined into a single Committee on Children. As Chicago Judge Hastings Hart's comments on this occasion suggest, delegates felt that any limitations on institutional placement would bind not only the institutions, but the court as well:

> Dependent, Delinquent, and Defective children are not divided into separate classes by hard and fast lines, and we cannot prescribe definite treatment in advance for each separate class of children.
>
> The action recognizes that the Juvenile Court is not simply a branch of the Criminal Court, to administer justice to children of the criminal class, but that it is a great social agency, to inquire with discriminating insight into the conditions of the children of all classes which may be brought to it. (Hart 1906, 87)

These purely definitional innovations stand in clear contrast to the more substantive innovations associated with the reformatory. Further examination of Figures 4 and 5 shows that there is a difference not only in the content of these changes, but in their functional form as well. Recall that the data examined in Chapter 3 revealed a series of necessary, but not sufficient, relationships between the reformatory and the legal changes associated with it: the legal changes came either simultaneously or shortly after the establishment of an institution in almost all states. These figures show a contrary association: simultaneous enactment was the rule, but many states defined delinquency and neglect without establishing juvenile courts. There is obviously a close association between the definition of delinquency and the creation of a juvenile court—the simple correlation between the two innovations is .76. But note that some states defined delinquency in the period 1900–1920 whether they had a juvenile court by name or not—a phenomenon that suggests that the juvenile court movement influenced partial adoption of its institutional package. In Figure 5, the distribution of lags is remarkable: six states had defined neglect by 1894, well before the juvenile court movement; three states waited between ten and fifteen years after establishing a juvenile court to define neglect; and one did not do so until 1971. Even with this case removed from the sample, definition of neglect and creation of juvenile courts are correlated only at .35.

So far the data show no direct implications of juvenile court legislation for the treatment of different types of juvenile offenders. In many states the timing of these definitional reforms is only loosely associated with the establishment of juvenile courts, and in almost all states the definition of delinquency and neglect had no practical consequences for court decision making. Further discussion will show that the same pattern of cosmetic reform appears in the other court-related innovations.

SEPARATE DETENTION AND TRIALS. The requirements that children under detention before trial be confined apart from adults and that children's trials be held apart from adult trials are straightforward extensions of the segregative tendencies of nineteenth-century juvenile justice. In the refuge and reformatory movements, reformers were concerned to prevent hardened criminals from corrupting children in prisons. Juvenile court reformers sought to extend the principle of aseptic segregation to preadjudicatory and adjudicatory stages of court processing.

Legislation addressed itself to the detention issue in a variety of ways, but in general, statutes placed only weak constraints on the incarceration of children before trial. Juvenile court laws often authorized, but seldom required, the construction of separate juvenile detention facilities, and most acts contained safety valve clauses that permitted commingling under a wide variety of circumstances. In Arkansas, for example, authorities were prohibited from sending juveniles to jail only if there was a juvenile detention facility available (1911 Arkansas *Acts*, no. 215, §11). Some states imposed more categorical limits: Iowa prohibited the detention of juveniles in facilities with adults (1904 Iowa *Acts*, ch. 11, §12), and Colorado simply forbade the detention of juveniles in jails or lockups (1903 Colorado *Laws*, p. 101, §6). Many other jurisdictions allowed juveniles to be detained with adults but required separate rooms. For the purposes of this analysis, all such restrictions are considered separate detention.

The residual plot in Figure 6 shows the relative timing of legislation requiring juvenile courts and separate detention for juveniles. Again, despite the close graphic relationship between these reforms, their statistical association is only moderate—the correlation coefficient is .49. The distribution of extreme lags is striking. The most interesting of these are the left lags that indicate that the trend toward separate juvenile detention began in the nineteenth century. For example, Vermont and Ohio distinguished between juveniles and adults at detention over forty years before the first juvenile court; New York did so in 1873, and Pennsylvania and Rhode Island, in the 1890s. In thirteen other cases, separate detention preceded the juvenile court in varying degrees. Again, because most of the changes in juvenile detention laws occurred between 1900 and 1920, the effect of the juvenile court ideology cannot be denied. But it is apparent that the formal adoption of the juvenile court was not a prerequisite for the preadjudicatory separation of juveniles and adults.

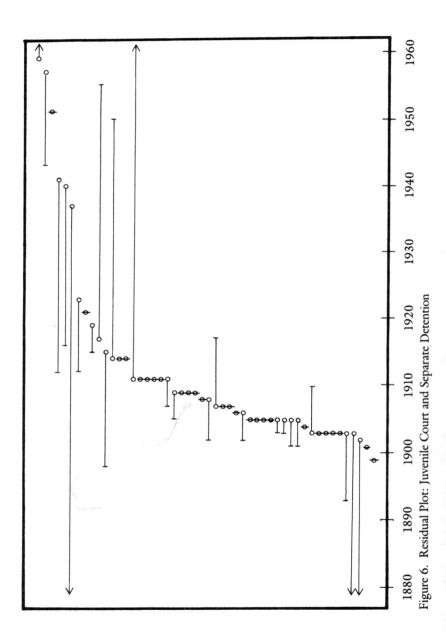

Figure 6. Residual Plot: Juvenile Court and Separate Detention

Figure 7 shows the relationship between the requirement of a separate trial, docket, or record for juvenile cases and the juvenile court. Strictly speaking, a docket is a court schedule, and a record is a written summary of court proceedings; but for coding purposes the three terms are taken as synonyms. There are three justifications for this. First, the concept of a separate trial was interpreted in several different ways. In some cases it meant a hearing in the judge's chambers; in others, a special day or hour set aside for juvenile cases; and in a few, a separate room outfitted and used only for juvenile hearings. Second, the designation of a separate docket and record implies separate hearings—as signified, for example, in the common distinction between civil and criminal dockets. Third, the literature of the juvenile court movement shows that all three forms of separation had the same purposes—to avoid mixing adult and juvenile offenders and to assure the privacy of juvenile hearings.

The residuals in Figure 7 again show a fair number of cases in which the legal innovation preceded the institution. In four states shown in the plot, separate trials were required before 1899. Massachusetts required separate juvenile trials in 1874. The majority of cases show simultaneous establishment of a juvenile court and separate trials, and only three states lagged in requiring separate hearings. Even with conspicuous outliers included in the sample, there is a high correlation of .79 between the dates of the two reforms.

JUVENILE PROBATION. Probation was the means by which juvenile court reformers sought to reduce the number of juveniles being committed to institutions and to provide professional social work expertise to wayward children and their families. But like the other innovations reviewed here, probation did not originate with the juvenile court. As Julian Mack (1909) noted, Massachusetts provided formal probation services to adults for forty years before the juvenile court. Court reformers simply included juvenile probation as part of their comprehensive reform package.

These data do not record when probation became a dispositional

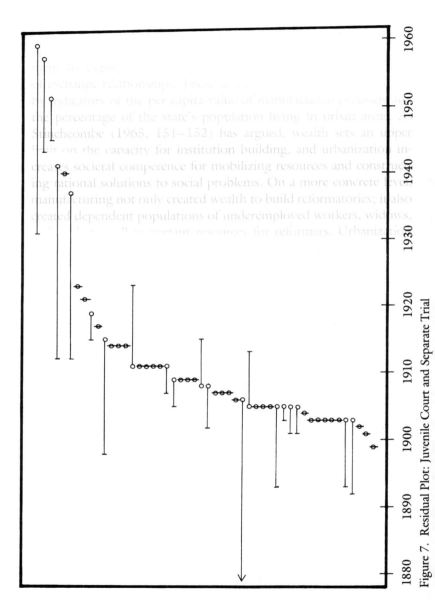

Figure 7. Residual Plot: Juvenile Court and Separate Trial

option for judges because probation, either formal or informal ("home placement"), was part of the juvenile court legislation of every state. Judges were authorized to suspend cases indefinitely, to review them at will, and to recommend sanctions at any time if the offender's behavior did not come up to expectations. Thus probation as such implied a tremendous increase in the judge's discretionary authority, which was synonymous with the juvenile court itself. For this reason I focus more specifically on the authorization of a specialized probation staff. The data record the year in which appointments were authorized and whether officers were to serve on a paid or volunteer basis. However, these data must not be taken as indicators of the extent of probation services actually offered because in many cases it was left up to judges or other local officials to employ as many officers as they wanted, and in others only one paid officer was authorized, with others to serve voluntarily. And as Rothman (1980) has shown, probation staffs have never been adequate to provide services other than cursory surveillance. These data record only the first year in which *any* volunteer probation officers were provided for and the first year in which *any* paid probation officers were authorized.

Twenty-one states established volunteer probation services before paid staffs were authorized, but most of these quickly established paid probation services. Twenty-seven states set up probation on a professional basis at the outset, and two states have made no provision for specialized juvenile probation units.[6] Because of the generally strong trend toward professional probation, subsequent analysis does not distinguish between paid and volunteer probation services.

Figure 8 shows the timing of probation and the establishment of juvenile courts. Little comment need be made here because the

6. Two states—New Jersey and Wyoming—never set up distinct juvenile probation services by statute (they appear in Figure 8 as extreme right lags), but that does not mean there is no juvenile probation. In New Jersey, there is a single centralized state probation agency that is required to provide juvenile services; officers were never formally attached to the juvenile court. Presumably, some similar arrangement prevails in Wyoming.

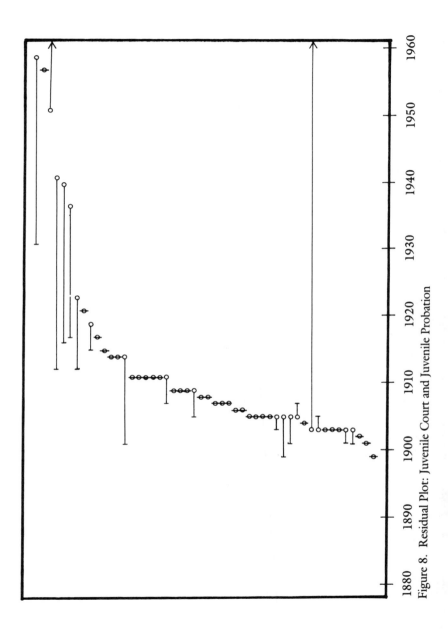

Figure 8. Residual Plot: Juvenile Court and Juvenile Probation

pattern is similar to those seen already. With two obvious outliers removed, the adoption of juvenile courts and probation are correlated at .83. In most cases juvenile court legislation included provisions for the appointment of probation officers, but in 14 states probation came before a juvenile court was established by name. Of the states that ever had juvenile probation, only two established juvenile courts without probation services, and they fell into line within two years. Again, states that had set up probation before they established juvenile courts tended to do so during the peak years of the juvenile court movement, presumably on the strength of the movement's ideology.

In summary, although the juvenile court is conventionally associated with important changes in the legal status of children, indeed with the "invention" of delinquency itself, it did not inaugurate the "new era in our criminal history" that its proponents foresaw (Fox 1970, 1229). This was in large part a result of the ambiguity of the juvenile court concept. Much of the impetus for the new court came from repugnance for juvenile reformatories and a desire to limit the commitment of children; yet within the charity organization movement the court became the partner rather than the enemy of the institution. The juvenile court "codified the shift from congregate to family penology; it did not shift the underlying rehabilitative aim of all juvenile penology" (Fox 1970, 1212).

Close examination of statutes revealed that the juvenile court was a piecemeal affair—in one sense really no more than the sum of its parts. It was distinct neither as the embodiment of an original philosophy of juvenile deviance nor as an organization. States varied idiosyncratically in the scope and status they gave their juvenile courts and in most cases were content to set up the court as a ritual affair, conducted one or two days a week by judges who were primarily concerned with other matters. The legal changes associated with the court—the labeling of delinquent and neglected children, the requirement of separate detention and trials for juveniles, and the appointment of specialized probation officers—were without exception pioneered independently of a general reform program and later incorporated into a comprehensive institutional package. Unlike the reformatory, the juvenile court did not inaugurate these changes, and it was not a necessary condition for their enactment, but it drew them together and promulgated them nationwide. As an anonymous author wrote in 1911,

> These features are not . . . entirely new, as is sometimes thought, but rest on principles long recognized. What is new in these laws consists mainly in providing improved administrative machinery for the application by the court of established principles and recognized powers, such as the suspension of sentence. (Note 1911, 302)

But the juvenile court was important simply because it was the sum of its parts. As its ideology became solidified and as juvenile courts proliferated among the states, the elements that made it up became more lustrous as they became associated elements of a model reform. For example, even in states where there was no felt need to provide special institutional care for neglected children, delinquency and neglect were defined because that was the normative pattern of juvenile court legislation. No matter that there was overall no less punitive treatment of neglected children; no matter either that probation was a facade for extended surveillance rather than a substitute for incarceration. The achievement of the juvenile court was the elaboration of an institutional myth: by forging a link between the movement for charity reform and the law, the juvenile court extended the basic premises of the reformatory movement within a more rational and legitimate framework. The linkages described so far are symbolic and ideological. The next section explores how political linkages were formed and in which direction they flowed. Specifically, I ask whether the juvenile court rode on the coattails of the charity organization movement or whether it diffused through some unique impetus of its own.

The Dynamics of Juvenile Court Reform

Support and Opposition

For the remainder of this chapter, I am concerned with discovering those factors that led to the acceptance of the juvenile court outside of Illinois. One prominent hypothesis, offered most forcefully by Platt (1969) and developed in the preceding chapter, is that the juvenile court was accepted because of its relationship with the charity organization movement. It will be worthwhile at this point to outline the history of that relationship.

The first mention of the court before the National Conference of Charities and Correction was the announcement by Illinois delegates of the creation of the Chicago court (*PNCCC* 1899, 53). The *Proceedings* record this announcement without fanfare, and it appears to have been regarded at first as an item primarily of local significance. The Illinois law was not a product of a national movement, but rather a practical, even ad hoc response to problems in the local child-care system (Fox 1970; Mennel 1973, 127–128). The NCCC did not immediately endorse the court or make it part of its child-saving program. Ohio delegates reporting on the progress of legislation in their state in 1902 made no mention of the juvenile court law that had been passed that year (*PNCCC* 1902, 89–91) and mentioned it only in passing in the next year's report (*PNCCC* 1903, 93). In the 1902 meetings, Ben Lindsey took the floor in informal discussion to advocate nationwide juvenile court legislation, describing the Chicago and Denver courts and urging subscriptions to their respective publications (*PNCCC* 1902, 423–425, 448–449).

In 1903, Lindsey made a special presentation on the subject of the juvenile court in the NCCC section meeting on juvenile delinquents (Lindsey 1903a). That same year, *Charities* magazine devoted an entire issue to the juvenile court in which it was reported that a special juvenile court exhibit had been set up at the St. Louis Exposition (*Charities* 1903, 395). Clearly, the juvenile court's time had come. In contrast to the nonchalance of the Ohio delegates to the NCCC two years earlier, the Texas delegates at the 1904 meetings had discovered a conspicuous need for juvenile courts in that state, and the West Virginia committee simply and reluctantly reported, "We have no juvenile court" (*PNCCC* 1904, 100, 109). At the same meetings a special section was devoted to juvenile courts. A permanent subcommittee on juvenile courts was established in 1905, and the ubiquitous Lindsey, serving as chair, delivered the progress report (Lindsey 1905).

The NCCC's adoption of the juvenile court as an officially sanctioned cause was undoubtedly an important step toward national legitimacy. Questions of power and influence aside, it is apparent that within the charity organization movement the rather raw notion of a court for children was elaborated into a coherent institutional model that reflected the broader ideals of the movement. Further, the NCCC in particular was a formidable communications network for disseminating reformist ideology, distributing model juvenile court acts, and lobbying state legislatures through its constituent state conferences of charities and correction. Thus at the very least the charity organizers provided a rationalized vocabulary through which the juvenile court was made part of a larger doctrine and promulgated from the urban centers to the nation's periphery.[7]

The evangelical promotion of the juvenile court became a common task of prominent activists. Timothy Hurley, president of the Chicago Visitation and Aid Society, reported that Illinois reformers had been invited to other states in the wake of the 1899 juvenile

---

7. A good example of center-periphery diffusion is found in the remarks of Oklahoma activist Kate Barnard in 1908. She reported that a major task of the territorial charities association was to help write planks for the pending constitutional convention and to keep the press informed on such social problems as child labor, sweat shops, and tenements (Barnard 1908, 38–39). That this laundry list of urban-industrial social problems is applicable to a predominantly rural state is assumed. For more on Ms. Barnard's struggle to modernize Oklahoma's charity institutions, see Bryant (1968).

court act to "explain the measure and the method of administering the law in Cook County" (Hurley 1903, 424). Hurley himself spoke on behalf of the court at the 1904 meetings of the Minnesota State Conference of Charities and Correction (*Charities* 1904–1905, 275), and Judges Tuthill and Mack of the Chicago court visited Minnesota as well (Lindsey 1905, 160). There were pilgrims as well as evangelists: Judge George Stubbs of Indianapolis visited Chicago, and Kate Barnard, the prominent reformer from Oklahoma, went to both Chicago and Denver to see the court in action (Collins 1932, 1–2; Bryant 1968, 369).

Lindsey was by far the most active evangelist. In 1904, he and Julia Lathrop went to state charities conferences in Washington and Oregon. While Lathrop stumped for charity organization, Lindsey spoke on behalf of the juvenile court. Lindsey went on to the California charities meeting as well, thus visiting three states in a single month (*Charities* 1904, 270–278). Perhaps encouraged by Lindsey's efforts, Oregon and Washington passed juvenile court laws in 1905. California already had a juvenile court, but in 1905, it amended its legislation to add probation officers. A juvenile court bill was passed in Iowa after Lindsey addressed the legislature and the Iowa Congress of Mothers lobbied on its behalf (*Charities* 1904, 405), and Lindsey was given credit for the 1906 Massachusetts juvenile court law (*PNCCC* 1906, 36). In 1907, he visited Oklahoma at the expense of the Russell Sage Foundation with a custom-drafted juvenile court bill in hand (Bryant 1968, 370). When Washington, Oregon, Nebraska, Kansas, and Utah all passed juvenile court laws in 1905, one commentator remarked, "They are all scalps for the belt of Judge Lindsey" (*Charities* 1905, 649).

This evangelical effort may explain the consistency among state rules affecting the labeling, detention, trial, and probation of children in their juvenile court acts. States often copied their juvenile court bills from acts already in force in other states, and the two normative models were those of Colorado and Illinois. Legislators were usually presented with draft bills by local reform groups; thus which model act was adopted may have been a simple function of propinquity and who visited town last. The Missouri juvenile court law of 1903, sponsored by the Humanity Club of St. Louis, was largely copied from the 1899 Illinois law (*PNCCC* 1903, 69–70). The Oregon charities conference passed a resolution after Lindsey's visit calling for an act "to include the special features of the Colorado juvenile court law" (*PNCCC* 1904, 94). The Nebraska act, already noted as one of Lindsey's triumphs, was a complete adoption of "the Colorado system" (*Charities* 1905, 649). The Washington law was modeled after both the Illinois and Colorado laws (*PNCCC* 1905, 84). Finally, in an interesting example of reverse diffusion, Illinois revised its juvenile court act by borrowing a provision from the Colorado law that held parents responsible for the dependency or delinquency of their children (*PNCCC* 1905, 45). Through cross-fertilization and the borrowing and reborrowing of statutory language, there was eventually a general convergence on the major points that characterized the juvenile court.

But the work of these evangelists does not explain why many states were such willing converts to the juvenile court gospel or why some were more receptive than others. According to one writer, the strength of the movement was in its breadth: "The men who are interesting themselves in it are not of one group nor of the type which can be called perennial reformers." Thus, he continued, the idea spread "spontaneously": "In the South, especially, the idea is spreading like a philanthropic boll weevil" (*Charities* 1905, 871). Lindsey credited "the press, the pulpit, the educational and charity organizations generally throughout the country" for publicizing the juvenile court and noted Theodore Roosevelt's endorsement of the court in 1904 as a sign of the movement's universal appeal (Lindsey 1905, 151).

Remarks of this sort are the purest boilerplate. They are intended to encourage solidarity among rank-and-file participants and to assure them that their day-to-day efforts are part of a universal, even transcendent, undertaking. But I would argue that this self-aggrandizement contains an element of truth. Although the juvenile court offered little in the way of clear, substantive reforms, it did fit quite well with broader Progressive trends toward rationalized administration and socialized jurisprudence. Unlike more controversial Progressive reforms such as mothers' pensions and workmen's compensation, it cost nothing to enact and threatened no property interests. In short, the court could accommodate a broad base of support precisely because little about it was controversial.

The literature reviewed here provides only fragmentary evidence of the court's broader base of support, but in general it appears that the same sorts of groups were influential in the diffusion of juvenile court laws as were prominent in Illinois—that is, voluntary civic associations, especially women's clubs. The influence of such groups in Iowa and Missouri has already been mentioned. The California Club, "a San Francisco organization of women of high standing," was credited with originating the drive for a juvenile court in that state (*PNCCC* 1903, 29–30). The women of the New Century Club were given credit for the first Pennsylvania juvenile court act and for a second one that was adopted after the original bill was declared unconstitutional (*PNCCC* 1901, 90; Schoff 1903, 426). After visits to Nebraska by NCCC representatives, women's clubs lobbied for juvenile court and child labor legislation (*PNCCC* 1907, 557) with apparent good effect: the juvenile court bill passed without "a dissenting voice in either branch of the legislature" (*PNCCC* 1905, 65). In Boston the Civic League supported reform (*PNCCC* 1907, 548); in Louisiana the Prison Reform Association, the women of the Era Club, and the Society for the Prevention of Cruelty to Children were influential (*Charities* 1905, 758); and the Kentucky juvenile court law was credited to "the influence of the men's and women's clubs of the state" (*PNCCC* 1906, 30).

Opposition to the new court was diffuse and largely mute. Some opposition to probation and parole reforms came from rank-and-file police officers (Rothman 1980, 78–79), but reform police administrators such as August Vollmer (1923) were anxious to jump on the delinquency prevention bandwagon. Movement literature itself is curiously vague on the reasons for occasional legislative setbacks. The failure of a proposed bill in Washington was blamed on inadequate lobbying (*Charities* 1903, 396), and "much opposition" was reported to a failed attempt to extend the juvenile court in Ohio beyond Cleveland (*PNCCC* 1904, 91). In neither case is any organized opposition described. Similar reticence is found in reports of juvenile court bills that failed to pass in New Hampshire, North Carolina, Maine, and Tennessee, and one killed by governor's veto in South Carolina (*PNCCC* 1905, 67–68, 73; 1908, 469; 1911, 460).

Where did legal professionals stand on the issue of the juvenile court? The Chicago Bar Association was active in lobbying for the Illinois act, but movement sources mention no support by legal organizations in other states. In Oklahoma and Indiana, some judicial officials viewed the court as an incursion on their proper domain (Collins 1932, 4; Bryant 1968, 369). This resistance appears not to have delayed enactment, however, and it is not clear how common such resistance was. Appeals judges tended to support the court on the basis of the 1838 *Crouse* case and the *parens patriae* doctrine. In the few cases where juvenile court legislation was struck down, it was always for technical reasons. In the Georgia case mentioned previously, a juvenile court law was found to have unevenly extended the jurisdiction of the superior courts. The first Pennsylvania juvenile court law was declared unconstitutional because it had too many separate subjects; the same law was subsequently reenacted in a series of separate bills (*PNCCC* 1903, 96). The first Nebraska law passed by the legislature was unconstitutional because of a "technical defect," "a little clause discovered by the Attorney General when it was too late to be corrected" (*PNCCC* 1904, 67).

Criticism of the court on constitutional due process grounds was slow to appear and was heard regularly only after the juvenile court was thoroughly institutionalized. Timothy Hurley (1905), a Chicago court reformer, voiced reservations about the discretionary latitude the court had received. A Pennsylvania judge criticized the juvenile court in 1914 for the questionable legal principles on which it was based, for discriminating against the poor, and for overreaching its appropriate jurisdiction by considering cases of simple dependency as well as misbehavior (Lindsey 1914). Jurist Roscoe Pound portrayed the court as the exemplar of socialized law that had reached and breached the "limits of effective legal action": "In modern law not only the duties of care for the health, morals and education of children, but even truancy and incorrigibility are coming under the supervision of the juvenile courts." Such duties, he wrote, "morally are of great moment but legally defy enforcement" (Pound 1917, 162; cf. Mead 1918). A thirty-year retrospective article by Murphy (1929) accused the juvenile court of every shortcoming that has been rediscovered since: for being unjust, discriminatory, overloaded, understaffed, imperialistic, and a general failure at both preventing delinquency and keeping children out of harmful institutions. Yet the juvenile court by that time was a "success" and has persisted in every state since.

In summary, it appears that the juvenile court movement was driven from the top by a national organization of charity reformers and fueled from the bottom by local civic groups that seized on it as an inoffensive focus for their varied efforts to do good. Documentary evidence suggests that charity organizers were particularly effective as an information network promoting uniformity in the language of state acts but provides only anecdotal proof that they hastened the enactment of juvenile court laws in a systematic way. Subsequent quantitative analysis addresses this issue.

Bivariate Effects on the Diffusion of the Juvenile Court

This analysis explores several general explanations for the diffusion of juvenile court legislation. The first of these, parallel with the analysis in Chapter 3, is the legal evolution model. According to this approach, a specialized children's court is a further example of structural differentiation in the realm of law. Again following Turner

(1980), the analysis pays special attention to three types of variables, all of which represent aspects of societal complexity: economic development, measured by per capita manufacturing output and percentage living in urban areas; educational development, measured by the percentage of the school-age population attending school and the percentage distribution of literacy in the population over age ten; and political centralization, measured by ratios of state government employees per ten thousand population.

A second major hypothesis, introduced in the previous section, is that the "moral entrepreneurs" of the charity organization movement induced a felt need for juvenile justice reform independent of structural conditions. Measuring the strength of a social movement is a risky business; to test this hypothesis, I examine collateral areas of reform agitation to see whether the general legitimacy of the charity agenda was conducive to the early adoption of juvenile courts. First, a series of three dummy variables will indicate whether states established centralized boards of charities and correction (1) by 1900, (2) between 1900 and 1910, or (3) after 1910 or not at all.[8] If the social movements hypothesis is correct, the first dummy variable should have a strong positive effect because it suggests that charity organizers were influential before the emergence of the juvenile court; the second should have a mild positive effect or none at all because it represents influence that was either prior to or concurrent with the court; and the last, representing states that tended most to resist the charity program, should have a negative effect. Second, I examine per capita expenditures on charities, hospitals, and corrections; here a positive effect is expected. Third, the percentage of manufacturing employees under age sixteen—a measure of reliance on child labor—is treated as a negative indicator of child welfare. Enactment and enforcement of child labor laws were high on the agenda of charity

8. Ideally, this variable would be treated as continuous. There are two reasons for not doing so, however: the distribution is extremely uneven; and data, drawn from the *PNCCC*, were not published after 1911. At that point seventeen states had no charity boards.

reformers. Insofar as high levels of child labor imply a lack of movement influence, they should be inversely related to rates of juvenile court adoption.

The analysis also examines some substantive hypotheses drawn from the literature on Progressive reform. Two of these specify causal effects endogenous to the legal system. Many writers have suggested that reform legislation was incited by judicial conservatism (see Bowman 1906; Pound 1907; James 1913; Smith 1914; Friedman and Ladinsky 1967; Nonet 1969)—in other words, that legislatures provided substantive remedies to problems of poverty, disability, and industrial exploitation because courts refused to abandon their rigid adherence to nineteenth-century laissez-faire doctrines. Canon and Baum (1981) have developed a composite index of state court innovativeness for 1902–1938 that allows a test for an expected negative relationship between judicial and legislative innovation. Fox (1970) has suggested, in concurrence with movement sources, that the juvenile court was intended to reduce commitments of juveniles to institutions.[9] If we assume that a desire to reduce commitments is related to high levels of commitments in a given state (not necessarily a valid assumption, of course), then a variable consisting of the ratio of committed delinquents per hundred thousand juvenile population will permit a test of that relationship. It has further been suggested that Progressive reform in general (Schiesl 1977) and the juvenile court in particular (Platt 1969) were, like Jacksonian reforms, aimed at the control and socialization of immigrants. If this is the case, states with higher percentages of foreign-born residents should have been more amenable than others to the court.

Finally, I again explore three kinds of effects from an institutional perspective: patterns of associations that depart from functional hy-

9. Mennel (1973, 125n) further observes that several late nineteenth-century court decisions released children held in reform schools. He suggests that these cases reflected a general public skepticism toward institutions and may have helped usher in the juvenile court. See *People v. Turner*, 55 Illinois 280 (1870); *State v. Ray*, 63 New Hampshire 405 (1886); *Ex parte Becknell*, 51 Pac. Rep. 692 (California, 1879); and *Angelo v. the People*, 96 Illinois 209 (1880).

potheses and point toward more historically specific interpretations; time-dependent trends in adoption rates that suggest legitimation processes; and regional diffusion effects that identify comprehensible reference group patterns among the states.

As I have already pointed out, whether a state did or did not have a juvenile court at a given time was a matter of some confusion, and the formal definition I have chosen for this discussion is somewhat arbitrary. It may be argued that such a definition will bias the analysis: we should not be surprised to find that a purely nominal reform was accepted without regard to functional requisites or social movement influence. As a check on such definitional bias, I present parallel analyses on two adoption processes: the enactment of juvenile court laws and of laws requiring separate juvenile trials. I chose the latter innovation because it lies at the core of the movement's ideology, because it seems to represent the minimum commitment necessary for a state to consider itself to have a functioning juvenile court, and because it is the most binding and substantive of the six innovations described.

Table 4 shows parameter estimates of the bivariate relationships between the independent variables and rates of adoption for juvenile courts and separate trials. Here all independent variables are assigned their value in 1900 unless noted otherwise in the table; for convenience it is assumed that relative values remain constant throughout the observation period and that relationships are not time dependent.

The most striking finding shown by the table is the lack of strong relationships. Only three measures are significantly related to the observed adoption rates: urbanization shows a weak positive effect on juvenile court diffusion, which may be read to indicate a 2 percent increase in adoption rates for each percentage increase in urban habitation. Two region dummies have strong effects on both innovations: juvenile court adoption rates for New England states are 66 percent below the norm, and those for North Central states are 335 percent above. The associations are similar in the case of separate trials, where North Central states appear as eager innovators and

Table 4.   Bivariate Effects on Rates of Establishing Juvenile Courts
          and Separate Juvenile Trials

	Juvenile Courts	Separate Trials
Societal Complexity:		
Value manufactured products per capita (hundreds)	1.08	1.06
Percent urban	1.02*	1.01
Percent school-age population attending school	1.03	1.03
Percent literate	1.02	1.02
State government officers per 10,000 population	.95	.97
Social Movement:		
Charity board by 1900	1.20	1.29
Charity board, 1900–1910	1.60	1.59
No charity board by 1911	.62	.58
Social welfare spending per capita, 1903	1.04	1.21
Percent manufacturing employees under 16	.97	.95
Legal:		
Judicial innovation, 1902–1938	1.00	1.00
Delinquents in institutions per 10,000 youths, 1904	1.00	1.00
Immigration:		
Percent foreign born	1.02	1.02
Regions:		
New England	.34*	.41*
North Atlantic	2.35	.80
North Central	4.35**	6.66***
Midwest	2.02	2.30
South	.62	.61
South Central	1.12	1.20
Mountain	.99	.78
Pacific	1.34	2.68

*p < .05
**p < .01
***p < .001

New England states as reluctant. The estimates for the North Central states suggest a regional diffusion of the juvenile court from a point of origin in Chicago to neighboring states, which are also states in which Progressive ideology was strong. The New England estimates suggest that states may emulate their neighbors by resisting innovations as well as by adopting them.

All other relationships are insignificant, although almost all are in the expected directions. Only two items bear mention. State government size has a negative, but insignificant, effect on adoption rates, contrary to the hypothesis offered previously, and charity board dummies perform somewhat differently than expected. States that established charity boards between 1900 and 1910 were more receptive to the reforms than those that established boards earlier. This does not suggest a causal influence but rather a process of coincident diffusion: both charity boards and juvenile court reform spread most rapidly in the first decade of the century.

Summary statements are difficult, given the lack of strong associations. The data suggest that urbanization may have increased state receptiveness to juvenile court acts and that contrary regional influences were important in both reforms. The nearly identical effects shown for both adoption processes suggest that the estimates are not artifacts of the way in which the innovations were operationalized. Fortunately, multivariate findings turn out to be more revealing.

A Multivariate Model of Juvenile Court Reform

I built multivariate diffusion models in four steps. First, I entered three legal evolution variables into equations predicting juvenile court and separate trial laws as a block: urbanization, school attendance, and size of state government. I chose urbanization as the indicator of economic development because of its significant bivariate effect on juvenile court adoption; tests revealed that it outperformed the manufacturing item in both multivariate models. Similar tests using alternative specifications determined the choice of school attendance over literacy as an indicator of educational development. I discuss the significance of these choices later.

Second, because of the promising results of the bivariate analysis, I added each region dummy to the equation and tested the significance of its contribution using likelihood ratios. Third, I tested the resulting relationships for time dependence by dividing each into two periods. Some preliminary examinations showed that 1910 is the most revealing dividing line. This makes intuitive sense; because the median date of juvenile court adoption is 1908, the year 1910 approximately distinguishes early innovators from late adopters. Fourth, I tested the remaining social movement, legal, and immigration measures for both time-independent and time-dependent effects.

Table 5 displays results from the analysis of juvenile court adoption rates. Model I shows results from the first step of the analysis. It is a single-period equation that estimates the effects of the legal evolution variables only. In model II we see that, when regional effects are tested against this baseline model, only the New England dummy adds significantly to its predictive power. Model IIIa tests whether adoption rates vary from one time period to another, independent of the effects of exogenous measures. The difference in the constant terms shows that adoption rates more than doubled after 1910, and likelihood ratio tests indicate that the difference is significant (at $p \leq .05$). Model IIIb shows the results of time-dependence tests carried out on specific variables. The only difference from model IIIa is that the effect of the state government measure is shown to vary over time. This specification is a significant improvement over both models II and IIIa (for both tests, $p \leq .05$), which suggests that the observed time dependence is indeed the result of change in the effect of the variable. Finally, model IV shows that, of all the other variables tested, only the juvenile incarceration rate makes a significant contribution to the model ($p \leq .05$).

Results from model IV may be summarized briefly. In general, the multivariate models reveal effects that were latent in the bivariate analysis, and the relationships are richer and more complex than

Table 5. Multivariate Effects on Rates of Establishing Juvenile Courts

		Percent Urban	Percent Attending School	State Government Officers	New England	Delinquents in Institutions	Constants	X²
I		1.02***	1.02	.93			.025***	7.39
II		1.02***	1.04***	.94	.18***		.011***	21.07***
IIIa	1900	1.03***	1.06***	.91	.12***		.004***	25.43***
	1910						.009***	
IIIb	1900	1.03***	1.07***	.98	.11***		.002***	29.90***
	1910			.60**			.011***	
IV	1900	1.06***	1.08***	.98	.17***	.99**	.001***	33.87***
	1910			.62**			.011***	

**p < .01
***p < .001

those observed in the analysis of reformatory adoption (cf. Table 2). Urbanization and school attendance are positively and significantly related to early adoption of juvenile courts, lending some support to the legal evolution model. But contrary results are shown by the state government measure, which has no effect before 1910 and a significant negative effect thereafter. This finding suggests, contrary to functionalist imagery, that less centralized states were more rapid adopters of juvenile court legislation, at least after 1910. The New England dummy shows an even stronger negative association in the multivariate model than it did when considered alone. Juvenile incarceration rates are negatively associated with juvenile court enactment: the coefficient shows that an increase of one per hundred thousand in the incarceration rate is related to a 1 percent decrease in the adoption rate. The interpretation of this statistically significant finding is unclear, but it belies the hypothesis that states adopted juvenile courts to reduce commitments. None of the other variables added significantly to the model. Thus no evidence suggests that the juvenile court was propelled by the strength of the charity organization movement, judicial conservatism, or fear of immigrants.

Results from the parallel analysis of separate trial legislation are shown in Table 6. The modeling process here developed along quite similar lines as those shown in Table 5, even though the procedure itself was intended to permit models to diverge in whatever directions the data suggested. Models I through IIIb represent equivalent specifications in both tables. As model II in Table 6 shows, the New England dummy was the best regional predictor of the adoption of separate trial laws, net of structural effects. One difference here, not shown in the table, is that the North Central dummy is also a powerful predictor that has a significant positive effect on the adoption of separate trial laws. The two region variables could easily be switched with little impact on the rest of the model; the New England variable is shown here for the sake of consistency with Table 5 and because it yields a slightly more efficient model in terms of comparative X^2 values.

Table 6. Multivariate Effects on Rates of Establishing Separate Juvenile Trials

		Percent Urban	Percent Attending School	State Government Officers	New England	Constants	X^2
I		1.01	1.03	.94		.024***	3.75
II		1.01	1.04**	.94	.27***	.013***	9.84*
IIIa	1900	1.01	1.05***	.93	.22***	.007***	12.39*
	1910					.013***	
IIIb	1900	1.00	1.08***	.96	.24***	.002***	20.52**
	1910			.49***		.013***	

*p < .05
**p < .01
***p < .001

Constant terms in model IIIa suggest that there are time-dependent trends in the data, but this specification is not a significant improvement over model II. As in the earlier analysis, model IIIb shows that state government employment has a significant and time-dependent negative effect on adoption rates. School attendance again has a strong positive effect, which emerges as the model becomes more complex. Finally, three differences in the two sets of models may be observed: first, urbanization has no apparent effect on the adoption of separate juvenile trials. Second, none of the other variables tested, not even juvenile incarceration rates, added significantly to the equation shown in model IIIb. Third, as shown by relative X^2 values, the models do not fit the data as well as their counterparts in Table 5. This is because fewer states enacted separate trial laws than created juvenile courts during the observation period, thus yielding fewer transitions on which to build a model.

Findings from both analyses lend no strong support to any general theory of legal change but are compatible with the hypothesis that the juvenile court was accepted because its institutional ideology was isomorphic with the least radical aspects of national Progressivism. No evidence suggests that the juvenile court was propelled by the direct influence of the charity organization movement. Although documentary evidence shows that charity organizers helped standardize the wording of legislation and perhaps influenced the passage of juvenile court acts in particular cases, in general, prior movement influence is unrelated to adoption rates. Indeed, the data are compatible with a reverse interpretation, that is, that the juvenile court was seen as a means to increase the legitimacy of organized charity.

The legal evolution approach fares somewhat better but permits no simple interpretation. The negative effect of state political centralization is contrary to the hypothesis in that it suggests that more decentralized states were more receptive to reform. This makes sense given the essentially local nature of the juvenile court, but the data do not reveal whether smaller state governments are associated with stronger local administrations. It is also interesting that urbanization—offered as an indirect measure of economic development—performed well as a predictor of juvenile court adoption, but manufacturing output—a more direct measure—did not. The insignificance of manufacturing output implies that differences in state wealth did not substantially affect the diffusion of the juvenile court. Given this conclusion, the positive effect of urbanization can be interpreted in two ways. Urbanization may have raised the demand for reform independent of resource constraints by heightening the perception of social ills, increasing the need for social services, and creating more complex networks of communication and mobilization. Or it may be that legislators saw the juvenile court as particularly appropriate for urban areas on grounds of efficiency.[10] Informal means of separating adults and juveniles may have proved inadequate as crime and juvenile caseloads increased, and urban court systems could more easily achieve economies of scale by formalizing the separate administration of juvenile justice. Both "demand" and "efficiency" interpretations are compatible with a general functionalist model, and they are not mutually exclusive.

But this argument breaks down when we look at the adoption of separate trial legislation. This is a more substantive reform than the nominal certification of a juvenile court, for it is likely to involve real costs, it appears to be an active response to constituents' concerns, and it promises long-run efficiency. Thus we might expect its adoption to depend on both the availability of resources and the concentration of demand. Instead we find that no effects are associated with either the manufacturing output or urbanization variables. This lack of association undermines a functional interpretation because the more instrumental of the two reforms is less influenced by functional constraints. It suggests instead that the social demand for juvenile justice reform may reflect symbolic more than instrumental concerns. If the juvenile court was seen, as I have argued, as an ideological

10. Data from a 1918 survey support the notion that juvenile courts were seen, contrary to reformers' aims, as urban phenomena (Belden 1920). Abbott (1925, 273) observed that rural judges often resisted implementation of juvenile court laws.

component of the urban-based drive for administrative reform, it is plausible to assume that legislators in the more urbanized states sought to demonstrate the same commitment to Progressive ideals as their colleagues in states that they took as referents. If this commitment was purely symbolic, it is not surprising to find that it erodes completely when the reform at issue has practical rather than symbolic implications, as is the case with separate trial legislation.

The distinction between resource and demand constraints has more straightforward implications for the effects of educational development. Enrollment ratios suggest a resource constraint insofar as they measure collective commitment to, and support for, formal public means of child socialization. The resources at issue here, however, are institutional and ideological rather than directly economic. Literacy suggests a demand constraint. It measures more directly than urbanization the collective capacity for learning and shared discourse and hence for mobilization and institution building. In these analyses, as with the reformatory, the two have empirically distinct effects on rates of reform. Educational capacity increases adoption rates in both cases, but literacy has no effect in either. As with the reformatory, the simplest and most satisfying interpretation is that states with large sunk costs in institutions for children are predisposed to make further, more specific commitments such as those represented by the juvenile court and separate trial legislation.

The findings regarding the education items suggest further that the effect of urbanization not be interpreted instrumentally. The conventional functional imagery that links social problems, concentrated resources, and an articulate public with formal policy solutions in a smooth causal chain appears not to apply to the diffusion of the juvenile court. If it did, we would expect urbanization and literacy to show positive effects on the substantive and the symbolic components of reform. What we see instead is the coevolution of two historical reform trends: in the nineteenth century, neither the common school nor the reformatory was primarily an urban-industrial institution. Educational reform in particular was traditionally rural based, localistic, and pietistic in tone. At the turn of the century, the common school gave way to the urban school system and the reformatory to the juvenile court as foci of reform energy. Both institutions went through similar stages of development, becoming more professionalized and more formalized. Thus the most straightforward interpretation of these relationships is that urbanization, educational development, and juvenile court adoption are all manifestations of a nationwide Progressive trend toward the rationalization and expansion of administrative capacities.[11]

Finally, the data show some limited regional diffusion effects. Both analyses show that New England states were reluctant converts to the juvenile court cause. North Central states, as noted previously, were conspicuously rapid in providing for separate juvenile trials, but their apparent eagerness to establish juvenile courts, shown in Table 4, disappears when other factors are controlled. The general receptiveness of the North Central states to reform is clearly a mimetic response: Illinois, Indiana, Michigan, Ohio, and Wisconsin were all self-consciously Progressive states, and juvenile court reform spread outward from Chicago by propinquity and ideological affinity. The negative association for New England is more difficult to interpret. Massachusetts and New Hampshire were early adopters of both reforms; Connecticut, Vermont, and Maine were among the last ten states to establish juvenile courts and were nearly as resistant to separate trials. Why this should be so is unclear: examination of charity association proceedings, charity board reports, and bar association literature has so far yielded no hint of organized intra- or interstate resistance. On the contrary, scattered references suggest that the New England region had an exemplary reputation for child welfare efforts (see, e.g., Kelso 1922). All states but Vermont and Maine had centralized charity boards before 1900; in fact, Massachusetts established the first board of charities and correction in 1863. It is tempting to

---

11. For a more thorough discussion of the interrelationships of educational development, urbanization, and general bureaucratization, see Meyer et al. (1979) and Tyack and Hansot (1982).

speculate, along with the NCCC delegate quoted earlier, that precisely because welfare services were already well developed, New England legislators considered the juvenile court as "not radical enough," but support is lacking for any such generalization. Despite the difficulty of firm interpretations, this finding reemphasizes the independence of charity organization and juvenile court reform.

Conclusion

This analysis has made two general points in support of a ceremonial interpretation of juvenile court history. The first point is descriptive: the court should not be understood as a sweeping change in the treatment of children, but as a manifestation of a national trend toward administrative reform and as an institutional compromise between law and social welfare. As enacted in state laws, the juvenile court implied no major changes in the legal treatment of children and required no significant, consistent deployment of human or fiscal resources. It was primarily a shell of legal ritual within which states renewed and enacted their commitment to discretionary social control over children.

The second point is causal. Quantitative analysis yielded only tentative, equivocal support for hypotheses generated by an evolutionary systems theory of legal change. The data give no support at all to hypotheses that juvenile court reform was accelerated by the professional achievements of charity reformers, by the obduracy of legal institutions, or by the felt need to control and socialize immigrants. The data show that the most rapid innovators were states outside New England with large urban populations (and even urbanization ceases to be important when the more practical aspects of juvenile court reform are considered), well-developed educational systems, and relatively decentralized political systems. Rapid innovation by urban, educationally oriented states lends some support to a functional argument, but the findings as a whole are also compatible with a simpler ideological diffusion argument.

This conclusion permits some further specification of the institutional model introduced in Chapter 3. In the case of both the reformatory and the juvenile court, the same very general causal argument is appropriate: identifiable reform groups focused their energies on a specific institutional innovation and upon a set of changes in juvenile law that would legitimize and facilitate the operation of that institution. These groups forged cogent, legitimate reform messages that gathered political momentum as they ripened. In both analyses, reform progressed most quickly in states committed to education. But the differences between the two reforms and the institutions they sponsored are more interesting than this general similarity. First, I suggested that reformatories were "moral institutions" in that they embodied a set of particularistic values about childhood and deviance that were ultimately reflected in law. It must also be remembered that the separate incarceration of juveniles involved the construction of *physical* institutions consisting of buildings, an inmate population, and staff. The juvenile court was an institution defined by ceremony whose main function was to preserve inherited patterns of discretionary control. Although the term "juvenile court" connotes a special place, a special time, and specialized personnel, historical data show that in practice the juvenile court did not necessarily deliver any of these.

A second point of comparison has to do with the dynamics of the reform process. The very originality and tangibility of the reformatory provided a foundation upon which colliding groups could negotiate a rationalized blueprint for their rehabilitative machine and upon which state legislatures could construct enabling statutes. As the reformatory spread among the states, it caused a thorough reinterpretation of children's legal status. The first juvenile court emerged as a response to the excesses of the reformatory and as a means to protect it. The court was an expedient and was therefore not a fertile source of new conceptions; rather, it was assembled from the bits and pieces of child welfare reforms that had existed in the states for years, in some cases for half a century. It did not generate new ideas.

Instead, it absorbed old ones, domesticated them, and projected an aura of legitimacy about them.

Precisely because of its ideological character, however, the juvenile court had important implications for the treatment of deviant children and for wider patterns of control and social welfare. As Fox (1970) argues, the court gave the reform school a new lease on life and encouraged the expansion of a variety of public and private child-care institutions throughout the Progressive era. Resurgent penological reformers looked approvingly at juvenile justice agencies and spoke of them as the proving ground for their successful campaigns for adult probation, parole, and indeterminate sentence laws (McKelvey 1936).

Perhaps most important, juvenile courts in some states played a role in the adoption and administration of mothers' pension laws, which provided the dominant means of public welfare assistance in the period before the New Deal. Prominent juvenile judges such as Ben Lindsey, Merritt Pinckney in Chicago, and E. E. Porterfield in Kansas City supported pensions as a means to keep children with their destitute but otherwise able mothers, and juvenile courts were frequently given authority to determine eligibility and distribute relief (Lubove 1968, ch. 5; Tishler 1971, ch. 7). Ironically, the charity organization societies and private agencies that had supported the juvenile court opposed mothers' pensions vociferously. Although they had hoped that the court would serve as a comprehensive social service agency, they had principled objections to unsupervised means of "outdoor relief" and a self-interested concern for the future of their institutional clientele. Despite professional opposition, mothers' pension laws swept the country in the second decade of the century. Thus true to form, a major consequence of the juvenile court was almost wholly unanticipated by its staunchest advocates.

6

In Need of Supervision

The juvenile court went about its business largely unchallenged for the first half of the twentieth century. In the mid 1960s, a new wave of reform began to crest, and once again the existing system of child regulation came under widespread attack for arbitrariness, excessive severity, and ineffectiveness. In the ensuing years state juvenile codes have been overhauled and new programs aimed at preventing and curing delinquency have proliferated. More specifically, legislation in the period from 1965 to 1980 has identified the noncriminal or status offender—under a variety of euphemistic and acronymic labels—as the focus of a renewed delinquency prevention effort and as a category of offender worthy of special treatment at every point in the juvenile justice process. In this chapter I characterize briefly the challenges raised to the legitimacy of the juvenile justice system and describe contemporary legislative innovations as a set of strategic responses to these challenges.

The changes I describe consist generally of attempts to provide alternative processing techniques designed to relieve as many juveniles as possible from the stigma associated with the "traditional" system. These techniques include programs to "divert" offenders from the juvenile court and to "deinstitutionalize" or "decarcerate" juveniles who would otherwise be confined, especially status offenders. It should immediately become apparent that this reform drive has much in common with previous reforms already discussed in this book. The refuges, the reformatories, and the juvenile court were all offered as means to "divert" children from more punitive forms of treatment, reduce stigma, and provide more effective preventive services. In the same fashion the contemporary decarceration movement is intended to prevent crime by removing children from the juvenile court and secure detention and correctional facilities.

Also like previous reforms, the most recent permutation of juvenile law is not *sui generis*. Much of the rhetoric and rationale for the change was borrowed from a parallel critique of custodial mental institutions and of excessively informal commitment procedures (see Scull 1977). Further, like prior reforms, the national movement for juvenile decarceration was preceded by a pioneering reform that was local in origin. In 1961, California revamped its juvenile code to distinguish more thoroughly among types of juvenile offenders, to rationalize the application of treatment alternatives, and to specify increased due process rights (1961 California *Laws*, ch. 1616). As Lemert's (1970) thorough analysis shows, this reform was a response to a confluence of circumstances unique to that state—including rapid and uneven population growth in the post–World War II period, leading to expanding caseloads and pressures for bureaucratization in an archaic and variegated juvenile court system, which led in turn to the perception of "anomalies" in juvenile court practice by a few concerned and strategically placed attorneys, judges, chief probation officers, and correctional administrators. It is significant that this reform was, in Lemert's terms, a "revolution from within" the existing system: it was an attempt by motivated participants to rationalize the administration of juvenile justice, not a response to public outrage or movement-generated pressure for change. Thus in terms of both the content of the legal change and the process by which the reforms were achieved, the California experience was an exemplar for states lacking its distinguishing characteristics.

The Parameters of the Juvenile Decarceration Movement

In this chapter I neither discuss the broader decarceration movement nor, as I have in previous chapters, explore the micropolitics of reform at the state or social movement level. This is in part because the literature is too vast and the webs of influence too complex to permit ready generalizations. But a more important and related reason is, as I intend to show throughout the discussion, that reform was catalyzed primarily at the federal level. The characteristic feature of this reform is that it took shape not from the internal negotiations of voluntary associations, nor from the interactions of moral entrepreneurs and state legislatures, but from the equivocal challenges posed by the national state to traditional local juvenile justice institutions.

This transformation is, in short, a reform that lacks an identifiable social movement base. Although its origins appear unusually diffuse, it is possible to describe some contributing factors, more to characterize the reform than to provide a genetic explanation. One such factor surely has to be the growing perception of crime—especially juvenile crime—as a national issue in the 1960s. This perception was aided and abetted by quickening presidential action: special commissions and task forces on delinquency met in 1950, 1961, and 1966; in 1961, Congress passed the Juvenile Delinquency and Youth Offenses Control Act. Candidates Goldwater and Nixon made crime an explicit issue in their presidential campaigns, and in 1968, Congress passed both the Juvenile Delinquency Prevention and Control Act and the Omnibus Crime Control and Safe Streets Act, the latter of which was the crowning achievement of President Nixon's "war on crime."[1]

A second, and only partially independent, trend was a growing critique of traditional strategies of social control, coming largely from academic quarters. One early example was Paul Tappan's (1946) attack on the abusive discretion of the juvenile court. Subsequently codified societal reaction and labeling theories of deviance (e.g., Lemert 1951; Becker 1963) and sociological analyses of the disabling effects of incarceration (e.g., Goffman 1961) provided an imagery of "stigma" and "total institutions" that could easily be vulgarized and absorbed into the standard ideological repertoire of juvenile justice. Soon sociologically informed critiques were appearing in volumes of reports by official commissions (e.g., Lemert 1967; Vinter 1967). Meanwhile, treatment programs were established and evaluated to demonstrate the superiority of "alternative" technologies to the traditional system. Such exemplary programs included the Highfields Project, begun in 1950 (McCorkle, Bixby, and Elias 1958), the Provo Experiment, begun in 1959 (Empey and Rabow 1961; Empey and Erickson 1972), and the California Community Treatment and Probation Subsidy Programs, begun in 1961 and 1965, respectively (Palmer 1971; Lerman 1975).

I mention a third trend briefly here and explore it more fully in the course of this chapter. Legal arguments for civil rights were applied to the treatment of children as they had been so effectively used on behalf of minorities. These arguments were informed by social science thinking on the inadequacies of the juvenile justice system but were carried on in the specialized institutional context of legal jour-

---

1. For a summary of federal activity in regard to juvenile crime, see U.S. Department of Justice (1974, 1–2). The 1968 enactments are especially important because they mark the first effort by the federal government to fund local crime control activities in partial response to widespread urban disorder. The Safe Streets Act further created the Law Enforcement Assistance Administration (LEAA) within the Justice Department to centralize federal efforts and symbolize the administration's commitment to "law and order."

nals and courts. Because state and local judges tended to resist frontal attacks on the *parens patriae* doctrine and because most state juvenile codes prohibited direct appeals of juvenile cases, however, the impact of this trend was not crescive, but delayed and ultimately explosive.

By the mid 1970s, the movement for decarceration had assumed the proportions of a "social fad" (Klein et al. 1976). An entire book could be devoted to a detailed account of the rise—and apparent decline—of the decarceration fad, but it is important here to identify two of its salient characteristics.[2] First, decarceration reforms not only lacked an identifiable, bounded movement base, but they also accommodated quite dissimilar political bedfellows under the same set of covers. Conservatives incensed by increasing crime tended to favor both more punitive treatment of offenders and a narrower, more legalistic interpretation of juvenile court jurisdiction that would potentially limit official controls over neglected and incorrigible children. Liberals, meanwhile, were once again under attack for the failure of humanitarian attempts to rehabilitate delinquents, but by assuming a civil libertarian posture they could agree with the conservatives on the need to limit the discretion of the juvenile court. Thus "support for the diversion of less serious delinquents [was] often accompanied by demands for stringent measures applied to felony-level violations" (Hellum 1979, 304). The conceptual linchpin that bound the humanitarian and get-tough positions together was skepticism about the distinction between adult and juvenile offenders, and this in turn threatened the core preventive ideology of the juvenile court.

Both sides stopped short of demanding that the juvenile court be abolished or made to resemble criminal courts, or even that jurisdic-

---

2. Four references provide mileposts of intellectual opinion on the evolution of decarceration policies. Lemert (1971) followed up his earlier (1967) critique of the juvenile court with a thoughtful proposal of alternative "models" for diversion programs. Empey (1973) attempts to bring order out of chaos by providing a conceptual analysis of the several, sometimes contradictory, themes that are brought together in the drive for "diversion, due process, and deinstitutionalization." Hellum (1979) offers a more politically and empirically informed update on the progress of the "second revolution in juvenile justice," and Lemert (1981) brings the discussion full circle with a rueful appraisal of the unanticipated consequences of reform.

tion over noncriminal offenders be rescinded. Such suggestions have been made but have not been taken with any great seriousness. Instead, decarceration policies arose to fill the vacuum left between conservative severity and the "decline of liberal optimism" (Bayer 1981). As Cohen (1979, 342) suggests, these policies rest on two questionable deductions: first, institutions do not work or do harm; therefore community treatment works better or does no harm. Second, theories of labeling and stigma suggest that more treatment is bad; therefore less treatment can be good. Using the same odd *post hoc* logic as the reformatory and juvenile court reformers, decarcerationists proposed that reduced official contact could become an edifying experience if it were supplemented by an affirmative preventive policy carried out by quasi-official community agencies.[3] Hence an irony observed by Scull (1977, 42): the abolition of the asylum has been accompanied by the same "millennial expectations" as its founding.

This brings us directly to the second characteristic of decarceration in juvenile justice, which involves its outcomes. There is now a mountain of evidence to show that diversion and deinstitutionalization policies have not been effective in reducing either the number of children under official control or the crime rate. Apologists maintain that decarceration is a good idea that could yet work if only it were better funded, more thoughtfully implemented, and more carefully monitored (see, e.g., Levine 1977). But more sophisticated analyses yield evidence that these policies have not just fallen short of humanitarian expectations, but seem designed to preserve and perhaps increase official discretion. Studies of juvenile court procedure have found that compliance with due process mandates is uneven at best and that more than token compliance is rare (Lefstein, Stapleton, and Teitelbaum 1969; Sosin and Sarri 1976; Clarke and Koch 1980). In most states diversion does not complement due process,

3. Massachusetts's "radical experiment" in juvenile corrections is a spectacular example of the *post hoc* logic that characterizes juvenile justice reforms. The first step in the reform was to empty the institutions; only later was thought given to a new system of alternative treatment (Scull 1977, 52–53; for the official account see Bakal 1973).

but rather subverts it, because treatment alternatives are typically available only on admission of guilt (Cohen 1979, 351). Treatment programs lack any new or distinctive theories and instead continue to invoke the family as the ambiguous and unproven source of delinquent behavior (Blomberg 1980).[4] The most serious indictment is that by "thinning the mesh" of social control activities and "widening the net" of behaviors that can lead to official intervention (Cohen 1979, 346–347), decarceration has led to an increase in the official social control of juveniles. Numerous studies find just such effects (see, e.g., Blomberg 1977; California Youth Authority 1976; Dunford 1977; Klein 1974, 1979; Klein et al. 1976; Lerman 1975; Mattingly and Katkin 1975; Morris 1978; Rutherford and Bengur 1976; Vinter, Downs, and Hall 1975; Vorenberg and Vorenberg 1973). The biggest single reason for this appears to be that most diversion programs are administered, contrary to their ideology, from within the official system (Bullington et al. 1978, 65–66). The tendency is for police (Klein et al. 1976) and probation officers (Blomberg 1977, 276) to treat such programs as opportunities to expand their informal surveillance activities. Because most diverted juveniles continue to be under court jurisdiction, such extralegal criteria as program rules and client demeanor can be used to justify subsequent incarceration (Lerman 1975); in programs involving families, unindicted siblings can become vulnerable to legal control as well (Blomberg 1977). Thus decarceration is a defense of the status quo—as Bullington et al. (1978, 65) remark, "The widespread popularity of diversionary programs is due to the fact that they offer the appearance of significant reform without any major modification of values."

But all is not entirely consistent under the new regime. It appears to be a significant departure from the past that while official agencies

4. A federal commission maintains, with startling originality: "Involvement in delinquency can often be traced to inadequate socialization and the lack of family cohesion" (National Advisory Committee on Criminal Justice Standards and Goals 1976, 88).

are maintaining or expanding their total capacity for surveillance and control, they are divesting themselves of more mundane board-and-care responsibilities by turning clients over to private agencies. Scull (1977) and Lerman (1980) present convincing evidence that private facilities are absorbing a large and increasing share of the deviant population generally and of juvenile offenders in particular. This shift is encouraged by federal policies for funding out-of-home placement of children: in 1975, funding primarily for private child welfare facilities under the Social Security Act outstripped funding for state correctional agencies through LEAA by a ratio of more than four to one (Lerman 1980, 287–289). The consequences of this shift may be profound, even though they are consistent with the time-honored strategy of therapeutic discretion, and they apply most forcefully to the noncriminal offender.

One such consequence is the further muddying of legal and therapeutic decision rules. Lerman (1980) notes increases in the voluntary commitment of juveniles to private mental hospitals in the 1970s and suggests that these increases have resulted from court coercion—that is, under diversion policies, officials may defer adjudication if a child seeks private treatment. For adjudicated offenders who are referred to mental hospitals by the court, Lerman argues that discretionary psychiatric judgments may result in longer terms of confinement than they would have received under a formal sentence to a public institution. At the same time private agencies receiving public clients are drawn closer to official patrons and gradually alter their classification, accounting, and evaluation procedures to meet official needs (Cohen 1979, 353–356). And finally, the most humble reform goals may be defeated by the use of such mental health terms as "milieu therapy" and "residential treatment in a structured setting" as euphemisms for incarceration (Lerman 1980, 286–287).

In summary, diversion and deinstitutionalization are the juvenile court and the reformatory turned inside out. Threatened from left and right, a stodgy system of social control has rid itself of its most troublesome duties while clinging stubbornly to its traditional clientele and antique preventive philosophy. The result may be a recutting of the social control pie between public and private agencies, but certainly the pie has grown no smaller. As Cohen (1979, 358) has written:

> It is, eventually, the sheer proliferation and elaboration of these other systems of control—rather than the attack on the prison itself—which impresses. What is happening is a literal reproduction on a wider societal level of those astonishingly complicated systems of classification—the "atlases of vice"—inside the nineteenth century prison. New categories and subcategories of deviance and control are being created under our eyes. All these agencies—legal and quasi-legal, administrative and professional— are marking out their own territories of jurisdiction, competence and referral. Each set of experts produces its own "scientific" knowledge: screening devices, diagnostic tests, treatment modalities, evaluation scales. All this creates new categories and the typifications which fill them.

On Theory

The research issue in this chapter, as it has been in the discussion so far, is one of legal differentiation: how have states chosen to distinguish between the status offender and more serious delinquents? What factors determine whether states adopt such differentiating policies and how fast they do so? As before, a major issue is whether such changes are related to economic, educational, and political development, as legal evolution theory would predict. I have already suggested that the decarceration movement has not resulted in any practical increase in rights or reduction in arbitrariness. Subsequent discussion of the statutory innovations themselves will show that reform did not fail simply because of maladministration or inadequate funding, but because the laws themselves create new opportunities for discretionary action— as in the past, more laws have not created more law, contrary to functionalist predictions. Causal analysis will begin by exploring whether a functional model contributes to our understanding of rates of reform.

A second and more substantive model is offered by Scull's (1977) analysis of decarceration. Scull and other analysts (e.g., Blomberg 1977; Cohen 1979; Warren 1981; Estes and Harrington 1981) emphasize that decarceration is above all a strategy of control that extends the interventionist logic of the nineteenth- and early twentieth-century institutional reformers, albeit through more subtle and diffuse means. In the particular context of juvenile justice, this approach suggests that the apparent legalization of the juvenile court is a trivial phenomenon and that the extension of informal surveillance through diversion and other related programs is not just an unanticipated consequence of an otherwise well intentioned reform, but in fact the real goal of reform. The driving force behind deinstitutionalization, Scull argues, is the "fiscal crisis of the state" (cf. O'Connor 1973): as social welfare expenditures ballooned in the 1960s and 1970s, policymakers turned away from institutions in search of more cost-effective means of maintenance and control. Extrainstitutional treatment appeared cheaper, the more so because it was often underwritten by federal funding, and private agencies emerged to fill the social control gap by "recommodifying" the deviant (Scull 1981). Scull offers provocative evidence based on data from selected states on institutional commitment rates and public welfare expenditures. In this analysis I attempt to specify this model and apply it to rates of statutory change in all fifty states.

These models differ markedly: the legal evolution approach is relatively abstract and structural. It generates dubious predictions about the content of reform; yet it generates quite clear hypotheses about the factors that should affect rates of adoption. The decarceration model, by contrast, is more substantively oriented to contemporary juvenile justice reforms. It deals more convincingly with the content of those reforms but is rather vague about the factors that may be expected to influence adoption rates. But it is important to note that these models share one important theme: both are in some sense instrumental interpretations. In both cases legal change is assumed to serve some functional need, whether that of society as a whole or of its constituent political units. They fail to attend seriously to the distinctive and broadly legitimate institutional character of the juvenile justice system itself and to the conservative, inertial effect that that character can have on externally induced pressures for reform. The institutional argument developed in this chapter overlaps in places with Scull's model yet is distinct from it: it emphasizes the loosely coupled nature of juvenile justice policy-making and implementation, which makes the system poorly suited for fiscal management but well suited to absorbing criticism, making cosmetic adaptations, and maintaining the overall status quo. The analysis will suggest that Scull and other critics are correct in saying that the promise of deinstitutionalization is fraudulent and that the success of the movement depends significantly on the actions of the national state. The pace of reform seems to be driven not by fiscal crisis, however, but by the need for legitimacy in the face of federal challenges. In the next section I survey those challenges as they have come from federal courts and Congress, and show how they affected state-level decarceration policies.

Challenge and Response in Juvenile Justice Legislation

Federal Initiatives

I have suggested that, although there was a general convergence of interest in the juvenile justice system in the 1960s, federal action was the immediate prod that led to the reforms that are currently under way. In this discussion I argue that the mandates issued by the Supreme Court and Congress were characteristically weak and ambivalent, but nonetheless placed unprecedented constraints on state and local juvenile justice policy and initiated a series of strategic legislative reforms at the state level. For reasons I have already indicated, I ignore the diffuse societal pressures that contributed to federal involvement. Rather, I hope to show that a distinctive feature of decarceration policies, as compared to earlier reforms, is that their specific content resulted almost entirely from political negotiations among official agencies in federal and state government.

The first federal initiative in the area of juvenile justice came in a series of decisions by the U.S. Supreme Court between 1966 and 1971. These decisions simultaneously opened the juvenile court to constitutional scrutiny and limited the amount of change that could be expected in court procedures. The first of these decisions, *Kent* v. *United States* (383 U.S. 541 [1966]), was for our purposes a straw in the wind: it required that certain procedural safeguards be provided to juveniles in hearings to determine whether their cases should be transferred to an adult court. But in 1967, the *Gault* case (*In re Gault,* 387 U.S. 1) carried the same logic into routine juvenile hearings, with far-reaching results for state juvenile justice codes.

The specific facts of the *Gault* case need not be recited here; it will suffice to observe that it involved a juvenile, accused of a minor crime, who was tried without benefit of any ordinary due process guarantees and given an indeterminate sentence to a state juvenile institution. Although the case was egregious in its particulars, it was probably not atypical of most juvenile cases, nor was the state juvenile code under which it was heard at all unusual. Because appeal was prohibited under the code, the juvenile's parents filed for a writ of *habeas corpus* to the state supreme court, charging that the state juvenile code was unconstitutional and that the defendant had been denied due process. The writ was denied. The parents appealed this decision to the U.S. Supreme Court, where the state court decision was reversed, the state juvenile code was declared unconstitutional, and Gerald Gault's case was referred back for rehearing.

Three points about *Gault* are salient to this discussion. First, it was the first case in which the Court had directly confronted the issue of whether the Bill of Rights is applicable to the adjudication of minors. Second and more specifically, the Court expressly upheld the appellant's right to be notified of the charges against him, to be given counsel, to confront and cross-examine witnesses, and to refuse self-incrimination. Third and most important, despite the apparent breadth of the decision, its applicability was carefully circumscribed. The Court's opinion carefully avoided judgment on "the totality of the relationship of the juvenile and the state" (387 U.S. at 13), and it mandated no changes in pre-judicial process (arrest) or dispositional proceedings (sentencing). Moreover, the Court shied away from applying its decision to all juvenile cases. Only in cases where the juvenile is charged as a "delinquent" and where he or she is potentially subject to institutional commitment are these due process protections guaranteed. Subsequent decisions further delineated the limits of due process in juvenile cases: *In re Winship* (397 U.S. 358 [1970]) granted delinquents the right to proof "beyond a reasonable doubt," but *McKeiver* v. *Pennsylvania* (403 U.S. 528 [1971]) denied juveniles the right to a jury trial. In this latter case the Court reaffirmed its commitment to the juvenile court as a forum in which the therapeutic benefits of informality might be balanced with the fairness and sobriety of adversarial procedures.

Although *Gault* and its progeny placed pressures on the juvenile court, they also created safety valves. In 1967, almost all states permitted noncriminal offenders to be sent to the most severe juvenile institutions. *Gault,* by making due process mandatory upon risk of incarceration, threatened to deprive the court of such minor cases where the statutes are so vague and the evidence so weak that they would not stand up to the pressures of an adversary proceeding. But at the same time the decision implicitly suggested strategies whereby discretionary control over this important clientele could be maintained. By explicitly refusing to apply due process considerations to preadjudicatory and dispositional proceedings, the Court implicitly encouraged the expansion of diversion programs, especially for minor offenders, and also suggested that dispositional hearings be distinguished from adjudication hearings and reserved as an occasion where otherwise inadmissible evidence could be considered (Sosin and Sarri 1976; Lefstein, Stapleton, and Teitelbaum 1969). I suggest further that the restricted applicability of the decision to "delinquents" liable for incarceration was an implicit invitation to the states to create new labels for status offenders, provide "alternative" dispositions, and continue to treat them as if *Gault* and *Winship* had never occurred. As the data will show, these decisions encouraged the emergence of the status offender as a differentiated category of deviant.

The second federal initiative, the Juvenile Justice and Delinquency Prevention Act of 1974 (P.L. 93–415), accelerated this trend. The general purpose of the act was to provide grant funds for the development of state and local delinquency prevention programs, with an emphasis on diversion and deinstitutionalization, and to establish a federal agency (the Office of Juvenile Justice and Delinquency Prevention) to administer the grants. Some notes on the history of this legislation provide useful insights on its eventual reception and impact.

One goal of the law was to centralize the funding of delinquency programs, which until 1974 were being administered from several places in the federal bureaucracy. The Department of Health, Education and Welfare had been given such responsibility in 1961 under the Youth Offenses Control Act, and LEAA began funding some delinquency projects out of its crime-fighting budget when it was created in 1968. In 1972, Congress attempted to divide responsibility cleanly by making HEW the funding source for programs outside the official law enforcement system and LEAA the source for official agencies (*Congressional Quarterly* 1974, 279). Thus the major controversy that arose was over what agency was to be the sole overseer of a large and growing federal spending program. The unsuccessful 1972 version of the act (Senate bill 3148) and the first draft of the bill that was eventually passed (S. 821) both placed the Office of Juvenile Justice and Delinquency Prevention (OJJDP) in the Office of the President (for texts, see U.S. Congress 1973, 7–42, 309–356). While the Nixon administration and its allies sought to have the office located within LEAA, Senator Birch Bayh, the bill's major sponsor and chair of the

Subcommittee to Investigate Juvenile Delinquency, was openly skeptical of LEAA's commitment to delinquency prevention.[5] The debate over the location of OJJDP was essentially a debate over how delinquency was to be defined as a social problem: whether as a preventive effort oriented toward social welfare concerns or as an extension of the administration's policy of aiding local crime control strategies. This is made clear, for example, in the hearing testimony of Senator Hruska, who argued that funding formulas should be made as discretionary as possible and that they should be handled within LEAA in order to dramatize the linkage between adult and youth crime (U.S. Congress 1973, 633–635). A similar plea was made by an LEAA administrator (U.S. Congress 1973, 668–669). The House clearly shared Bayh's skepticism because in a companion bill they authorized funding through HEW; the bill eventually reported out of the Senate subcommittee followed suit (U.S. Department of Justice 1974, 2–4). While the bill was in the Judiciary Committee, however, an amendment was attached, authored by Senator Hruska, that placed funding responsibility in LEAA and created an agency to study adult corrections. For its part HEW appeared remarkably unaggressive in pursuit of delinquency funds (see the exchange of letters in U.S. Congress 1973, 762–770). The final version reported out of the conference committee, then, placed administration of the act under LEAA and left only funding for runaway youth programs under HEW (*Congressional Quarterly* 1974, 278–282).

A few of the act's more substantive provisions, all of which restricted expenditures for diversion and deinstitutionalization, should be mentioned briefly. The 1972 version of the bill required that 75 percent of all block grant funds be expended on prevention, diversion, and deinstitutionalization programs and that noncriminal of-

5. See, for example, the hearing testimony of Richard Velde, associate administrator of LEAA, in which Bayh attacks LEAA's (and therefore the Nixon administration's) record and claims the support of a range of private agencies, from the Girl Scouts to the YMCA to the National Council on Crime and Delinquency (U.S. Congress 1973, 635–662).

fenders be totally separated from accused or convicted delinquents. The next, successful, version kept the 75 percent formula and added a requirement that 50 percent of all funds be passed to local governments. Funding became contingent on a state placing noncriminal offenders only in "shelter facilities" (undefined in the bill) within "a reasonable period." In the version that became law, the time period for compliance was specified as two years (Sec. 223[a][12]), the local share of block grant funding had been raised to two-thirds (Sec. 223[a][5]), and a provision that guaranteed private agencies a minimum 20 percent share of funds expended directly by OJJDP on exemplary projects (Sec. 224[c]) had been added.

Thus congressional action provided a complement to Supreme Court requirements. Whereas *Gault* had served the states with several ambiguous and open-ended mandates, the 1974 act provided incentives for the use of diversion and other alternatives to court processing and for the decarceration of status offenders and neglected children—in effect, it sanctified and encouraged a strategy for circumventing due process, assured that programs would stay in the discretionary hands of local officials, and encouraged the privatization of long-term social control. Subsequent amendments passed in 1977 (P.L. 95–115) further weakened the act: at the insistence of state officials, standards for compliance were changed[6] by extending the time period from two years to three and by requiring that only 75 percent of status offenders be removed from juvenile prisons (U.S. Congress 1978, 164; *Congressional Quarterly* 1977, 569). Nowhere in the act did Congress question the basic premises of American juvenile justice. It did not suggest, for example, that noncriminal juveniles should not be within the jurisdiction of the legal system at all. In the end the act revitalized the core juvenile justice ideology of discretionary control, albeit in the form of what it referred to as "advanced technology" and "alternative" programs. In

6. Several states were reluctant to participate in the act's funding program. The General Accounting Office reported that participation rates ran from a low of thirty-nine in 1975 to a high of forty-six in 1978 (U.S. Congress 1978, 163).

the next section I describe the legislative changes that have followed upon these federal initiatives.

State Responses

This discussion presents only a few aspects of the many changes that took place in American juvenile justice beginning in the 1960s. Here I am concerned primarily with the formal rules by which noncriminal offenders were distinguished from criminal offenders. I do not, for example, present data on the changes in formal court organization that reflected the Supreme Court's distinction between adjudicatory and dispositional hearings (see Stapleton, Aday, and Ito 1982), nor do I describe the frequency with which states toughened up the penalties that could be applied to delinquents. Further, I ignore the case of neglected, abused, or abandoned children—deserving of analysis on its own—and focus instead on the status offender. Specifically, incorrigible juveniles were distinguished from criminal juveniles at four points in the juvenile justice process: in the labels applied to them, in the options available for pretrial detention, in the due process rights they are guaranteed, and in the types of institutions to which they can be sent after conviction. I discuss these distinctions in turn; then I give a general sense of their interrelationships.

As shown in Chapter 5, the typical Progressive era juvenile court law included incorrigible juveniles under the definition of delinquency. By 1982, a total of forty-six states had redefined delinquency to exclude noncriminal offenders. This reclassification was accomplished in three different ways. First, nine states repealed juvenile court jurisdiction over incorrigibles entirely—one in 1963 and the rest between 1973 and 1979.[7] Second, seven states at one time or

---

7. Here I refer only to omnibus status offense categories such as beyond control, waywardness, and incorrigibility. No state has given up jurisdiction over more substantive, but nonetheless age specific, offenses such as running away, violating curfew, and possessing alcohol. Subsequent analysis of rules regarding the labeling, detention, adjudication, and disposition of status offenders refers to the former omnibus category, but in most cases substantive minor offenses are treated in the same fashion.

another moved status offenders out from under the delinquency label and subsumed incorrigibility under neglect. Two of these states later repealed status offense jurisdiction entirely, leaving a total of five states as of 1982. One state redefined incorrigibles in this way in 1913, and the rest did so between 1973 and 1978. The third and most popular option has been to create a special offense category for incorrigibles. Thirty-six states have created such a category, usually labeled something like PINS, MINS, or JINS (for Persons, Minors, or Juveniles In Need of Supervision). Massachusetts defined "wayward" children in 1906, and Kansas defined both "miscreant" and "wayward" children in 1957. The remaining states created such labels between 1961 and 1982. Two of these states later included incorrigibles under the neglect label, and one repealed its incorrigibility law, leaving thirty-three states with a special status offense label as of 1982. As of that year, finally, four states continued to place status offenses under the delinquency label.

By 1982, thirty-four states had established different detention standards for criminal and noncriminal juveniles. The statutes appear designed for minimal compliance with federal funding requirements: in no case are the two types of offenders required to be physically separated; rather, the tendency has been to reserve one most severe form of detention for alleged criminal offenders. A 1971 Georgia juvenile code revision is a typical example (1971 *Acts,* pp. 709, 724). The statute requires that "a child alleged to be delinquent" be detained in a foster home, a licensed child welfare facility, a court-supervised detention center, "any other suitable place or facility, designated or operated by the court," or "any appropriate place of security," as long as the child is separated from adults. A child alleged to be "deprived" or "unruly" may be placed in any of the above *except* a detention center or "place of security."

I coded procedural distinctions between status offenders and delinquents for this study in an open-ended fashion. That is, whenever any form of due process was explicitly guaranteed to one group but not to another, I treated it as a procedural distinction regardless of its specific content. Yet there is remarkable uniformity in the pattern of procedural reform: only in a very few cases have states guaranteed any procedural rights in statutes that were not already awarded in the *Gault* and *Winship* decisions. Twenty-eight states have specified different levels of rights for alleged criminal and status offenders, almost all since 1967. A recent Tennessee law (1970 *Laws*, ch. 600, §§ 24, 26, 27, and 29) provides a good example. Under this statute all juveniles are guaranteed the right to introduce evidence and to cross-examine witnesses, but only juveniles accused of criminal offenses (delinquents) are guaranteed the right to counsel, immunity from self-incrimination, consideration of only legally seized evidence, and conviction only upon proof beyond a reasonable doubt. Neglected and "unruly" juveniles can be convicted on the lower standard of "clear and convincing" evidence. In this case procedural standards for delinquents are higher than required by the Supreme Court, but the observed distinctions are all nonetheless discriminatory, and all relax constitutional guarantees in cases involving noncriminal offenders.

Of the innovations discussed here, the most commonly adopted is one that provides different standards for incarcerating criminal and status offenders. Again, the most common means of making this distinction is by reserving one most severe alternative for criminal offenders. For example, a North Dakota statute (1969 *Laws*, ch. 289, §1) permits "delinquents" to be sentenced to probation, a local institution for delinquents, the state industrial school, or another state department (such as the state social welfare agency). "Unruly" children may be sentenced to any of these except the state industrial school. Some states prohibit commitment of noncriminal juveniles to certain institutions as a general rule but also contain elastic clauses that permit such commitments in extraordinary cases. The exemplary California statute (1961 *Statutes*, ch. 1616, §2) provides that a status offender may be committed to the Youth Authority only after a special proceeding for modification of a court order, and an Ohio law (1969 *Laws*, vol. 133, ch. H320) permits "unruly" juveniles to be sentenced as delinquents if less severe alternatives are unsuccessful. In short, this dispositional reform, like the new detention policies, imposes minimal restrictions on local discretion. Only the most penitentiarylike of state juvenile institutions are typically set off limits to status offenders, and even these can be made live options through the exercise of various elastic clauses. Even before the recent reforms, such institutions absorbed a small minority of convicted delinquents and undoubtedly an even smaller proportion of status offenders. The reforms leave undisturbed the much more extensive networks of county "ranches," "forestry camps," and other institutions, which resemble, if not penitentiaries, medium-security adult prisons. This means that within the new laws most status offenders and delinquents can be given the same dispositions, despite their different levels of procedural rights.[8]

The interrelationships among these innovations are complex. Unlike previous juvenile justice reforms, there is no pattern of causal priority; that is, no single innovation is either a necessary or sufficient condition for any of the others. But the creation of a special status offense label appears to be a common feature of almost any reform. In nearly every case where states established differential standards for incorrigibles and delinquents at detention, adjudication, or disposition, they created a special status offense label in the same statute. The point here is a simple one—that the creation of discriminating rules, however weak, is typically accompanied by the discovery of identifiable offender categories, however poorly defined. The most important substantive distinction, however, is the dispositional one that addresses the fate of the noncriminal offender in juvenile prisons: it was encouraged by *Gault, Winship,* and the 1974 Juvenile Justice Act; it attracted the most attention and sympathy; and it was enacted with the greatest frequency.

It will be illuminating to examine the timing of these innova-

8. For examples of ways in which states may subvert the intent of their own deinstitutionalization statutes, see Gilman (1976) and the GAO's assessment of the impact of the 1974 Juvenile Justice Act (U.S. Congress 1978, 161–169, especially 166).

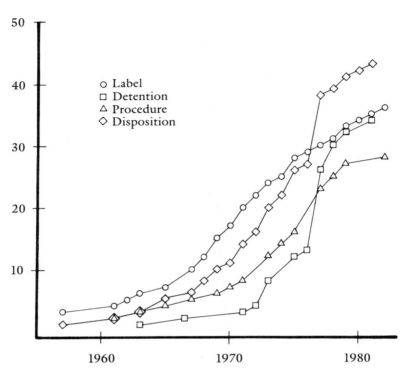

Figure 9. Cumulative Frequency Polygons: Numbers of States
          Distinguishing Status Offenders and Delinquents by Label,
          Detention, Procedure, and Disposition

tions as they occurred among the states. Figure 9 presents cumulative frequency polygons showing the rates at which a special status offense label was created and the rates at which incorrigibles and delinquents were differentiated at detention, adjudication, and disposition. The nominal priority of the special status offense label is suggested by its relatively higher frequency up until 1977. The fact that more states ultimately made dispositional distinctions than created a status offense label simply reflects the fact that some states made dispositional distinctions by repealing status offenses or redefining them as cases of neglect.[9] Close examination of Figure 9 lends some support to the hypothesis that federal initiatives decisively influenced the rate of enactment. The effect of *Gault* is discernible in the increasing rates of differentiation at adjudication and disposition after 1967. These data suggest that many states avoided application of the *Gault* mandates to status offenders by limiting the severity of their commitments and that several of these states followed by specifying lower procedural standards for status offense hearings. Finally, the sharp rise in the number of states making distinctions at detention and disposition after 1974 appears to reflect the impact of the Juvenile Justice Act.

In summary, descriptive evidence suggests that *Gault, Winship,* and the 1974 Juvenile Justice Act have had complex, but generally additive, impacts on the emergence of the status offender as a separate statutory category. Both federal initiatives had implications for the disposition of offenders, and it is at that point that a differentiation between incorrigibles and delinquents is most commonly made. The specification of differential procedural standards appears to be a defensive strategy designed to protect the court's discretionary control over its noncriminal juvenile clientele. The growing rate of differentiation at detention reflects the growing emphasis on community-based facilities subsidized by federal grant funds.

Two tasks remain. The first is to determine which states were most eager to adopt these measures. Are the most innovative states those with the most complex social systems, as the legal evolution model would suggest, or those with the most expansive social welfare systems, as the decarceration model would suggest? The second task is to build an integrated quantitative model that includes not only these factors, but also the effects of federal action.

9. For detention, procedural, and dispositional reforms, states were coded as having made a distinction if they repealed jurisdiction over status offenses or if they subsumed incorrigibles under a neglect label, and different standards applied to delinquent and neglected juveniles.

The Diffusion of Deinstitutionalization Laws

Bivariate Analysis

For the sake of brevity and simplicity, I present the analysis of exogenous variables only as it applies to innovations in dispositional rules. I chose this innovation because it is ideologically and politically central to the movement as a whole and because the frequency of its adoption suggested it would be the easiest to model. Parallel analyses show, however, that the findings regarding dispositional changes hold for innovations in labeling, detention, and procedural rules as well.

As in previous analyses, adoption of legislative innovations is treated here as an event-history process occurring in a continuous time frame, in this case extending from 1960 to 1981. Independent variables for 1960 and 1970 are taken from decennial censuses and related special reports. The relative wealth of these data permits a much more thorough specification of the relevant models than has been the case in previous chapters. To begin with the legal evolution model, indicators of societal complexity still fall under the conceptual headings of economic, educational, and political development. Manufacturing productivity per capita and percentage urban persist as indicators of economic development, and educational development is represented by three variables: enrollment ratios, education spending per capita, and spending per $1000 personal income, to control more directly for variation in wealth. Political development is approached from four different directions, in part because of the difficulty of disentangling state and local authority. Variables include total (state and local) government revenue per capita and as a ratio to income, the rate of state employment per ten thousand population, and the ratio of state employees to all (state and local) government employees. These items are intended to capture dimensions of general government resources, state-level bureaucratization, and the relative balance of state and local authority.

Scull's model suggests that two conceptually distinct factors are at work in the movement for decarceration. The first such factor is a "fiscal crisis" internal to the state's economy, engendered by an over-loaded public welfare system, and the second is the transfer of fiscal responsibility for social control activities to a higher level of government, in this case to Washington.[10] A measure of the percentage of total government revenues coming from the federal government will indicate the extent of intergovernmental dependence. Other variables capture the size of the state's welfare burden in various ways. General measures include the number of public welfare employees per ten thousand population as an indicator of bureaucratization and public welfare spending per capita, per $1000 personal income, and as a percentage of total spending. More specific measures germane to the issue of juvenile justice include the size of the state correctional bureaucracy and the ratio of incarcerated delinquents per hundred thousand juvenile population. Positive relationships between any of these items and the adoption rate of deinstitutionalization laws would lend support to Scull's model. Finally, region variables are tested in the familiar manner. Results of the bivariate analysis are shown in Table 7.

The findings are simple to summarize: there are no apparent effects. No parameter is significant; half of them show a perfect lack of association, and others fare little better. Region variables show only the average order of adoption—with Pacific states the most avid innovators, followed by South Central and Midwest states—but no significant effects, no regional clusters, and no apparent patterns of center-periphery diffusion. There are two possible reasons for these results short of the conclusion that state characteristics do not affect adoption rates. First, it might be that real effects emerge only when

10. Most decarceration analyses, including Scull's (1977), focus on transfers be-tween state and local governments, as in California's Probation Subsidy Program (Lerman 1975). It seems reasonable to extend this argument to federal-state ex-changes as well, especially because federal funding is cited as a key factor. The discus-sion here is limited to that particular level of analysis; no inferences are drawn about lower-level exchanges.

Table 7.   Bivariate Effects of Independent Variables on Adoption
             Rates of Deinstitutionalization Statutes

Variable	Antilog Parameter
Societal Complexity:	
Value added by manufacturing per capita (hundreds)	.98
Percent urban	1.00
Percent school-age population attending school	1.01
Education spending per capita	1.00
Education spending per $1000 personal income	1.00
Government revenue per capita	1.00
Government revenue per $1000 personal income	1.00
State employees per 10,000 population	1.00
State employees as percent of state-local total	.99
Decarceration:	
Percent of revenues from federal government	.99
Public welfare employees per 10,000 population	1.00
Public welfare spending per capita	1.01
Public welfare spending per $1000 personal income	1.01
Public welfare spending as percent of total	1.03
Corrections employees per 10,000 population	1.07
Delinquents institutionalized per 100,000 population age 10–20	1.00
Regions:	
New England	.59
North Atlantic	1.09
North Central	.72
Midwest	1.20
South	1.02
South Central	1.27
Mountain	.88
Pacific	1.62

other effects are controlled, as was the case in both the reformatory
and juvenile court analyses. Second, a dynamic effect might be present whereby the real effect of a variable is reduced or even reversed
from one period to another. This seems to be a plausible extension of
the decarceration model: if, as Scull argues, deinstitutionalization
results from the additive effects of local fiscal crisis and incentives

from the federal government, we would expect fiscal variables to have their strongest effects late in the diffusion period, particularly after *Gault* and the Juvenile Justice Act. In other words it might be argued that both stick and carrot are required to motivate legislative innovation.

To examine these possibilities, I tested multivariate models using variables that seem most salient to the evolutionist and decarceration arguments and that are relatively orthogonal to each other. Specifically, three variables—value added by manufacturing, percentage attending school, and welfare spending per capita—were entered into an equation in a block; then all other variables from Table 7 were added one at a time and their effects examined. Neither partial relationships nor X^2 tests on entire models were significant or even interesting. I tested dynamic effects using the same set of three variables. I estimated three models in which the effects of each item were allowed to vary from the period 1960–1970 to the period 1970–1981. In every model, X^2 values were significant (at $p \leq .001$), but no partial relationship was significant. The data (not shown) demonstrate that, indeed, adoption rates were higher in the second decade of the diffusion process, but not because of differential effects of any of the variables tested. Substantively, this suggests that although federal initiatives might have accelerated adoption, they did so across the board and not among any subset of states identified so far.

Dynamic Models of Adoption

The analysis to this point belies both evolutionist and decarceration models. It points suggestively toward federal action as a decisive factor, but not in a fashion that accords with Scull's imagery of instrumental fiscal exchange. The next logical step is to estimate the federal effect, but this poses difficult problems of measurement. One might hypothesize, for example, that Supreme Court decisions would have their greatest effect in states with high levels of juvenile justice litigation in the appellate system. In this sense the reforms would serve, as they did in California, as rationalizing measures, bringing order to an overgrown and underattended area of law. Unfortunately, no known reference—such as the *American Digest System*—provides counts of cases that are reliable from state to state.[11] Along these same lines, it could be argued that, in states with doctrinally conservative judiciaries, legislative action was required to formalize *Gault* and bring primitive juvenile courts up to date. Canon and Baum's (1981) judicial innovation index for 1950–1970 is a good, although general, inverse measure of conservatism. It was tested as a predictor of adoption rates both in bivariate models and in conjunction with the three variables tested previously, and no effect was revealed. Further problems are apparent in the case of the Juvenile Justice Act. Here it would be important to have information on federal funding levels over time and to estimate interactive models in which, perhaps, initial funding encouraged tentative policy innovation, which assured eligibility for further funding, and which in turn encouraged further innovation. If, and only if, it were assumed that federal funding decisions and state policies are tightly linked—through, for example, an efficient and detailed monitoring system—and that states base their decisions strictly on their own experience and not at all on others', such a model might be estimated. These are insupportable assumptions, and in any event there is no known source of complete funding data.

The foregoing time-dependence tests suggested the more parsimonious, but less precise, approach of estimating models containing time period effects only and no exogenous variables. Time periods were divided at points where federal initiatives occurred, in 1967 and 1974. If it is hypothesized that these initiatives accelerated innovation without regard to characteristics of individual states, transition rates should be significantly higher after these time periods than before. Moreover, examination of models with different time period

----

11. It is also likely that a single explosive case, rather than a quantity of cases, could threaten the legitimacy of a state's juvenile code and promote revision. My own fairly detailed examination of case reports found no relationships between such cases and early reform.

Table 8. Period-Specific Adoption Rates for Four
          Deinstitutionalization Laws

	Label	Detention	Procedure	Disposition
I.				
Time-homogeneous	.047***	.038***	.032***	.059***
X^2	0.0	0.0	0.0	0.0
II.				
1960–1967 Period	.022***	.006***	.012***	.015***
1967–1981 Period	.067***	.059***	.044***	.096***
X^2	7.97**	20.24***	7.59**	22.64***
III.				
1960–1974 Period	.040***	.012***	.021***	.035***
1974–1981 Period	.071***	.122***	.062***	.172***
X^2	2.14	41.42***	7.82**	23.95***
IV.				
1960–1967 Period	.022***	.006***	.012***	.015***
1967–1974 Period	.065***	.018***	.031***	.060***
1974–1981 Period	.071***	.122***	.062***	.172***
X^2	8.02*	43.75***	10.43**	32.63***
Likelihood Ratio X^2	0.0	2.32	2.60	8.68**

*$p < .05$
**$p < .01$
***$p < .001$

specifications on all four innovations ideally should suggest which federal action influenced which innovation. These models are presented in Table 8.

The table contains four alternative specifications of each adoption process. The first set of time-homogeneous models presents estimates of the constant rates of transition for each innovation. These parameters represent the null hypothesis to which alternative models are compared. The second row of models estimates the temporal effect of *Gault* by dividing the diffusion process into two periods at 1967 and allowing adoption rates to vary on either side. The third row contains similar two-period tests of the impact of the Juvenile Justice Act; here the dividing line is 1974. Models in rows II and III can be compared directly in terms of their relative X^2 values because the degrees of freedom are the same. Models in row IV test whether *Gault* and the Juvenile Justice Act had cumulative effects: three time periods are specified, with divisions in 1967 and 1974. Because these models add parameters to those in rows II and III, likelihood ratio tests are appropriate for comparison. Likelihood ratio tests shown in Table 8 compare the three-period models with the better fitting of the two-period models.

There are three observations to be made about Table 8. First, the existence of time trends in the data is undeniable. Almost all the time period models are significant at $p \leq .01$. The only exceptions to this are labeling models III and IV. Further, time trends are consistent: all show an increase in adoption rates over time, regardless of the innovation being modeled or which time periods are specified. The second observation involves comparison of the two-period models. Chi-square values suggest that *Gault* had the strongest effects on innovations in labeling: adoption rates after 1967 were three times higher than before. Innovations in detention rules appear to have been more strongly influenced by the Juvenile Justice Act: adoption rates increased by a factor of ten after 1974. Parameters show almost as great a before-after difference when the detention model is split at 1967, but X^2 values indicate that the specification in row III achieves a tighter fit with the data. Procedural and dispositional distinctions appear to have been affected equally by *Gault* and the Juvenile Justice Act; the relative fit of the two pairs of models is too close to call. This leads directly to a third observation: according to likelihood ratio tests, the only three-period model that achieves significance (at a cutoff of p ≤ .05) is that for the adoption of new dispositional rules. These data suggest that in this case the two federal initiatives had cumulative effects.

Substantively, these results are compatible with what we know about the content of the federal reforms. The *Gault* decision encouraged formalization of the relationship between procedural rules and dispositional options in juvenile courts, so it is reasonable that innovations in these areas increased after 1967. The Juvenile Justice Act encouraged state and local officials to demonstrate a commitment to a broader range of institutions for the detention and commitment of offenders; thus reform in these areas accelerated after 1974. The rate of procedural differentiation did not increase as much after 1974 as it did after 1967. The act's apparent effect on procedural distinctions is probably indirect, via the linkage between procedure and disposition made by *Gault*. In other words, federal legislation accelerated adoption of both policies invited by the Supreme Court, though Congress's manifest target was juvenile institutions. The creation of new deviant labels is less closely linked to any particular event. The trend toward differential labeling appears to have been initiated by *Gault*, then borne along as a certificatory mechanism used to further codify any of the other innovations and to signify that there are indeed "types of people" who receive appropriate "types of treatment."

Conclusion

This analysis suggests that two factors have influenced the legislative trend toward the decarceration of juvenile offenders that has occurred over the last twenty years. The first factor is the institutional inertia of the juvenile justice system itself. That inertia has provided a legitimate and historically consistent ideological rationale for the reforms that have been enacted. Again, the goals of prevention, rehabilitation, and maintenance of the family unit are cited as the objectives of juvenile justice. These objectives justify the maintenance of a model of substantive justice in which the imagery of diagnosis and treatment is dominant, and preserve an arena in which formal due process considerations are poorly accommodated. What has changed is that this ideology of informality is now more formally and narrowly focused: as juveniles were once distinguished from adults, so now the noncriminal offender is reserved for treatment, and the delinquent is consigned to punishment.

The second important factor is the influence of the federal government. In this sense deinstitutionalization is an important departure from previous reforms. Although the refuges and reformatories emerged from local voluntary associations and gradually became an accepted component of state government, and while the juvenile court spread from state to state with the blessing of national-level Progressive reform organizations, the locus of energy in the recent past has been at the federal level. This is not to say that the national state has preempted all other agencies in determining policies of social control. The actions of various interest groups and of plaintiffs such as Gerald Gault in raising issues to the federal level are obviously crucial, and policy changes still require ratification at the state level. The road to reform does not end in Washington, but it runs through it.

Indeed, the characteristic quality of federal initiatives in juvenile justice is their weakness rather than their strength. The limitations of federalism prevent the Supreme Court and Congress from dictating delinquency policy, and the institutional legitimacy of the juvenile justice system further renders their initiatives conservative and diffuse. The Court abhors the practices of the juvenile court while it endorses its philosophy, and Congress must entice policy changes rather than enforce them.

The analysis has implications for theories of legal change that deserve a final word. In the first place, no evidence that supports a legal evolution approach was observed. Neither the content of the reforms nor their rate of adoption among the states fulfilled the predictions of functionalism. The implications for Scull's decarceration model are more complex. It is possible to suggest, for example, that the models presented here are misspecified and that other variables would be more indicative of state-level fiscal crisis. Because the formal models depend entirely on temporal relationships and therefore fail to specify the mechanics of the adoption process, they may appear more gross than simple. I contend, however, that the *pattern* of temporal relationships shown by the various innovations is more important than any individual relationship: policy changes are temporally and substantively linked to appropriate federal initiatives.

A bigger problem might be a difference in the outcomes that are considered to be of interest. Although this discussion has been concerned with the proliferation of rules, Scull bases his argument on an analysis of decarceration rates. It might be that fiscal variables explain much of the variance in deinstitutionalization rates, although Downs (1976) found evidence only for more microlevel bureaucratic and ideological factors. But the relationship between rules and rates is still at issue. I have argued that the observed policies are important largely because they are loosely coupled to agency practice. This means that policies do not directly determine behavior, but it does not assume that they are totally independent. If it is to be argued that deinstitutionalization is a qualitatively new strategy for expanding social control over children and not, as I have argued, primarily a defense of the status quo, the linkages between policy and practice must be explicated further. Whether these rule changes set the stage for a consistent, convergent behavioral response by juvenile justice officials—in the direction of either the expansion or privatization of social control—or whether state and local agencies continue to maintain divergent and often ad hoc agendas is an issue that requires further empirical analysis.

7

Reflections on American Child Control

In the preceding chapters I have described the growth of American child control institutions as occurring through a series of developmental stages. Within each stage I emphasized two dynamic aspects of the reform process: the crises and negotiations that led to the construction of reform programs and the structural factors that influenced the diffusion of new policies of control. My task in this last chapter is to amplify this dynamic interpretation by drawing these findings together—not to summarize, but to offer a retrospective frame through which these reforms can be seen as episodes in an ongoing drama of institution building.

I approach this task in two ways. First, I attempt to generate some empirical inferences about the changing patterns of reform over the three-hundred-year history of American juvenile justice. The point here is to identify consistent features that recur across all reforms, as well as secular trends. The second and longer part of the chapter is a detailed exploration of various theoretical approaches to these results. Returning to the issues raised in the Introduction, I describe the relative strengths and weaknesses of conventional models of social control and describe in more formal terms the institutional model that has informed my interpretations throughout this book.

Empirical Inferences

The most obvious inference to be drawn from this study concerns the consistently political nature of reform. Contrary to the ideology of progress advanced by reform activists, American child control strategies did not grow in an evolutionary pattern, driven by the incremental advance of knowledge and legal competence. Rather, they grew through recurrent conflicts and struggles for authority over institutional turf. There is a pattern of struggle that is remarkably similar across all reforms. At each stage of growth, reform was incited when externally generated legitimation crises threw a fairly stable institutional order into disequilibrium. The content of each reform emerged from reformers' attempts to preserve inherited institutional patterns in the face of these external threats. Change typically began with expedient proposals designed to neutralize criticism and patch together the existing system. In each case, however, political negotiations brought new players into the reform game, which led to a partial reorientation of the growth process, the elaboration of a myth of rehabilitative control, and the diversification of the institutional system designed to exemplify that myth. Each stage of growth was complete when potentially divisive interest groups were successfully contained, the new model of control was accepted as legitimate nationwide, and a temporary equilibrium was reasserted.

The remaining three observations are concerned with long-term changes in the reform process. First, we have seen a long-term shift in the sources of reform, in terms of both the social location of important actors and the ideological justifications they gave for their actions. From the Puritan divines to the Jacksonian gentleman philanthropists, to networks of Progressive social workers, to contemporary private and public child welfare bureaucrats, change has increasingly been generated by specialized personnel in occupational roles devoted exclusively to the social control of children. Reform ideologies have grown into well-rationalized professional myths: as occupational roles and routine ways of doing business have become institutionalized, interest group boundaries that define a range of legitimate discourse have emerged, and that discourse has become consensually validated as an expert body of knowledge, something approaching a scientific paradigm.

This is simply to say, at one level, that juvenile justice is an institutionalized domain of activity that has gradually become differentiated from law and social welfare in general. But a more important observation can be made that over time the systemic criticisms that eventuate in legislative change have tended to come less from sources external to the system than from deep within it. To be sure, abiding public skepticism and plaintiffs in landmark appeals cases help initiate crises, but the task of articulating system inequities and their solutions is now a function of the bureaucratic agencies that compose the system. For example, while gentleman amateurs distilled the ideology of the refuges from a broad set of class-based moral prejudices and pseudoscientific notions, correctional bureaucrats in California invented juvenile decarceration, and a network of academic specialists and state and federal policy experts promoted it nationally. In the decarceration movement even the actions of Congress and the Supreme Court were deferential to established institutional prerogatives. In short, reform has become an internally self-reciprocating process.

The second inference is about the content of successive reforms. As the therapeutic model of child control has become reified, policy debates have been confined to a narrowing range of discourse, and reforms have become less substantive and more symbolic. The most obvious example of this is the changed emphasis on physical institutions at successive stages of development. The refuges and reformatories occupied real time and space; they redefined the legal meaning of childhood, and needless to say they had real consequences for the treatment of deviant children. Although they were in some sense elaborations of the prison, they hold a justifiable claim as technical, theoretical, and legal innovations. The juvenile court was in practice often a grand legal fiction, but it at least implied the existence of a specialized forum that convened at specified times, it eventually developed in most urban centers into a formidable bureaucracy, and it contributed in unexpected ways to early programs of relief for poor families. The decarceration movement, like the juvenile court, derives much of its impetus from an anti-institutional backlash, but it makes little pretense of offering a formal structural equivalent to the routine technology of control. Instead, it ingenuously claims only to "deinstitutionalize" and almost as an afterthought to refer offenders to community agencies presumed already to exist. In short, reform is increasingly concerned with cosmetic adaptations at the margins of the system. Ironically, these latter-day reforms have left the core of the system—the juvenile prisons—untouched, and indeed have allowed them to prosper.

All these reforms arose in part from complaints about the abuse of official discretion and may be understood as attempts to control, direct, and ultimately preserve that discretion. This is a difficult task in a complex administrative system. Rosett and Cressey (1976, 170) have observed in their study of plea bargaining that the criminal justice system "has a remarkable capacity to accommodate itself to . . . attempts to structure it rigidly. Like a closed tube of toothpaste, if squeezed in one spot it merely pops out in another." What we observe in juvenile justice is not a "popping out" of discretion, but the systematic migration of discretion from core to peripheral agencies in the system. The juvenile court was a rebuke to reformatory managers and police court judges because it claimed to absorb some of their latitude in making decisions about the treatment of offenders. Contemporary reforms claim to front-load the decision process further by diffusing the discretion of judges and probation officers among referral agencies. This is not to say that any of these reforms have actually eliminated discretionary behavior—as discussed in Chapter 5, for example, juvenile court laws were too weak to bind private child-care agencies, and Chapter 6 showed that deinstitutionalization programs are largely controlled by system incumbents. I argue, on the contrary, that the movement of legitimate discretion to the system's frontier is a strategy for preserving informal discretion in the system as a whole.

A third inference may be made about the changing configurations of causal forces that appear to affect adoption rates from reform to reform. In examining the three major reform episodes, I explored different sets of hypotheses about diffusion rates, holding constant a baseline model of societal complexity. The most important finding from these analyses is the consistent role of educational expansion in the adoption of reformatories and juvenile courts. Education data on school enrollment and literacy rates were initially intended only as indicators of more general and abstract modernization processes. The available literature did not suggest any direct interdependence between education and juvenile justice; rather, there was every reason to expect that receptivity to juvenile law reform would be contingent on the development of the legal and organized charity systems. When these relationships were tested directly in the analysis of the juvenile court, results ran counter to expectations: the expansion of education *as an institution* stands apart not only from other indicators of societal complexity, but also from education per se, as measured by literacy rates; and neither law nor social welfare measures had any discernible effects on the diffusion of reform. It is readily apparent that education and juvenile law grew isomorphically throughout this period. Both, after all, focus on children; both aim toward broad goals of nation building through institutional regimes of socialization and control; and both experienced major transitions of bureaucratization and professionalization around the turn of the century. Given these broad similarities, what causal significance can we attribute to this relationship?

There are two possible general explanations for the relationship between educational expansion and juvenile justice reform. One is that the two movements were directly linked through the participation of influential activists or the formation of alliances. This was certainly the case in the early years of the refuge movement. As Chapter 2 showed, many of the refuge reformers were also active in the common school movement, from which they drew a legitimating ideology of moral training. But my own fairly detailed exploration of the education literature shows that, by the latter half of the nineteenth century, the two domains were becoming increasingly segregated. Although educational and child welfare reformers spoke appreciatively of each others' programs, I find no evidence of a common network that transcended professional boundaries or of other forms of direct mutual support. A second and, I think, more convincing explanation is that education and juvenile justice both exemplify in a rather pure form the ideological contours of the emergent American welfare state. This interpretation builds on arguments by Janowitz (1976) and Heidenheimer (1981) that education in the United States was a functional substitute for the integrated social welfare systems in contemporary European states. They suggest that mass schooling provided a means to incorporate members and allocate social benefits in an apparently egalitarian manner while still remaining faithful to American notions of individual initiative and decentralized authority. Education, in short, is a fundamental strategy of state building in the United States (Meyer et al. 1979). Therapeutic responses to delinquency and dependency should be seen as an extension of this state-building strategy. Here the focus was on children who had already deviated from the normal path of socialization, but the basic link between morality and citizenship was maintained. It is therefore reasonable, on ideological grounds alone, that juvenile justice reform followed educational expansion in the United States.

The fairly consistent pattern of causal effects on the diffusion of reformatories and juvenile courts appears to have changed decisively in the case of the decarceration reforms discussed in Chapter 6. The analysis revealed no differences across states in rates of reform, only differences over time that imply states were responding primarily to federal initiatives. The prominent role played by federal mandates appears to set decarceration policies apart from earlier reforms. But I think that decarceration is more of a continuation than a decisive break with the past in that it culminates a long-term trend toward the centralization of reform. Progressive charity activists sought to expand their influence relative to their nineteenth-century predecessors by absorbing a variety of local reform groups, building a powerful national organization and a persuasive cosmopolitan ideology, and seeking federal recognition for their child welfare program. Decarceration in this sense completes the Progressive agenda. Moreover the national state has not usurped the role of state governments and professional associations in generating and implementing reform. The federal role is to endorse rather than enforce change:[1] it detects anomalies and articulates justice claims; it arbitrates between those claims and demands for professional discretion and issues a rationalized model of reform; and it certifies legitimate participants on the basis of professional credentials.

Social Control Theory and Juvenile Justice Reform

What implications do these findings have for theories of social control and legal change? As I suggested in the Introduction, such theories fall into two broad classes—what Humphries and Greenberg (1981) refer to as "systems" and "agency" theories. These theories approach the question of change from opposite directions: in the systems view, societies evolve solutions to their problems; in models

---

1. The distinction between "endorsed" and "enforced" authority is drawn from Dornbusch and Scott (1975).

that emphasize historical agency, entrepreneurial movements invent social problems to fit their preconceived solutions. The results of this analysis suggest that these approaches have complementary weaknesses that limit their applicability to the development of American juvenile justice.

A major theme in this study has been that juvenile justice reforms are best understood as symbolic efforts to dramatize an ideal vision of social order rather than instrumental attempts to control children's misbehavior. Case studies of American social movements have fruitfully emphasized this aspect of reform, but as a general account of modern social control strategies, they fall short. The imagery of the entrepreneurial approach implies that reformers were socially marginal cranks and on-the-make professionals who used a nostalgic vision of moral order to promote themselves and their ideals. This raises a logical problem: if reformers lacked social status and political power, how did their schemes succeed?

This study presents two challenges to the entrepreneurial approach. First, child control reformers were not outsiders; rather, they were relatively powerful incumbents who used sophisticated strategies to publicize their causes, develop networks of influence with potential allies, and apply pressure to legislators. The promoters of the houses of refuge, for example, were careful to incorporate both educators and politicians into their movement, and later juvenile court activists forged links with sympathetic leaders in law and social welfare in the context of charity organization societies. Second and more important, child control reformers did not "invent" the concept of delinquency *de novo*. Rather, they built their programs on a fairly stable and broadly legitimate set of assumptions about childhood and deviance that originated in the Puritan ideal of family discipline. The motivating principle of American juvenile justice is the Puritan vision of the family as the bulwark against vice and of the law as the guarantor of social virtue. Each generation of reformers adapted this basic theme to meet emergent political contingencies, to address the practical failures and preserve the institutional successes of the generation before. In short, child control reform is deeply embedded in the historical and institutional context of the welfare state.

It is exactly this structural context that classic systems theories claim to illuminate. Theories posed at the social system level—whether motivated by a Durkheimian "consensus" argument or a Marxian "conflict" argument[2]—suggest that official controls arise as traditional affective controls are swept away under the disintegrating pressures of modernity. Mainstream functionalist arguments, from Maine (1917) and Durkheim (1933) to Parsons (1964a) and Schwartz and Miller (1964), all argue that the dominant tendency in legal development is the secular evolutionary trend toward generality and formal rationality—a shift, in Maine's (1917) famous phrase, "from status to contract." The expectation here is that, as societies become more complex, they will evolve more rule-bound, universalistic, and structurally differentiated mechanisms for maintaining social order. At a superficial level, the development of juvenile justice institutions seems to fit this schema. Watershed policy reforms tended to emerge first in the nation's shifting cosmopolitan centers, where deviance and the resources for attacking it were most plentiful. These reforms contributed to the gradual differentiation of various types of offenders and of specialized agencies designed to treat them.

But the analysis of the invention and adoption of reform policies does not sustain the functionalist argument beyond this very abstract level. Successful reform policies were not efficient technical solutions to problems of crime and poverty as much as they were effective strategic responses to assaults on institutional autonomy. Juvenile justice legislation did not strengthen the application of the rule of law to children; on the contrary, reforms were designed to blur the fine line between public and private conduct and to strengthen the hand of discretionary authority. Moreover, the adoption of reform

2. For systematic comparisons of consensus and conflict approaches, see Hopkins (1975), Chambliss (1976), Hagan, Silva, and Simpson (1977), Hagan (1980), and Meier (1982).

innovations was not governed by functional logic. From the 1850s through the 1970s, states enacted reforms independent of any demonstrable social system imperatives. In terms of functionalist theory, the rise of a therapeutic model of law generally, and of juvenile justice in particular, is an anomaly—it signifies a move away from contract imagery and toward a system of sanctions based on professionally maintained status distinctions.[3]

Much of this critique applies as well to Marxian inspired left-functional theories. From the conflict perspective, official controls operate not in service of society as a whole, but of its dominant elites; as capitalist economies develop, control becomes not only more formal, but also more harsh, coercive, and oriented toward the repression of lower-class disorder (see Quinney 1974; Chambliss 1976; and especially Platt 1974). The most compelling feature of the conflict argument is that it looks beneath the progressivist, evolutionary discourse of reformers and Whig historians to probe the class and ethnic biases that influence the administration of sanctions. Nineteenth- and early twentieth-century reformers explicitly directed much of their attention to the perceived failings of immigrant families, and some of the more punitive reforms of the recent past appear motivated by a fashionably unspoken fear of urban blacks. Young women of all ethnic backgrounds have suffered disproportionately from the system's obsessive concern with their moral—and especially sexual—rectitude. But it does not follow from these effects that the American pattern of juvenile justice is efficiently caused by capitalist economic imperatives.

This instrumental logic raises the same problems for conflict theory as it does for the consensus argument. If juvenile justice is

3. This shift affected the emergent pattern of American economic regulation as well, and its historical significance was clear to Progressive era legal thinkers: "If Sir Henry Maine's interpretation of legal and political history is sound, from 'status to contract,' all of this means we are traveling backward, for legislation is putting disabilities upon employers and employees, as well as on common carriers and others engaged in public employments, which are not imposed upon the rest of the community" (James 1913, 774). For a related view of English legislation, see Dicey's (1905, 236, 283) remarks on the Landlord and Tenant Acts and the Workmen's Compensation Act of 1897.

simply a means of repression, how do we explain the elaborate discourse of treatment and rehabilitation? If this discourse is nothing
but an ideological smokescreen for punishment, how do we explain
the vast network of penal, psychiatric, and welfare agencies through
which control is administered? An orthodox Marxian model, as
Kolko (1963, 291–293) has observed, cannot account for reformist
legislation that is either contrary or irrelevant to the economic interests of capitalist elites. This approach treats as epiphenomenal the
very features that I would argue constitute the juvenile justice enterprise: the repeated—and generally successful—attempts to remove
children from adult institutions, the gradual development of an extraordinarily broad and flexible range of sanctions, the creation of a
deliberately informal style of decision making, the persistent inclusion of private interests in the official control process, and the over-
weening concern for noncriminal (and typically intrafamilial) misbehavior. To treat these as residual outcomes of an underlying punitive
impulse is to ignore the thing that needs explaining.

   There are two more specific points on which a simple class control
model is suspect. The first has to do with the effect of sanctions on
offenders. A key link in the conflict argument (and of consensus
theory as well) is that social control produces individual conformity,
either by transforming offenders or by deterring potential deviants.
Most notably, Platt (1969) argues that the reformatory produces
docile and abstemious workers by socializing children to the rhythms
of industrial life.[4] Assertions of this sort closely resemble the more
extreme fantasies of reformers; they conspicuously lack any support-
ive data. In this study I have argued repeatedly that the primary
effects of child control reforms are institutional rather than individual: reforms produce agency charters that may form new centers of
bureaucratic power but wherever possible leave routine decision making undisturbed. These reforms create neither consistent attitudes

   4. Platt's explanation of delinquency control thus resembles the allocation model
of public education offered by, for example, Bowles and Gintis (1976). For an institutional critique of such approaches, see Meyer (1977).

nor behavior; rather, they define deviant labels that evoke societal responses independent of individual attributes.[5] In this sense social control agencies produce deviants not by socialization, but by certification of the officially dependent, delinquent, and insane.

An important corollary to this instrumental argument is the assumption that official agencies were all-powerful and that the children and families that became entangled in the social control web were passive victims. These simplistic interpretations echo the self-important accounts left by reformers themselves. Research on the impact of industrial labor, disease, and economic dislocation on family structure shows that families were more resilient, and institutional reforms were less powerful, than conventional assumptions suggest (e.g., Tilly and Tilly 1980; Tilly and Cohen 1982). In a similar way, institutional histories of reformatories, schools, and the welfare system in the United States reveal that the immigrant poor actively negotiated their fate with whatever leverage they could muster (e.g., Brenzel 1983; Tyack and Hansot 1982; Katz 1983). These studies show that, in times of unemployment, illness, or death of a breadwinner, child-saving institutions in particular frequently provided a temporary alternative to the permanent desolation of the family.

This is not to suggest that lower-class life was smooth, rather, that it was a struggle in which the poor were to some degree empowered by the exercise of collective political strategies. Nor do I suggest that the formation of the American juvenile justice system was the outcome of naive pluralism. Upper-class and professional elites have held the upper hand in the generation of reform policies; and because I have been primarily concerned with official policy innovations, the narrative underplays the insurgent strategies of lower-class families and communities. We would expect these strategies to have more conspicuous effects on the outcomes of reform, but even in this

5. This interpretation is generally supported by research on correctional policy that finds no consistent socialization effects. For a policy-oriented review see Martinson (1974); for a more theoretically oriented discussion see Pontell (1984, chapters 2 and 3).

study their impact is apparent. The most conspicuous example of this is in the discussion of juvenile court reform. There it appeared that the charity organizers' critique of the patronage system was an expression of a much wider assault on the emergent political power of the immigrant community. Ironically, the civil courts have also provided a means by which persons who were supposed to be the objects of control were able to influence policy. In a recurrent barrage of cases running from *Crouse* in the 1830s to *Gault* in the 1960s and beyond, system incumbents were forced to defend themselves and their discretion against the legal claims of children and their families. Whether these suits were successful or not, they encouraged reformers repeatedly to develop more sophisticated legitimating ideologies and to seek more expansive legislative guarantees of institutional autonomy.

In short, the American juvenile justice system is a *negotiated* order—negotiated, to be sure, among unequal participants—not one determined exclusively or even largely by the economic priorities of a single class. Recognizing this fact, a number of conflict-oriented theorists have begun to revise the basic Marxian model to incorporate an explicitly political dimension and to account for the rise of more co-optive, subtle, and ameliorative control strategies. Kolko's (1963) research on business regulation is an early exemplar; more recent examples include Spitzer (1975) and Humphries and Greenberg (1981) on criminal justice, Scull (1979) on psychiatry, and Abel (1981) on the legal system generally. These writers have portrayed the social control sector less as a simple instrument of control by dominant classes than as a potentially autonomous arena for interest group conflict, and have called attention to the variables that have proved important in this research: the reifying effect of institutionalized ideologies of deviance, the strategies of organized professional groups, and the self-legitimizing activities of the state and its constituent agencies.

But adding qualifiers to a fundamentally instrumental model does not go far enough in dealing with these policy-shaping influences. The findings from this study suggest that child control reforms are

not in any meaningful sense expressions of social or economic instru-
mentalities but rather are primarily institutional and political in nature. By this I mean, following Stinchcombe (1968, 101–129), that
the social control system at any point in time reflects the value prefer-
ences of powerful groups in society, that structural reforms are
strongly influenced by incumbents' attempts to maintain legitimate
control over the system, and that the major effect of the system is to
preserve and perpetuate a repertoire of deviant roles that faithfully
reproduces a normative conception of the social order. The problem
now is to describe a general theoretical approach that will illuminate
the growth of American juvenile justice from this perspective.

An Institutional Theory of Social Control Reform

Max Weber's sociology of law provides the most general foundation
for an institutional theory of control. Weber charted a middle course
between pure agency and systems theories: unlike agency theorists,
he argued that legal development must be understood in the wider
context of political domination. Unlike systems theorists, he argued
that legal change is ultimately driven by the strategic actions of situ-
ated individuals and is relatively autonomous from economic development. His key insight, for our purposes, is that the structure of
obligation and control is determined not only by the distribution of
power in society, but also by the ways in which power is organized
and justified so that it appears to be legitimate.

However, Weber's model is not very useful for helping us understand the emergence of a specifically therapeutic style of control. His
argument turns out to be one-sided in another direction: he saw
formally rational law as the dominant institutional paradigm for order in modern Western societies, and he anticipated that, over the
long term, legal development would become increasingly autonomous and self-sustaining. The trend toward formalism implies the
exclusion of ethical imperatives, policy goals, and distributive concerns—claims of the sort Weber termed "substantive"—from the

legal order, and the progressive dominance of a style of logical reasoning based on abstract principles and controlled by legal professionals (Kronman 1983, 84–95).[6] The difficulty with this prediction is that it leaves us with only one kind of variation to study. Modern societies may have more or less formal legal systems, but they cannot deviate far from the path of formalism without forfeiting the claim to legality as such. Our problem is to develop a more flexible institutional model, one that permits the legal order to be vulnerable to exogenous normative claims and allows legal development to have qualitatively different outcomes.

Weber's more sympathetic critics have begun to work toward such a model from within the Weberian agenda. Schluchter (1981, 114), for example, points out that even the most highly developed formal-legal order must legitimize legal behavior with reference to ethical norms, and that particular regimes may vary widely in the weights they give to the substantive and procedural components of law while still staying within a general legal-rational context. Kalberg (1980) argues that modern societies can, and typically do, accommodate a number of discrete and substantively rational systems of action that may compete with law for normative dominance. This has relevance for legal development in two ways. First, formal law is vulnerable to criticism when it violates the ethical principles in which it is grounded—as may occur, for example, when procedural technicalities are seen as impeding the effective prosecution of crime or the equitable distribution of social goods. Second, because law is only one among several highly rationalized institutional spheres in contemporary society, pressure for more substantively oriented law is likely to come not just from transient demands for economic or political advantage, as Weber (1978, 894) anticipated, but also in the form of sustained demands for normative reorientation launched by legitimate institutional interests. The problem-solving approach of

6. Thus Weber (1978, 895) wrote, "Inevitably the notion must expand that the law is a rational technical apparatus, which is continually transformable in the light of expediential considerations and devoid of all sacredness of content."

modern welfare states implicates the sciences and the professions in particular as likely carriers of substantive norms (Schluchter 1981, 117). Because of their high prestige and collegial organization, such groups are capable of transforming ethical imperatives into rational patterns of action and thus are likely to have erosive effects on the purely logical integrity of formal law. In short, the revisionist program reminds us that formal rationality is an ideal type only, not the inevitable goal of modern systems of control, and encourages us to treat formal and substantive rationalization as interactive processes in the analysis of modern societies.

These themes have not been taken up with much enthusiasm in the mainstream literature on the sociology of law. There the tendency has been, following Weber, to define official social control exclusively as *legal* control, to analyze official behavior in terms of the degree to which it conforms to formal rules, and to treat antiformal tendencies as pathologies.[7] In order to understand the development of qualitatively different styles of control in the modern United States, this study has turned repeatedly to a set of institutional models that have become prominent in the study of organizations. The value of an organizational approach for these purposes is that it shifts attention upward, from an exclusive focus on the legal domain to the generic issue of how control is administered and legitimized. Thus it speaks to the central concerns of Weber's sociology of domination but allows a more open-ended consideration of outcomes.

Three implications of this approach are particularly relevant to the findings from this study. First, institutional theories argue that modern societies are structured around multiple institutional "orders" (Meyer and Rowan 1977), "fields" (DiMaggio and Powell 1983), or "sectors" (Scott and Meyer 1983) that offer highly rationalized mod-

---

7. There are, of course, exceptions. Most notably, Unger (1976) and Nonet and Selznick (1978) have offered macrotheoretical accounts of the decreasing autonomy of the legal order in modern welfare states. These studies are ultimately disappointing, however, because they treat Western law in global terms: they make little effort to describe variation among legal systems or to identify specific institutional structures that may influence law in specific ways.

els for collective organizing efforts. Depending on the analytical problem at hand, the notion of sectors may denote quite general distinctions—as between the public and private or manufacturing and service sectors—or more fine-grained distinctions such as those commonly made among industrial organizations, hospitals, or religious groups. Whatever the level of detail, the models embodied in institutional sectors are both cognitive and normative: they generate taken-for-granted expectations of how activities will be organized, and they convey a sense that some forms of organizing are intrinsically more right and legitimate than others. As a result, administrative structures that conform to existing models are more likely than others to emerge and to persist.

Social control policies are unusually vulnerable to institutionalizing pressures because they almost entirely lack a practical technical foundation. By this I mean that American approaches to deviance and social welfare are structured more by deeply entrenched beliefs about the nature of crime and poverty than by any empirically valid theories. These beliefs are not free floating but instead are anchored in wider religious, political, or professional ideologies. Once these ideologies are embodied in an administrative regime, they become reified: participants develop material and normative commitments to established patterns, and legislators and others who control access to resources are likely to favor familiar policies, ones that build on past achievements or that imitate policies perceived to be successful elsewhere.[8]

Juvenile justice policy in particular has shown a recurrent dependence on legitimating ideologies drawn from the environment. Since the 1820s, the practical heart of the system has been the simple expedient of incarceration. That expedient was originally justified by an ideology that combined Calvinist moralism with Enlightenment rationality. Subsequent reformers worked within this basic ideology and elaborated it by borrowing at various points from models in the

---

8. This argument is similar to that contained in Heclo's (1974) concept of "political learning," especially as employed by Orloff and Skocpol (1984).

spheres of law, education, and welfare. An important part of the reform process was the geographic diffusion of ideological models. Cosmopolitan American activists incorporated elements of European penal and educational experiments into their own more systematic programs, and once these programs were enacted in key states and publicized as successful, they were imitated by legislatures in peripheral states. As the data have shown, the driving force behind this diffusion process was ideological and political rather than instrumental, and ideology became more pronounced in successive reforms.

A second implication of this approach is that, as institutional environments vary over time and across social units, administrative systems must adapt to shifting norms. The most important long-term shift in the modern West has been toward the expansion and rationalization of institutional sectors, with a corresponding contraction in the scope of competitive markets. The result has been an increase in the proportion of administrative forms that are oriented primarily to normative concerns rather than technical efficacy. Di-Maggio and Powell (1983) argue that the state and the professions have superseded economic competition as the dominant "engines of rationalization" in modern society. These metasectors are repositories of organizational models, and they frequently act directly to charter certain forms of organizing through their regulatory and certificatory activities.

The development of official child control strategies has been punctuated by adaptations of exactly this sort. In America the secularization of civil society has been epitomized by the growing prestige of the sciences and professions. Generations of delinquency reformers responded to this trend by gradually deemphasizing the Calvinist imagery of spiritual conversion in favor of a more scientific ideology of rehabilitation, especially as codified in the individualistic treatment models of psychiatry and social casework. Conversion and rehabilitation models served as functional equivalents in different contexts, legitimizing discretionary control in terms of the wider normative order. State policies have defined the formal structure of the system through legislation that establishes child control agencies and delimits their jurisdiction. While administrative control of these agencies remains highly decentralized, over time the task of generating policy has been centralized, to the point where the federal government now bears major responsibility for chartering and funding local programs. The partial centralization of funding and the continued decentralization of control has led to three kinds of structural adaptations: overall, local juvenile justice systems have become more complex; they have developed patronage links with sponsors at progressively higher levels of government; and they have become more similar, at least in terms of formal structure.

This leads directly to the third implication. As an organization or system of organizations seeks to enhance its legitimacy by incorporating institutional models into its own structure, the link between structure and behavior becomes increasingly problematic. This occurs because any substantial change in system activity invites a considerable sacrifice of inertia—including sunk costs in materials, in collective learning, and in the authority of incumbents. Sacrifices of this sort are particularly costly when environments change frequently and in unpredictable ways because it is impossible to forecast how durable a given adaptation will prove to be. Under these circumstances, when survival necessitates some form of change, structural adaptations are likely to be confined to the margins of the administrative system, where they will be highly visible but will not interfere with routine work. The best-known example of this tendency is the educational system, in which administrators strive to maintain a consistent program and improve resource flows in the face of shifting public attitudes and political priorities. In systems of this sort, policies are announced but not implemented; offices are created with no command links to operational units of the system; and positions are staffed to display competence rather than to control activities. Such "loose coupling" (Weick 1976) is thus an adaptive response to environmental uncertainty.

This last point allows us to make sense of two perplexing and paradoxical questions about the history of American child control. How has the system survived, and even prospered, despite its well-perceived inability to prevent or otherwise reduce juvenile crime? How is it that the multiplication of juvenile justice statutes has not eliminated discretion, but rather has arguably expanded it? The answers to these two questions are indissolubly linked. The only technical claim reformers could make with any assurance was for their ability to confine deviant children. This is what the system does best, but it is also the point on which it is most vulnerable to criticism: liberals argue that the system incarcerates too much and too arbitrarily, and conservatives complain that it does not do enough. Because incarceration alone has never been an adequate means by which to define the system's purpose or justify expansion, reformers were forced repeatedly to claim legitimacy on wider ideological grounds.

When public criticism and adverse court decisions called these claims into question, the best defense was to advocate legislative reforms that gave the illusion of legality but offered no real controls over routine decision making. Again we saw this pattern inaugurated by the colonial Puritans, who enacted a legal code in order to camouflage their practical system of discretionary lay justice. Subsequent reforms likewise used legal measures to expand the formal structure of the child control system, with the avowed goal of bringing greater rationality and accountability to bear. But the real effect of this structural elaboration has been to seal off the system from criticism and to preserve a domain of discretionary action in which the routine work of classifying and sanctioning delinquents is legitimized by substantive claims of professional expertise. Thus the system's formal structure has become increasingly symbolic; indeed, the concept of a juvenile justice *system* is a polite euphemism that implies rationality while it obscures the fragmented nature of the social control process. The system is in fact made up of autonomous agencies that tend to pursue their own, often contradictory, priorities. Police, juvenile courts, probation agencies, and correctional bureaucracies have systematically different views of deviance and often regard each other as adversaries; but all must act as if such negotiable concepts as delinquency, due process, and treatment have technical meaning and practical consequences. In juvenile justice, as in education, a facade of structural integrity is maintained by a "logic of confidence" (Meyer and Rowan 1978, 101–103), a continual enactment by all participants of a good-faith assumption of competence.

This interpretation fits the findings of this study better than any of the alternatives we have considered. Yet in a sense it begs the question because it suggests only that the American pattern of child control was built upon and perpetuated by a complex of ideological structures that are embedded in the wider society. This leaves a more comprehensive issue to be addressed—namely, why did America take this early and decisive turn toward a therapeutic style of control? What institutional features of American society made this turn attractive? My discussion here must be in part speculative because this research has not established a comparative perspective through which to analyze cross-national differences. But it is clear that America was a pioneer in the kinds of policy reforms I have discussed: I argued that the roots of the modern concept of delinquency are to be found in Massachusetts Bay law and, since the time of Beaumont and Tocqueville, American institutional innovations have set the tone for policies in other nations. With these caveats in mind, my final comments should be viewed as a first approach to this issue.[9]

The argument starts with a return to Weber's views on the relationship between legal change and domination. Recall that in the basic Weberian model, any trend toward a substantively rational system of control in modern societies is precluded because of the superior efficiency and predictability of formal law. The keystone of Weber's argument is his conception of the modern state: autonomous and formally structured legal institutions emerged as the counterpart to strong, centralized states in which sovereigns claim author-

9. The following argument is spelled out in more comprehensive terms in Hamilton and Sutton (1983).

ity based on certain secular and universal norms. In the European regimes that he took as referents, the process of state formation implied the gradual structural differentiation of the political and legal orders. As law became autonomous from politics, responsibility for articulating substantive values and representing the public interest was increasingly borne by political agencies. The domains of law and politics became institutionally segregated but reciprocally interdependent: on the one hand, formal law derived its content only vicariously, from contests of values enacted in the political arena. On the other hand, political contests were constrained to follow ethically neutral "rules of the game" defined in law. The political and judicial, substantive and formal components of domination were yoked together and legitimized by the transcendent authority of the sovereign state (Schluchter 1981, 109).

But it is precisely this concept of unified sovereignty—and correlative notions of hierarchy, rulership, and obedience—that are lacking in American political discourse; indeed, the concept of domination itself seems to be an anathema.[10] Relative to European regimes, the United States is a weak state with strong law. The founders of the American state consciously rejected European patterns of state building based on the model of aristocratic hierarchy (Tocqueville 1945; Bailyn 1967; Huntington 1968; Wills 1979) and instead constructed a federal system in which sovereignty is divided and authority is diffused among levels of government. One consequence of this state-building strategy is that American government lacks a strong bureaucratic center and has typically relied instead on patronage-oriented political parties to administer distributive policies. At the same time, beginning in the 1790s and continuing at least through the nineteenth century, the U.S. legal system moved toward an exclusively formal style of jurisprudence. In theory, formalism meant that the law was a scientific, professional domain that was autonomous from politics. In

---

10. Weber (1978, 946) defined domination as "the authoritarian power of command." As Parsons (1964b, 152) points out, the German term for domination—*Herrschaft*, literally "the master's hand"—has "no satisfactory English equivalent."

practice, as Weber (1978, 891, 894) observed, American courts showed conspicuous antiformal tendencies. Formal doctrines provided grounds on which courts resisted pressure to intervene in social affairs and to adjust the manifest inequities caused by uncontrolled economic growth (Horwitz 1977). As a result, the American "state of courts and parties" (Skowronek 1982) is notoriously vulnerable to interest group pressures and resistant to top-down policy-making.

The problem of control is chronic in the United States because neither the authority of the state nor the majesty of the law is sufficient to mobilize citizens toward collective goals, achieve distributive justice, or manage economic growth. By the 1880s, disadvantaged groups—including industrial workers, farmers, immigrants, and consumers—had begun to find their political voice. In reaction to this growing trend, even economic elites began to support moderate reform policies concerned with crime, urban poverty, and industrial accidents. The courts, however, remained obdurate, and after 1900, state legislatures assumed the burden of achieving distributive justice (Friedman 1973; Friedman and Ladinsky 1967; Gilmore 1977). Support for reform legislation was plainly fueled by resentment of conservative courts and their bondage to formalistic legal dogma (White 1980, 60).[11] In view of all this, the task reformers set for themselves was a difficult one. They sought on the one hand to incorporate immigrants without strengthening the hand of the patronage system and on the other to enhance government's problem-solving capacity without invoking the imagery of centralized power. To build a rational, activist state within the confines of these institutional limitations, they adopted indirect strategies.

I see two main themes to their strategies. The first is ideological: rather than grounding their appeals in the authority of the state and

---

11. As one contemporary wrote, "The people are not interested in precedent. They have lost their primitive reverence for it. They are interested in justice, and a dogmatic adjudication that 'this is the law as settled by precedent' will not tend to counteract a fast developing prejudice to judges as a class of public servants and to courts as institutions" (Bingham 1912, n. 113–114).

the duties of citizens to obey, reformers identified society itself—which they conceptualized in terms of a complex web of obligations owed by citizens to one another—as the moral center of politics. We find this theme first in the colonial Puritan notion of the covenant and later in the voluntarist moral reform movements of the nineteenth century. But it is developed most thoroughly in the writings of turn-of-the-century American sociologists, who argued that individual identity, morality, and political authority are all rooted in the patterns of association and interaction that give form to social life.[12] Indeed, it was as part of this intellectual trend that E. A. Ross (1901) coined the term "social control" to denote a natural form of authority that is articulated through embedded roles rather than political hierarchy. Social control, in his view, was *self*-control (see also Mead 1924–1925).

The second theme is structural and institutional. Reformers sought to redefine the political problem of control as an administrative problem in order to emphasize the ethical universality of their proposals and, increasingly, to distance themselves from the patronage system. They did not attempt to implement their policies through direct bureaucratic centralization, however, but rather through the creation of functionally specialized, autonomous administrative agencies at all levels of government. This strategy has had several important consequences. It led to the further dispersion of governmental authority and ultimately to the permanent fragmentation of the welfare state (Skocpol and Ikenberry 1983; Orloff and Skocpol 1984). In the absence of a centralized bureaucracy, these agencies tended to subcontract important tasks to certified professional groups and other private interests (Silberman n.d.). In the absence of direct linkages to courts, decision making in these settings is informed not by adversarial proce-

12. Writings on this theme are too numerous to permit a representative listing. Key examples include Ward (1883), Cooley (1902), and Mead (1924–1925) on social psychology; James (1909) and Dewey (1922) on the pragmatic approach to ethics; and Holmes (1963) and Pound (1917) on jurisprudence. For an overview see Janowitz (1975).

dures and the rule of law, but by a combination of agency priorities and professionally informed diagnostic criteria.[13] These trends are not, of course, equally apparent in all agency settings; some conform more than others to the pure Weberian model of bureaucratic rationality. But to the degree that reformist agencies are closely tied to externally maintained value systems and loosely coupled to the authority of the state—as they are, most notably, in juvenile justice—the decision-making structure will tend to be substantive and therapeutic rather than formal, strict, and coercive.

If this expanded argument is correct, it suggests two important implications. The first is that the origins of a therapeutic system of control lie farther back in history than is conventionally thought. Although most of the recent literature on control—especially the writings of Foucault and those he has influenced—places the therapeutic revolution in the midst of the eighteenth-century efflorescence of scientific rationalism, I have argued that its origins lie in the American colonists' political experiments in the 1640s. A second implication concerns causation. Again Foucault and others have tended to equate the increasingly invasive potential of therapeutic control with the expansionist tendencies of the modern European state. In this view the prison, the reformatory, and the asylum are all aspects of a centralizing trend that also includes the modern army and governmental bureaucracies. I have argued on the contrary that, in the American case at least, therapeutic justice is an expression of the weakness and ambivalence of official authority.

Americans moved early and decisively toward a loosely coupled, discretionary style of control because they lacked the institutional infrastructure to support a more centralized, formally rational, and frankly coercive system. The fact that much of this energy has been

13. For historical discussions of the growth of diagnostic procedures in agency settings, see, for example, Pound (1914) on railway and public utility commissions, Freund (1923) on the Interstate Commerce Commission, and Nonet (1969) on workmen's compensation. For studies of contemporary social welfare, see Mashaw (1974), Dickson (1976), and especially Friedman (1981).

directed at children is not surprising. Humanitarian impulses aside, America has perennially seen itself as a young nation; we tend to see our future in our children and to see our worst fears realized in the children of others. Having rejected European patterns of mobilization and control, Americans sought means to directly instill proper feelings of obligation in individual consciences. The result was an original and subtle style of control, of which many elements have spread to other modern states but which remains fundamentally wedded to the American experience of authority and deeply rooted in the habits of American institutional life.

This conclusion offers little solace to those who are looking to make practical, humane alterations in our official responses to deviant and dependent children. The history of reform presented here suggests that to make those changes would require more than tinkering. Rather, it would require a thoroughgoing reallocation of legal responsibility, a sharp reduction of official discretion, and a radical pruning of the dense web of patronage exchanges between public and private sectors. Moves of this sort would be catastrophic for the individuals and groups that have a stake in the existing system. They will not occur because we lack the political will. We lack the political will because we are subservient to a set of attitudes that supports these institutional arrangements. Ultimately we care less for other people's children than we do for our own—all the more so when those children are of another color, live in a city we have never seen, or speak a different language.

Even more important, we have yet to resolve our fundamental ambivalence about the meaning of crime and poverty. How, if at all, are they related to each other and to the vast catalog of major and minor delicts we have learned to fear—from drunkenness, drug addiction, sexual abuse, and promiscuity to idleness, irreligiosity, and poor school attendance? To the medical eye all are symptoms of an underlying pathology. Are they products of misfortune or of vice? Both at once, we tend to believe. The therapeutic ideology informs an official response that cuts neatly between these alternatives and serves neither. In the modern "penal-welfare state" (Garland 1985), criminal punishment is disingenuously called treatment, and assistance to the economic casualties of society is accompanied by surveillance and stigma. In this sense we have not come far from Massachusetts Bay.

APPENDIX A:
METHODOLOGICAL NOTES

This appendix is designed as a brief introduction to the quantitative data and dynamic modeling techniques used in Chapters 3, 5, and 6 of this book. It is aimed at the general reader with, at most, a basic familiarity with the logic of linear regression. Interested readers will find more detailed accounts of event-history techniques in Tuma and Hannan (1984, pt. II).

I begin by describing the two types of quantitative data used here. One type of data records the timing of state-level reforms in laws that govern the classification, adjudication, and institutional treatment of juvenile deviants. Because the language and content of juvenile codes tend to be remarkably consistent across states, it was possible to summarize a great deal of legislative activity in terms of twenty-five discrete and specific innovations, fourteen of which I analyze explicitly.[1] The choice of these twenty-five salient reforms was guided in part by previous literature and in part by my own initial explorations into state statutes. Each of these innovations is treated as an outcome, and for each state I recorded data on the year in which each was adopted (if at all). I determined the year of adoption through a systematic search of the legislative histories of the juvenile codes in all fifty states. The second type of data, used as independent variables, consists mainly of indicators of aggregate state characteristics taken from decennial U.S. censuses and special reports by the Census Office and Census Bureau. A few additional items are drawn from social movement publications and from secondary sources; these are detailed in the text.

A key question throughout this study is why some states were more receptive to reform than others. Because most of the reforms studied here

1. A sample coding form is reproduced in Appendix B.

were eventually adopted by all fifty states, the question reduces to one of timing: what factors determine the rates at which reforms were adopted among the states? This question could be approached in several different ways using conventional cross-sectional analytic techniques. The most fruitful and efficient approach, however, is to treat data on the timing of statutory innovations as event-histories and to analyze them using explicitly dynamic methods. Event-history techniques are intended for the analysis of qualitative changes over time. These changes must be discrete, but otherwise may be of any sort and at any level of analysis, including marriages and divorces in a sample of individuals (Hannan, Tuma, and Groeneveld 1978), organizational failures (Carroll and Delacroix 1982), changes in the political structure of nations (Hannan and Carroll 1981) or cities (Knoke 1982), or, in this research, adoption of a legal innovation.

An event-history is a quantitative description of the time path of change. The first step in constructing an event-history is to conceptualize a complete and mutually exclusive set of conditions or "states" that a unit in a research sample can occupy and to identify all the logically possible transitions.[2] In a study of marriage, for example, we may wish to consider individuals as being (1) never married, (2) married, (3) divorced, or (4) widowed. Subjects can obviously move from 1 to 2 at any time by getting married; likewise they can move from 2 to 3 or 4, or even from 3 or 4 to 2 if they remarry. Clearly, they cannot move from 2, 3, or 4 to 1 or from 4 to 3. Individuals may experience no transitions, or they may experience all the logical possibilities, some more than once. When we have data on the times at which all sample members experience valid transitions—or events—we have complete event-histories on our sample. An event-history can be compactly recorded by coding the type and time of transition for an individual during the time period in which the individual is in the sample.

The transitions in this study are much simpler than those in this hypothetical example. Because each legislative innovation is analyzed separately, each of the U.S. states that compose the sample exhibits one of only two possible conditions: either it (1) has not adopted a given law or (2) such a law is in force. Because none of the reforms examined here is repealed within

2. It is conventional in the event-history literature to refer to the condition of individuals as "states" and to transitions as occurring from one state to another. In this study the unit of analysis is U.S. states. To avoid terminological confusion, I use the term "condition" rather than "state."

the time frame of the analysis, the only transition possible is from 1 to 2.[3] Data on legislative enactments are transformed into event-histories simply by assigning a state a code of 1 for every year before adoption and 2 for the year of adoption and after.

Most generally, event-history techniques are preferable to static models because they use all available information on the number, sequence, and timing of events that occur over time. Because the transition processes at issue here are relatively simple, it is possible that the information loss involved in using static models would be small.[4] Yet there are two specific reasons for preferring dynamic methods to model even such basic processes. The first is the problem of censoring. The most common type of censoring is "right-censoring," which occurs when a subject drops from the sample midway or does not experience a transition before the end of the research period. In a study of the effects of a surgical procedure on mortality, for instance, patients may move before the study is over or live on beyond the follow-up period. Investigators using static methods are forced either to fill in missing data with arbitrary values or drop such subjects from the sample; however, maximum likelihood estimators for event-history data can easily handle cases that are right-censored (see, e.g., Tuma and Hannan 1978). "Left-censoring" poses difficulties for both static and event-history methods. It occurs when there are data relevant for the transition rate of an individual prior to the start of the observation period for this individual. For example, data for a study of delinquency among high school students are left-censored if we lack information on the number of times an individual has been truant from school prior to the start of the study because individuals with high truancy rates may be expected to have a greater probability of subsequent delinquency.

These data contain examples of both types of censoring. Some states are right-censored because they never adopt a given reform; they simply remain "at risk" of adopting the reform during the observation period and are coded as a censored case at the end. A few states are so precocious that they originate a reform well in advance of the general trend and thus before the

3. A few of the reforms adopted in the late nineteenth and early twentieth centuries—and analyzed in Chapters 3 and 5—were repealed after 1960 and are treated explicitly as separate transitions in Chapter 6. These include, most conspicuously, the repeal of incorrigibility legislation.

4. For a systematic comparison of the findings from static and dynamic analyses of a single set of data, see Michael and Tuma (1983). For an earlier cross-sectional analysis of the data presented in Chapter 3 of this book, see Sutton (1983).

beginning of the observation period. To deal with this type of left-censoring, I have coded these states as having already adopted the reform in question at the first observation.

A related sampling issue arises when states are admitted to the Union after the start of the diffusion process. It is possible to include such states in the sample, but it makes analytic sense to do so only if data are available on independent variables. In Chapter 3, nineteen states had to be omitted from the analysis for lack of such data, but three states admitted to the Union after 1900 were included in the analysis in Chapter 5.

The second advantage of dynamic methods lies in their more realistic treatment of exogenous variables. In any causal process that occurs over an extended period of time, it is likely that relative values of independent variables will change, that the strength and direction of their effects will change, or that both will change. Static techniques are poorly suited to examining these possibilities—typically, they rely on a single baseline observation to model an evolving process. Where changing values of variables are left unmeasured, the variables become unreliable; where changing effects are ignored, models are misspecified. Event-history techniques invite the use of multiple observations. Ideally, observations on independent variables should be updated continuously—say, yearly—but this is seldom possible. Because census data are available only decennially and because correlations tend to be high from one census to the next, I have settled for much longer intervals between observations.

In order to interpret event-history models appropriately, it is important to highlight a few of their distinguishing features. I focus here on issues of sampling, the nature of the dependent variable, and the kinds of variation that enter into the model. First, it is crucial to recognize that, because time is an explicit feature of dynamic models, sampling involves the choice not only of a representative group of members, but of an appropriate and bounded period of time as well. The choice of beginning and end points for the observation period is only secondarily a data or statistical issue; like cross-sectional sampling, it is determined primarily by theory. Based on these considerations, I have chosen observation periods that include most of the diffusion process and that exclude only extremely early or late adopters. Beyond this basic constraint, my heavy reliance on census data suggested the use of decennial census years (i.e., those ending in 0) to bound the analysis.

In the analysis of juvenile court diffusion in Chapter 5, for example, the end of the observation period is set at 1930, and three states that passed juvenile court laws in 1937, 1940, and 1959 are thereby right-censored. I made this decision on the grounds that these states probably resisted reform for so long largely for idiosyncratic reasons. Thus extending the observation period to include them—and gathering the additional data that would be required—would result in a minimal analytic payoff. It is important to reiterate, however, that they are included in the sample, even though all we know about them is that they did not adopt juvenile courts by 1930.

The most crucial point to understand about event-history models is that the dependent variable—the instantaneous rate of transition from one condition to another—is not directly observable. Stated informally, a transition rate is the rate of change in the probability of moving from, say, condition 1 to condition 2, calculated across individuals in the sample and over time. Transition probabilities themselves are given directly by the data. To take the simple legal change data used here as an example, a graph showing the probability of a state moving to condition 2 (i.e., adopting a given reform) for every year is one of several functions that can be used to describe change in those probabilities. The transition rate is—again speaking informally—the continuous slope of such a function. To use an analogy from physics, transition rates are to transition probabilities as acceleration is to velocity: they describe change in the rate of change.

In dynamic models the null hypothesis of constant rates is tested by examining two kinds of effects: conventional population heterogeneity (i.e., systematic variation among members of the sample) and time dependence (i.e., variation in transition rates over time). When independent variables are added to a model of transition rates, the question being asked is, in effect, whether a single transition rate suffices to describe the sample or whether subgroups of the sample (or states that differ on an observed attribute) have rates that vary systematically from one another. Population heterogeneity can be illustrated with plots of cumulative survival probabilities, one kind of probability function that is directly related to transition rates. In Chapter 3, I introduce a dummy variable to represent states in the South with convict leasing systems, with the expectation that they will show lower rates of reformatory adoption. Figure A.1 shows survival probabilities—the declining probability that a state will "survive" or not adopt a reformatory in the

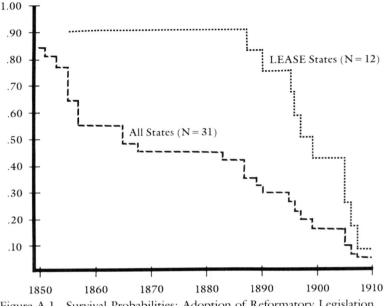

Figure A.1. Survival Probabilities: Adoption of Reformatory Legislation,
           All States and LEASE States

next time interval—estimated for the entire thirty-one-state sample used in
the analysis and separately for states with convict leasing systems.[5] It provides a graphic portrayal of the effect of the LEASE dummy variable, showing that the survival probabilities associated with leasing states are higher—
hence their transition rates are lower—than those of the sample as a whole.
The differences are, moreover, statistically significant. Confidence intervals
drawn around the estimates (omitted from Figure A.1 for simplicity) show
that the estimates are mutually exclusive at a 95 percent significance level.
The variation in transition rates is quite clear in this case because a dummy

5. I am grateful to Clifford Nass for writing an extraordinarily flexible program
for estimating survival probabilities from censored event-history data. The functions
in Figures A.1 and A.2 are based on standard Kaplan-Meier estimates.

independent variable is used to divide the sample categorically. The same basic logic extends to the analysis of continuous independent variables, but their relationships to transition rates cannot be drawn on a two-dimensional graph.

The notion of time dependence is slightly more difficult, but also amenable to graphic representation. There are many research situations in sociology where we might expect that rates of change vary systematically over time. One well-known example is Stinchcombe's (1965) hypothesis that younger organizations experience higher rates of mortality because of a "liability of newness" (see also Carroll and Delacroix 1982). Here time—measured in terms of the age of the organization—serves as a useful proxy for such intangible factors as legitimacy, inertia, and learning. In this study I repeatedly examine changes in adoption rates over historical time. The data consistently show that adoption rates accelerate over the course of the diffusion process, and I argue that this acceleration signifies a "bandwagon effect" resulting from the successful institutionalization of reform programs. Once again we can take the diffusion of reformatories as an example. In Chapter 3, I divide the observation period into two subperiods, 1850–1880 and 1880–1910, and show that adoption rates are higher in the latter period than in the former. This shift can be shown by extending our understanding of survivor functions slightly.

First, it is important to note that even when transition rates are constant, survival probabilities are not. In fact, constant rates yield survivor functions that decline exponentially. Thus the sample plot in Figure A.1 is useless for detecting time dependence because we would expect it to exaggerate changes early on and understate them later in the process. These estimates can be detrended in a fairly straightforward way, however. It turns out that the instantaneous transition rate is the negative of the slope of the log survivor function. Thus a drawing of the log survivor function is a useful diagnostic tool: where rates are constant, it will decline in an even stepwise fashion; where rates increase, its slope will decline more rapidly. The survivor function for reformatory adoption is plotted on a log scale in Figure A.2. Again the plot is compatible with the findings in Chapter 3: survival probabilities decline fairly evenly until just after 1880 and fall more rapidly after that, with only a brief pause around 1900.

In addition to using time dependence as a proxy for unobserved variables, it is possible to extend the model by specifying changes in the effects of

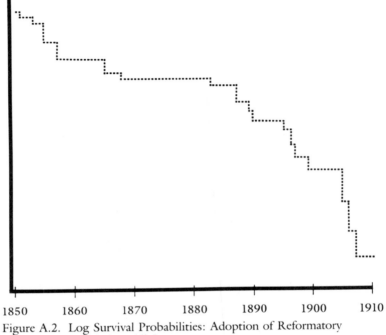

Figure A.2. Log Survival Probabilities: Adoption of Reformatory
           Legislation, All States

independent variables over time. The more realistic way to go about this is to model continuous changes in effects, but in this study I have taken the simpler route of testing for changes between time periods. When the model is specified to allow two time periods and the effect of a variable is examined in each, two parameters result: one that estimates the effect of the variable on transitions occurring before the split and another that estimates its effect on transitions that occur after.

I describe most of my modeling procedures in the text. For the most part the logic of dynamic model building is analogous to the logic of cross-sectional analysis. Models are estimated using maximum likelihood methods in the functional form

$$lnr(t) = a_0 + a_1X_1 + \ldots + a_nX_n,$$

where the dependent variable lnr(t) is the log of the instantaneous rate of transition at time (t). Otherwise the model is conceptually similar to a linear regression equation: a_0 is a constant, parameters a_1 through a_n are effects estimates, and Xs are values of the independent variables. In the models presented in this book, I report the antilogs of the a parameters, which indicate the multiplicative effects of a unit increase in the independent variables on the rate itself. In further analogy to regression, statistics are available to test the significance of entire models (using X^2), of partial relationships between independent variables (using F), and of nested models (using likelihood ratios). I describe the use of these statistics in the context of the analyses.

APPENDIX B:
SAMPLE CODING FORM
FOR LEGISLATIVE VARIABLES

This appendix contains a list of the legal innovations coded as variables for this study. Values coded are for the state of Kansas. For all variables coded as years, the value *8888* is a missing data code, signifying an innovation that was not adopted within the time frame of the study.

I.D. Variables

KS	V1	State PO code.
32	V2	State ID number.
1861	V3	Year of statehood.

Court Organization

1861	V4	Year state constitution authorized establishment of separate courts.
1972	V5	Year of constitutional court reorganization and unification.
1905	V6	Year juvenile court established as "designated court."
8888	V7	Year juvenile court established as "divisional court."
1957	V8	Year juvenile court established as "separate court."
8888	V9	Year juvenile jurisdiction included in separate "coordinated court."

Jurisdiction and Deviant Labels

1869	V10	Year incorrigibility came under the jurisdiction of any court.
1901	V11	Year dependency/neglect came under the jurisdiction of any court.
1905	V12	Year delinquents defined as specific offender group.

1905	V13	Year dependent/neglected defined as specific offender group.
1957	V14	Year incorrigibles defined as specific offender group.
8888	V15	Year incorrigibles subsumed under dependency/neglect label.
8888	V16	Year jurisdiction over incorrigibility repealed.

Probation

| 1901 | V17 | Year juvenile probation service established on volunteer only basis. |
| 1905 | V18 | Year paid juvenile probation officers authorized. |

Preadjudicatory Detention

1901	V19	Year children required to be detained separately from adults.
1978	V20	Year detention distinction made between neglected/dependent and delinquents.
1978	V21	Year detention distinction made between incorrigibles and delinquents.

Adjudication

1881	V22	Year summary or informal proceedings authorized for commitment of juveniles.
1901	V23	Year separate trials, dockets, or records required for juvenile hearings.
8888	V24	Year procedural distinction made between neglect and delinquency.
8888	V25	Year procedural distinction made between incorrigibility and delinquency.

Disposition

1869	V26	Year specialized children's institution first established.
1957	V27	Year dispositional alternatives for dependent/neglected different from delinquents.
1957	V28	Year dispositional alternatives for incorrigibles different from delinquents.

REFERENCES

Abbott, Grace. 1925. History of the juvenile court movement throughout the world. In *The Child, the Clinic, and the Court*, edited by Jane Addams, 267–273. New York: New Republic.

Abel, Richard L. 1981. Conservative conflict and the reproduction of capitalism: The role of informal justice. *International Journal of the Sociology of Law* 9:425–467.

Adams, Brooks. 1887. *The Emancipation of Massachusetts: The Dream and the Reality*. Boston: Houghton Mifflin.

Almy, Frederic. 1905. The economics of the juvenile court. *Charities* 13(14):337–339.

Bailey, Hugh C. 1969. *Liberalism in the New South: Southern Social Reformers and the Progressive Movement*. Coral Gables, Fla.: University of Miami Press.

Bailyn, Bernard. 1967. *The Ideological Origins of the American Revolution*. Cambridge, Mass.: Harvard University Press.

Bakal, Yitzak, ed. 1973. *Closing Correctional Institutions: New Strategies for Youth Services*. Lexington, Mass.: D. C. Heath.

Banner, Lois W. 1977. Religious benevolence as social control: A critique of an interpretation. In *The Many-Faceted Jacksonian Era: New Interpretations*, edited by Edward Pessen, 302–321. Westport, Conn.: Greenwood Press.

Barnard, Kate. 1908. Shaping the destinies of the new state. *Proceedings of the National Conference of Charities and Correction*: 36–41.

Barnes, Harry Elmer. 1927. *The Evolution of Penology in Pennsylvania*. Indianapolis: Bobbs-Merrill.

Barrett, Kate Waller. 1908. The need of state supervision for both public and private charities. *Proceedings of the National Conference of Charities and Correction:* 30–36.

Bates, Helen Page. 1905. Digest of statutes relating to juvenile courts and probation systems. *Charities* 13(14):329–337.

Bayer, Ronald. 1981. Crime, punishment, and the decline of liberal optimism. *Crime and Delinquency* 27:169–190.

Beaumont, Gustave de, and Alexis de Tocqueville. 1964. *On the Penitentiary System in the United States and Its Application in France.* Carbondale, Ill.: Southern Illinois University Press.

Becker, Howard. 1963. *Outsiders: Studies in the Sociology of Deviance.* New York: Free Press.

Belden, Evelina. 1920. *Courts in the United States Hearing Children's Cases.* U.S. Children's Bureau Publication 65. Washington, D.C.: U.S. Government Printing Office.

Bingham, Joseph W. 1912. What is the law? *Michigan Law Review* 11:1–25, 109–121.

Blomberg, Thomas G. 1977. Diversion and accelerated social control. *Journal of Criminal Law and Criminology* 68:274–282.

————. 1980. The mixed results and implications of the diversion and family intervention reform movement. Paper presented at the annual meeting of the American Society of Criminology, San Francisco, Calif. Mimeo.

Bodo, John R. 1954. *The Protestant Clergy and Public Issues, 1812–1848.* Princeton, N.J.: Princeton University Press.

Boli-Bennett, John, and John W. Meyer. 1978. The ideology of childhood and the state: Rules distinguishing children in national constitutions. *American Sociological Review* 43:797–812.

Boorstin, Daniel J. 1958. *The Americans: The Colonial Experience.* New York: Random House.

Bowles, Samuel, and Herbert Gintis. 1976. *Schooling in Capitalist America: Educational Reform and the Contradictions of Economic Life.* New York: Basic Books.

Bowman, Harold M. 1906. American administrative tribunals. *Political Science Quarterly* 21:609–625.

Bremer, Francis J. 1976. *The Puritan Experiment: New England Society from Bradford to Edwards.* New York: St. Martin's Press.

Brenzel, Barbara M. 1983. *Daughters of the State: A Social Portrait of the First*

Reform School for Girls in North America, 1856–1905. Cambridge, Mass.: MIT Press.

Bryant, Keith L. 1968. The juvenile court movement: Oklahoma as a case study. *Social Science Quarterly* 49:368–376.

Bullington, Bruce, James Sprowles, Daniel Katkin, and Mark Phillips. 1978. Critique of diversionary juvenile justice. *Crime and Delinquency* 24:59–71.

Butler, Amos W. 1908. The board of state charities and the people. *Proceedings of the National Conference of Charities and Correction:* 43–49.

Cable, George W. 1969 [1889]. The convict lease system in the southern states. In *The Silent South,* edited by George W. Cable, 115–182. Montclair, N.J.: Patterson Smith.

California Youth Authority. 1976. *The Evaluation of Juvenile Diversion Programs: Second Annual Report.* Sacramento, Calif.: CYA.

Canon, Bradley C., and Lawrence Baum. 1981. Patterns of adoption of tort law innovations: An application of diffusion theory to judicial doctrines. *American Political Science Review* 75:975–987.

Carleton, Mark T. 1967. The politics of the convict lease system in Louisiana: 1868–1901. *Louisiana History* 8:5–26.

Carroll, Glenn R., and Jacques Delacroix. 1982. Organizational mortality in the newspaper industries of Argentina and Ireland: An ecological approach. *Administrative Science Quarterly* 27:169–198.

Chambliss, William J. 1964. A sociological analysis of the law of vagrancy. *Social Problems* 12:67–77.

———. 1976. Functional and conflict theories of crime: The heritage of Emile Durkheim and Karl Marx. In *Whose Law? What Order?* edited by W. Chambliss and M. Mankoff, 1–28. New York: John Wiley.

Chandler, Alfred D. 1977. *The Visible Hand: The Managerial Revolution in American Business.* Cambridge, Mass.: Harvard University Press.

Charities (1897–1905). New York: Charity Organization Society of New York.

Chesney-Lind, Meda. 1978. Young women in the arms of the law. In *Women, Crime, and the Juvenile Justice System,* edited by Lee H. Bowker, 171–196. Lexington, Mass.: D. C. Heath.

Cicourel, Aaron. 1968. *The Social Organization of Juvenile Justice.* New York: John Wiley.

Clarke, Stevens H., and Gary G. Koch. 1980. Juvenile court: Therapy or crime control, and do lawyers make a difference? *Law and Society Review* 14:263–308.

Cohen, Stanley. 1979. The punitive city: Notes on the dispersal of social control. *Contemporary Crises* 3:339–363.

Cohen, Stanley, and Andrew Scull, eds. 1983. *Social Control and the State*. New York: St. Martin's Press.

Collins, James A. 1932. The juvenile court movement in Indiana. *Indiana Magazine of History* 28:1–8.

Congressional Quarterly Almanac. 1974. Vol. 30. Washington, D.C.: Congressional Quarterly, Inc.

———. 1977. Vol. 33. Washington, D.C.: Congressional Quarterly, Inc.

Cooley, Charles H. 1902. *Human Nature and the Social Order*. New York: Charles Scribner's Sons.

Davis, Edwin Vance. 1970. Christian understandings of the legislator and his responsibility in Puritan Massachusetts Bay and Quaker Pennsylvania. Ph.D. dissertation, Drew University.

Devine, Edward T. 1901. Principles and method in charity. *Proceedings of the National Conference of Charities and Correction:* 321–324.

———. 1903. Economic aspects of material relief. *Charities* 11(19):541–544.

Dewey, John. 1922. *Human Nature and Conduct*. New York: Henry Holt.

Dicey, A. V. 1905. *Law and Public Opinion in England*. London: Macmillan.

Dickson, Donald T. 1976. Law in social work: The impact of due process. *Social Work* 21:274–278.

DiMaggio, Paul, and Walter Powell. 1983. The iron cage revisited: Institutional isomorphism and collective rationality in organizational fields. *American Sociological Review* 48:147–160.

Donzelot, Jacques. 1979. *The Policing of Families*. New York: Pantheon.

Dornbusch, Sanford M., and W. Richard Scott. 1975. *Evaluation and the Exercise of Authority*. San Francisco: Jossey-Bass.

Downs, George W. 1976. *Bureaucracy, Innovation, and Public Policy*. Lexington, Mass.: Lexington Books.

Dunford, Franklyn W. 1977. Police diversion: An illusion? *Criminology* 15:335–352.

Durkheim, Emile. 1933. *The Division of Labor in Society*. New York: Free Press.

Ekirch, Arthur A. 1943. Thomas Eddy and the beginnings of prison reform in New York. *Proceedings of the New York State Historical Association* 61:376–391.

Emerson, Ralph Waldo. 1876. New England reformers. In *Essays by Ralph Waldo Emerson*, 2nd series, 251–285. Boston: Houghton Mifflin.

Empey, Lamar T. 1973. Juvenile justice reform: Diversion, due process, and deinstitutionalization. In *Prisoners in America*, edited by Lloyd Ohlin, 13–48. Englewood Cliffs, N.J.: Prentice-Hall.

Empey, Lamar T., and Maynard L. Erickson. 1972. *The Provo Experiment: Evaluating Community Control of Delinquency*. Lexington, Mass.: D. C. Heath.

Empey, Lamar T., and Jerome Rabow. 1961. The Provo Experiment in delinquency rehabilitation. *American Sociological Review* 26:679–695.

Erikson, Kai T. 1966. *The Wayward Puritans: A Study in the Sociology of Deviance*. New York: John Wiley.

Estes, Carroll L., and Charlene A. Harrington. 1981. Fiscal crisis, deinstitutionalization, and the elderly. *American Behavioral Scientist* 24:811–826.

Farrand, Max, ed. 1929 [1648]. *The Laws and Liberties of Massachusetts*. Cambridge, Mass.: Harvard University Press.

Flexner, Bernard, and Roger N. Baldwin. 1914. *Juvenile Courts and Probation*. New York: Century.

Floyd, Josephine Bone. 1946. Rebecca Latimer Felton, political independent. *Georgia Historical Quarterly* 30:27–31.

Folks, Homer. 1906. Juvenile probation. *Proceedings of the National Conference of Charities and Correction:* 117–123.

Foreman, Paul B., and Julien R. Tatum. 1938. A short history of Mississippi's state penal system. *Mississippi Law Journal* 10:255–267.

deForest, Robert W. 1904. The federation of organized charities. *Charities* 12(1):16–23.

Foster, Charles I. 1960. *An Errand of Mercy: The Evangelical United Front, 1790–1837*. Chapel Hill: University of North Carolina Press.

Foucault, Michel. 1977. *Discipline and Punish: The Birth of the Prison*. New York: Pantheon.

Fox, Sanford J. 1970. Juvenile justice reform: An historical perspective. *Stanford Law Review* 22:1187–1239.

Freedman, Estelle B. 1981. *Their Sister's Keepers: Women's Prison Reform in America, 1830–1930*. Ann Arbor: University of Michigan Press.

Freund, Ernst. 1923. Historical survey. In *The Growth of American Administrative Law,* edited by Ernst Freund et al., 9–41. St. Louis: Thomas Law Book Co.

Friedman, Kathi V. 1981. *Legitimation of Social Rights in the Western Welfare State: A Weberian Perspective.* Chapel Hill: University of North Carolina Press.

Friedman, Lawrence. 1973. *A History of American Law.* New York: Simon and Schuster.

Friedman, Lawrence, and Jack Ladinsky. 1967. Social change and the law of industrial accidents. *Columbia Law Review* 67:50–82.

Garland, David. 1985. *Punishment and Welfare: A History of Penal Strategies.* London: Heinemann.

Garrett, Philip C. 1900. The essential iniquity of the spoils system. *Proceedings of the National Conference of Charities and Correction:* 34–43.

George, Staughton, Benjamin M. Nead, and Thomas McCamant, eds. 1879. *Charter to William Penn, and Laws of the Province of Pennsylvania.* Harrisburg, Penn.: State Printer.

Gilman, David. 1976. How to retain jurisdiction over status offenders: Change without reform in Florida. *Crime and Delinquency* 22:48–51.

Gilmore, Grant. 1977. *The Ages of American Law.* New Haven, Conn.: Yale University Press.

Goffman, Erving. 1961. *Asylums: Essays on the Social Situation of Mental Patients and Other Inmates.* New York: Anchor.

Gray, Virginia. 1973. Innovation in the states: A diffusion study. *American Political Science Review* 67:1174–1185.

Green, Fletcher M. 1949. Some aspects of the convict lease system in the southern states. In *Essays in Southern History,* edited by Fletcher M. Green, 112–123. Chapel Hill: University of North Carolina Press.

Griffin, Clifford S. 1957. Religious benevolence as social control, 1815–1860. *Mississippi Valley Historical Review* 44:423–444.

———. 1960. *Their Brothers' Keepers: Moral Stewardship in the United States, 1800–1850.* New Brunswick, N.J.: Rutgers University Press.

Griffin, Stanley G. 1909. Relative functions of the state and private charities in care of dependent and neglected children. *Proceedings of the National Conference of Charities and Correction:* 55–57.

Gusfield, Joseph. 1963. *Symbolic Crusade.* Urbana: University of Illinois Press.

Haber, Samuel. 1964. *Efficiency and Uplift: Scientific Management in the Progressive Era, 1890–1920*. Chicago: University of Chicago Press.

Hagan, John. 1979. Symbolic justice: The status politics of the American probation movement. *Sociological Focus* 12:295–309.

———. 1980. The legislation of crime and delinquency: A review of theory, method, and research. *Law and Society Review* 14:603–628.

Hagan, John, John D. Hewitt, and Duane F. Allwin. 1979. Ceremonial justice: Crime and punishment in a loosely coupled system. *Social Forces* 58:506–527.

Hagan, John, and Jeffrey Leon. 1977. Rediscovering delinquency: Social history, political ideology, and the sociology of law. *American Sociological Review* 42:587–598.

Hagan, John, Edward T. Silva, and John H. Simpson. 1977. Conflict and consensus in the designation of deviance. *Social Forces* 56: 320–340.

Hamilton, Gary G., and John R. Sutton. 1983. The problem of control in the weak state: Domination in the U.S., 1880–1920. Revised version of paper presented at the 1982 meetings of the Law and Society Association. Mimeo.

Handlin, Oscar, and Mary F. Handlin. 1950. Origins of the Southern labor system. *William and Mary Quarterly* 7(ser. 3):199–222.

Hannan, Michael T., and Glenn R. Carroll. 1981. Dynamics of formal political structure: An event-history analysis. *American Sociological Review* 46:19–35.

Hannan, Michael T., Nancy Brandon Tuma, and Lyle P. Groeneveld. 1978. Income and independence effects on marital dissolution: Evidence from the Seattle-Denver Income Maintenance Experiment. *American Journal of Sociology* 84:611–633.

Hart, Hastings H. 1906. Report of Committee [on Children]. *Proceedings of the National Conference of Charities and Correction:* 87–93.

———. 1909. Unity of child helping work. *Proceedings of the National Conference of Charities and Correction:* 42–45.

———. 1910. *Preventive Treatment of Neglected Children*. New York: Russell Sage Foundation.

Haskins, George Lee. 1960. *Law and Authority in Early Massachusetts: A Study in Tradition and Design*. New York: Macmillan.

———. 1965. Reception of the common law in seventeenth-century Massachusetts: A case study. In *Law and Authority in Colonial America: Se-*

lected Essays, edited by George Athan Bilias, 17–31. Barre, Mass.: Barre Publishers.

Hawes, Joseph M. 1971. *Children in Urban Society: Juvenile Delinquency in Nineteenth-Century America.* New York: Oxford University Press.

Heale, Michael. 1968. Humanitarianism in the early republic: The moral reformers of New York, 1776–1825. *Journal of American Studies* 2: 161–175.

Hebberd, Robert W. 1907. State supervision and administration: Report of the committee. *Proceedings of the National Conference of Charities and Correction:* 18–23.

Heclo, Hugh. 1974. *Modern Social Politics in Britain and Sweden.* New Haven, Conn.: Yale University Press.

Heidenheimer, Arnold J. 1981. Education and social security entitlements in Europe and America. In *The Development of Welfare States in Europe and America,* edited by Peter Flora and Arnold J. Heidenheimer, 269–304. New Brunswick, N.J.: Transaction Books.

Hellum, Frank. 1979. Juvenile justice: The second revolution. *Crime and Delinquency* 25:299–317.

Henderson, Charles R. 1904. Theory and practice of juvenile courts. *Proceedings of the National Conference of Charities and Correction:* 358–369.

Heuisler, Charles W. 1903. Probation work in children's courts. *Charities* 11(19):399–401.

Hilkey, Charles J. 1910. *Legal Development in Colonial Massachusetts.* New York: Columbia University.

Hofstadter, Richard. 1955. *The Age of Reform: From Bryan to FDR.* New York: Vintage.

Holmes, Oliver Wendell, Jr. 1963. *The Common Law.* Cambridge, Mass.: Harvard University Press.

Holmes, William F. 1965. James K. Vardaman and prison reform in Mississippi. *Journal of Mississippi History* 27:229–248.

Hopkins, Andrew. 1975. On the sociology of criminal law. *Social Problems* 22:608–619.

Horwitz, Morton J. 1977. *The Transformation of American Law, 1780–1860.* Cambridge, Mass.: Harvard University Press.

Howe, Mark DeWolfe. 1965. The sources and nature of law in colonial Massachusetts. In *Law and Authority in Colonial America: Selected Essays,* edited by George Athan Bilias, 1–16. Barre, Mass.: Barre Publishers.

Humphries, Drew, and David F. Greenberg. 1981. The dialectics of crime control. In *Crime and Capitalism*, edited by David F. Greenberg, 209–254. Palo Alto, Calif.: Mayfield.

Huntington, Samuel P. 1968. Political modernization: America vs. Europe. In *State and Society: A Reader in Comparative Political Sociology*, edited by Reinhard Bendix, 170–200. Berkeley and Los Angeles: University of California Press.

Hurd, Harvey B. 1905. Juvenile court law: Minimum principles which should be stood for. *Charities* 13(14):327–328.

Hurley, Timothy D. 1903. Development of the juvenile court idea. *Charities* 11(19):423–425.

———. 1905. Necessity for the lawyer in the juvenile court. *Proceedings of the National Conference of Charities and Correction:* 172–177.

———. 1907. Juvenile probation. *Proceedings of the National Conference of Charities and Correction:* 225–232.

Hutchinson, Thomas. 1936. *The History of the Colony and Province of Massachusetts-Bay*, vol. 1. Cambridge, Mass.: Harvard University Press.

Ignatieff, Michael. 1978. *A Just Measure of Pain: The Penitentiary in the Industrial Revolution, 1750–1850*. New York: Columbia University Press.

James, Eldon R. 1913. Some implications of remedial and preventive legislation in the United States. *American Journal of Sociology* 18:769–783.

James, William. 1909. *A Pluralistic Universe*. New York: Longmans, Green.

Janowitz, Morris. 1975. Sociological theory and social control. *American Journal of Sociology* 81:82–108.

———. 1976. *Social Control of the Welfare State*. Chicago: University of Chicago Press.

Jewell, Harry D. 1910. The status of the juvenile court in the exercise of the functions of the state as the ultimate parent of its children. *Proceedings of the National Conference of Charities and Correction:* 149–152.

Johnson, Herbert Alan. 1965. The advent of the common law in colonial New York. In *Law and Authority in Colonial America: Selected Essays*, edited by George Athan Bilias, 74–91. Barre, Mass.: Barre Publishers.

Kalberg, Stephen. 1980. Max Weber's types of rationality: Cornerstones for the analysis of rationalization processes. *American Journal of Sociology* 85:1145–1179.

Katz, Michael B. 1983. *Poverty and Policy in American History*. New York: Academic Press.

Kelley, Florence. 1904. Review of Ben B. Lindsey, *The Problem of the Children and How the State of Colorado Cares for Them. Charities* 13(1):43.

Kelso, Robert W. 1922. *The History of Public Poor Relief in Massachusetts, 1620–1920.* Boston: Houghton Mifflin.

Klein, Malcolm. 1974. Labeling, deterrence, and recidivism: A study of police disposition of juvenile offenders. *Social Problems* 22:292–303.

———. 1979. Deinstitutionalization and diversion of juvenile offenders: A litany of impediments. In *Crime and Justice: An Annual Review of Research,* vol. 1, edited by Norval Morris and Richard Tonry, 145–201. Chicago: University of Chicago Press.

Klein, Malcolm, Kathie S. Teilmann, Joseph A. Styles, Suzanne Bugas Lincoln, and Susan Labin-Rosensweig. 1976. The explosion in police diversion programs: Evaluating the structural dimensions of a social fad. In *The Juvenile Justice System,* edited by Malcolm W. Klein, 101–119. Beverly Hills, Calif.: Sage.

Knoke, David. 1982. The spread of municipal reform: Temporal, spatial, and social dynamics. *American Journal of Sociology* 87:1314–1339.

Kolko, Gabriel. 1963. *The Triumph of Conservatism: A Reinterpretation of American History, 1900–1916.* New York: Free Press.

Konig, David Thomas. 1979. *Law and Society in Puritan Massachusetts: Essex County, 1629–1692.* Chapel Hill, North Carolina: University of North Carolina Press.

Kronman, Anthony T. 1983. *Max Weber.* Stanford, Calif.: Stanford University Press.

Labaree, Benjamin. 1979. *Colonial Massachusetts: A History.* Millwood, N.Y.: KTO Press.

Lefstein, Norman, Vaughn Stapleton, and Lee E. Teitelbaum. 1969. In search of juvenile justice. *Law and Society Review* 3:491–562.

Leiby, James. 1978. *A History of Social Welfare and Social Work in the United States.* New York: Columbia University Press.

Lemert, Edwin M. 1951. *Social Pathology.* New York: McGraw-Hill.

———. 1967. The juvenile court—quest and realities. In *Task Force Report: Juvenile Delinquency and Youth Crime,* edited by U.S. Task Force on Juvenile Delinquency, 91–106. Washington, D.C.: U.S. Government Printing Office.

———. 1970. *Social Action and Legal Change: Revolution in the Juvenile Court.* Chicago: Aldine.

———. 1971. *Instead of Court: Diversion in Juvenile Justice.* Chevy Chase, Md.: NIMH Center for Studies in Crime and Delinquency.

———. 1981. Diversion in juvenile justice: What hath been wrought. *Journal of Research in Crime and Delinquency* 18:34–46.

Lerman, Paul. 1975. *Community Treatment and Social Control: A Critical Analysis of Juvenile Correctional Policy.* Chicago: University of Chicago Press.

———. 1980. Trends and issues in the deinstitutionalization of youths in trouble. *Crime and Delinquency* 26:281–298.

Levine, Theodore. 1977. Community-based treatment for adolescents: Myths and realities. *Social Work* 22:144–147.

Lewis, W. David. 1965. *From Newgate to Dannemora: The Rise of the Penitentiary in New York, 1796–1848.* Ithaca, N.Y.: Cornell University Press.

———. 1970. The reformer as conservative: Protestant countersubversion in the early republic. In *The Development of American Culture,* edited by Stanley Coben and Lorman Ratner, 64–91. Englewood Cliffs, N.J.: Prentice-Hall.

Lindsey, Benjamin B. 1903a. The reformation of delinquents through the juvenile court. *Proceedings of the National Conference of Charities and Correction:* 206–229.

———. 1903b. Some experiences in the juvenile court of Denver. *Charities* 11(19):403–413.

———. 1905. Recent progress of the juvenile court movement. *Proceedings of the National Conference of Charities and Correction:* 150–167.

Lindsey, Edward L. 1914. The juvenile court from the lawyer's standpoint. *Annals of the American Academy of Political and Social Science* 52:140–148.

Lou, Herbert H. 1927. *Juvenile Courts in the United States.* Chapel Hill: University of North Carolina Press.

Lubove, Roy. 1968. *The Struggle for Social Security, 1900–1935.* Cambridge, Mass.: Harvard University Press.

Lundberg, David, and Henry F. May. 1976. The enlightened reader in America. *American Quarterly* 28:262–271.

McCorkle, L. W., F. L. Bixby, and A. Elias. 1958. *The Highfields Story.* New York: Henry Holt.

Mack, Julian W. 1906. The juvenile court; the judge and the probation officer. *Proceedings of the National Conference of Charities and Correction:* 123–131.

————. 1908. Juvenile courts as part of the school system of the country. *Proceedings of the National Conference of Charities and Correction:* 369–383.

————. 1909. The juvenile court. *Harvard Law Review* 23:104–122.

————. 1916. Legal problems involved in the establishment of the juvenile court. In *The Delinquent Child and the Home,* edited by Sophonsiba P. Breckenridge and Edith Abbott, 181–201. New York: Charities Publication Committee.

McKelvey, Blake. 1935. Penal slavery and Southern reconstruction. *Journal of Negro History* 20:153–179..

————. 1936. *American Prisons: A Study in American Social History Prior to 1915.* Chicago: University of Chicago Press.

McKelway, Alexander J. 1908. The need of reformatories and the juvenile court system in the South. *Proceedings of the American Prison Association:* 55–64.

Maine, Sir Henry. 1917. *Ancient Law.* London: J. M. Dent.

Martinson, Robert. 1974. What works?—Questions and answers about prison reform. *Public Interest* (June):22–55.

Mashaw, Jerry L. 1974. The management side of due process: Some theoretical and litigation notes on the assurance of accuracy, fairness, and timeliness in the adjudication of social welfare claims. *Cornell Law Review* 59:772–824.

Mattingly, J., and D. Katkin. 1975. The youth service bureau: A re-invented wheel? Paper presented at the meetings of the Society for the Study of Social Problems, San Francisco, Calif.

May, Henry F. 1970. The problem of the American Enlightenment. *New Literary History* 1:201–214.

————. 1976. *The Enlightenment in America.* New York: Oxford University Press.

Mead, George Herbert. 1918. The psychology of punitive justice. *American Journal of Sociology* 23:577–602.

————. 1924–1925. The genesis of the self and social control. *International Journal of Ethics* 35:251–277.

Meier, Robert F. 1982. Perspectives on the concept of social control. *Annual Review of Sociology* 8:35–55.

Melossi, Dario, and Massimo Pavarini. 1981. *The Prison and the Factory: Origins of the Penitentiary System.* Totowa, N.J.: Barnes and Noble.

Mennel, Robert M. 1973. *Thorns and Thistles: Juvenile Delinquents in the*

American States, 1825–1940. Hanover, N.H.: University Press of New England.

Meyer, John W. 1977. The effects of education as an institution. *American Journal of Sociology* 83:55–77.

Meyer, John W., and Brian Rowan. 1977. Institutionalized organizations: Formal structure as myth and ceremony. *American Journal of Sociology* 83:340–363.

————. 1978. The structure of educational organizations. In *Environments and Organizations,* edited by Marshall W. Meyer et al., 78–109. San Francisco: Jossey-Bass.

Meyer, John W., David Tyack, Joane Nagel, and Audri Gordon. 1979. Public education as nation-building in America: Enrollments and bureaucratization in the American states, 1870–1930. *American Journal of Sociology* 85:591–613.

Michael, Robert T., and Nancy Brandon Tuma. 1983. Entry into marriage and parenthood by young adults. Chicago, Ill.: NORC Economics Research Center. Mimeo.

Miller, Perry. 1965. *The Life of the Mind in America: From the Revolution to the Civil War.* New York: Harcourt, Brace, and World.

Morison, Samuel Eliot. 1930. *Builders of the Bay Colony.* Boston: Houghton Mifflin.

Morris, A. 1978. Diversion of juvenile offenders from the criminal justice system. In *Alternative Strategies for Coping with Crime,* edited by N. Tutt, 50–54. Oxford: Basil Blackwell.

Morris, Richard B. 1975. *Government and Labor in Early America.* New York: Octagon.

Moulton, W. B. 1910. Politics and civil service in state institutions. *Proceedings of the National Conference of Charities and Correction:* 308–315.

Mulry, J. M. 1899. The care of destitute and neglected children. *Proceedings of the National Conference of Charities and Correction:* 166–170.

Murphy, J. Prentice. 1929. The juvenile court at the bar. *Annals of the American Academy of Political and Social Science* 145:80–97.

National Advisory Committee on Criminal Justice Standards and Goals. 1976. *Task Force on Juvenile Justice and Delinquency Prevention: Report of the Task Force.* Washington, D.C.: U.S. Department of Justice.

Nonet, Philippe. 1969. *Administrative Justice: Advocacy and Change in a Government Agency.* New York: Russell Sage.

Nonet, Philippe, and Philip Selznick. 1978. *Law and Society in Transition: Toward Responsive Law*. New York: Harper & Row.

Note. 1911. Criticism of the juvenile court. *Journal of Criminal Law and Criminology* 10:302–303.

O'Connor, James. 1973. *The Fiscal Crisis of the State*. New York: St. Martin's Press.

Orloff, Ann Shola, and Theda Skocpol. 1984. Why not equal protection? Explaining the politics of public social spending in Britain, 1900–1911, and the United States, 1880s–1920. *American Sociological Review* 49:726–750.

Palmer, T. B. 1971. California's Community Treatment Program for delinquent adolescents. *Journal of Research in Crime and Delinquency* 8:74–92.

Parrington, Vernon Louis. 1927. *Main Currents in American Thought: An Interpretation of American Literature from the Beginnings to 1920*. 3 vols. New York: Harcourt, Brace.

Parsons, Talcott. 1964a. Evolutionary universals in society. *American Sociological Review* 29:339–357.

———. 1964b. Introduction to *Max Weber: The Theory of Social and Economic Organization*. New York: Free Press.

Patton, Clifford W. 1940. *The Battle for Municipal Reform: Mobilization and Attack, 1875 to 1900*. College Park, Md.: McGrath.

Pear, William H. 1906. The full measure of responsibility. *Proceedings of the National Conference of Charities and Correction:* 96–106.

Pickett, Robert S. 1969. *House of Refuge: Origins of Juvenile Reform in New York State, 1815–1857*. Syracuse, N.Y.: Syracuse University Press.

Pierce, Bradford K. 1869. *A Half Century with Juvenile Delinquents*. New York: D. Appleton and Company.

Platt, Anthony. 1969. *The Child Savers: The Invention of Delinquency*. Chicago: University of Chicago Press.

———. 1974. The triumph of benevolence: The origins of the juvenile justice system in the United States. In *Criminal Justice in America*, edited by Richard Quinney, 356–389. Boston: Little, Brown.

Platt, Rutherford. 1908. A consideration of state intervention in the field of charity. *Proceedings of the National Conference of Charities and Correction:* 18–30.

Pontell, Henry. 1984. *A Capacity to Punish: The Ecology of Crime and Punishment*. Bloomington: Indiana University Press.

Pound, Roscoe. 1907. Executive justice. *American Law Register* 55:137–146.

———. 1914. Justice according to law II. *Columbia Law Review* 14:1–26.

———. 1917. The limits of effective legal action. *International Journal of Ethics* 27:150–167.

Powers, Edwin. 1966. *Crime and Punishment in Early Massachusetts, 1620–1692: A Documentary History.* Boston: Beacon Press.

Prison Discipline Society of Boston. 1972 [1855]. Reports. First–29th June 1826–May 1854. 6 vols. Montclair, N.J.: Patterson Smith.

Proceedings of the National Conference of Charities and Correction. 1874–1916. Boston: George H. Ellis; and Fort Wayne, Ind.: Fort Wayne Printing Co.

Quinney, Richard. 1974. *Critique of Legal Order: Crime Control in Capitalist Society.* Boston: Little, Brown.

Radzinowicz, Leon. 1966. *Ideology and Crime.* New York: Columbia University Press.

Ramirez, Francisco O., and John Boli-Bennett. 1981. Global patterns of educational institutionalization. In *Comparative Education,* edited by Philip Altbach, Robert Arnove, and Gail Kelley, 15–38. New York: Macmillan.

Ramsey, Annie. 1906. Work of the probation officer preliminary to the trial. *Proceedings of the National Conference of Charities and Correction:* 132–136.

Reinsch, Paul S. 1907. The English common law in the early American colonies. In *Select Essays in Anglo-American Legal History, Economics, and Public Law,* vol. 1, edited by the Association of American Law Schools, 367–415. Boston: Little, Brown.

Richmond, Mary E. 1901a. Charitable co-operation. *Proceedings of the National Conference of Charities and Correction:* 298–313.

———. 1901b. The message of associated charities. *Proceedings of the National Conference of Charities and Correction:* 327–329.

Rogers, Helen W. 1904. The probation system of the juvenile court of Indianapolis. *Proceedings of the National Conference of Charities and Correction:* 369–379.

Rosett, Arthur I., and Donald R. Cressey. 1976. *Justice by Consent: Plea Bargains in the American Courthouse.* Philadelphia: Lippincott.

Ross, Edward A. 1901. *Social Control.* New York: Macmillan.

Rothman, David J. 1971. *The Discovery of the Asylum: Social Order and Disorder in the New Republic.* Boston: Little, Brown.

————. 1980. *Conscience and Convenience: The Asylum and Its Alternatives in Progressive America*. Boston: Little, Brown.

Rusche, George, and Otto Kirchheimer. 1939. *Punishment and Social Structure*. New York: Columbia University Press.

Rutherford, Andrew, and O. Bengur. 1976. *Community Based Alternatives to Juvenile Incarceration*. Washington, D.C.: National Institute of Law Enforcement and Criminal Justice.

Rutman, Darrett B. 1965. The mirror of Puritan authority. In *Law and Authority in Colonial America: Selected Essays*, edited by George Athan Bilias, 149–167. Barre, Mass.: Barre Publishers.

Schiesl, Martin J. 1977. *The Politics of Efficiency: Municipal Administration and Reform in America, 1800–1920*. Berkeley and Los Angeles: University of California Press.

Schlossman, Steven L. 1974. Juvenile justice in the age of Jackson. *Teachers' College Record* 76:119–133.

————. 1977. *Love and the American Delinquent: The Theory and Practice of "Progressive" Juvenile Justice, 1825–1920*. Chicago: University of Chicago Press.

Schlossman, Steven L., and Stephanie Wallach. 1978. The crime of precocious sexuality: Female juvenile delinquency in the Progressive era. *Harvard Educational Review* 48:65–94.

Schluchter, Wolfgang. 1981. *The Rise of Western Rationalism: Max Weber's Developmental History*. Berkeley and Los Angeles: University of California Press.

Schoff, Hannah Kent. 1903. Pennsylvania's unfortunate children: What the state is doing for them. *Charities* 11(19):425–428.

Schur, Edwin. 1984. *Labeling Women Deviant: Gender, Stigma, and Social Control*. New York: Random House.

Schwartz, Richard D., and James C. Miller. 1964. Legal evolution and societal complexity. *American Journal of Sociology* 70:159–169.

Scott, W. Richard, and John W. Meyer. 1983. The organization of societal sectors. In *Organizational Environments: Ritual and Rationality*, edited by J. W. Meyer and W. R. Scott, 129–153. Beverly Hills, Calif.: Sage.

Scull, Andrew T. 1977. *Decarceration: Community Treatment and the Deviant: A Radical View*. Englewood Cliffs, N.J.: Prentice-Hall.

————. 1979. *Museums of Madness: Social Organisation of Insanity in Nineteenth Century England*. Harmondsworth: Penguin.

———. 1981. A new trade in lunacy: The recommodification of the mental patient. *American Behavioral Scientist* 24:741–754.

Seward, Rudy Ray. 1978. *The American Family: A Demographic History.* Beverly Hills, Calif.: Sage.

Shurtleff, Nathaniel B., ed. 1854. *Records of the Governor and Company of Massachusetts Bay in New England, 1628–1686.* 5 vols. Boston: William White.

Sidman, Lawrence R. 1972. The Massachusetts stubborn child law: Law and order in the home. *Family Law Quarterly* 6:33–58.

Silberman, Bernard. n.d. State bureaucratization. Mimeo.

Skocpol, Theda, and John Ikenberry. 1983. The political formation of the American welfare state in historical and comparative perspective. *Comparative Social Research* 6:87–148.

Skowronek, Stephen. 1982. *Building a New American State: The Expansion of National Administrative Capacities, 1877–1920.* Cambridge: Cambridge University Press.

Slater, Peter Gregg. 1977. *Children in the New England Mind: In Death and in Life.* Hamden, Conn.: Archon Books.

Smart, George Thomas. 1905. The impetus and meaning of organized charity. *Charities* 14(18):951–953.

Smith, Jeremiah. 1914. Sequel to workmen's compensation acts. *Harvard Law Review* 27:235–259, 344–368.

Sosin, Michael, and Rosemary Sarri. 1976. Due process—reality or myth? In *Brought to Justice? Juveniles, the Courts, and the Law,* edited by Rosemary Sarri and Yeheskel Hasenfeld, 176–206. Ann Arbor: University of Michigan, National Assessment of Juvenile Corrections.

Spitzer, Steven. 1975. Toward a Marxian theory of deviance. *Social Problems* 22:638–651.

Stampp, Kenneth M. 1956. *The Peculiar Institution: Slavery in the Ante-Bellum South.* New York: Vintage.

Stapleton, Vaughan, David P. Aday, Jr., and Jeanne A. Ito. 1982. An empirical typology of American metropolitan juvenile courts. *American Journal of Sociology* 88:549–564.

Stinchcombe, Arthur L. 1965. Social structure and organizations. In *Handbook of Organizations,* edited by James G. March, 142–193. Chicago: Rand-McNally.

———. 1968. *Constructing Social Theories.* New York: Harcourt, Brace, and World.

Strickland, Charles. 1969. A Transcendentalist father: The child-rearing practices of Bronson Alcott. *Perspectives in American History* 3:5–76.

Stubbs, George W. 1904. The mission of the juvenile court. *Proceedings of the National Conference of Charities and Correction:* 350–357.

Sutton, John R. 1983. Social structure, institutions, and the legal status of children in the United States. *American Journal of Sociology* 88:915–947.

Tappan, Paul. 1946. Treatment without trial. *Social Forces* 24:306–312.

Taylor, A. Elizabeth. 1942. The abolition of the convict lease system in Georgia. *Georgia Historical Quarterly* 26:273–287.

Teeters, Negley G. 1960. The early days of the Philadelphia House of Refuge. *Pennsylvania History* 27:165–187.

Teitelbaum, Lee E., and Leslie J. Harris. 1977. Some historical perspectives on the governmental regulation of children and parents. In *Beyond Control: Status Offenders in the Juvenile Court,* edited by Lee E. Teitelbaum and Aidan R. Gough, 1–44. Cambridge, Mass.: Ballinger.

Thomas, John L. 1965. Romantic reform in America, 1815–1865. *American Quarterly* 17:656–681.

Thompson, E. P. 1975. *Whigs and Hunters: The Origin of the Black Act.* New York: Pantheon.

Tilly, Charles, and Louise A. Tilly. 1980. Stalking the bourgeois family. *Social Science History* 4:251–260.

Tilly, Louise A., and Miriam Cohen. 1982. Does the family have a history? A review of theory and practice in family history. *Social Science History* 6:131–179.

Tishler, Hace Sorel. 1971. *Self-Reliance and Social Security, 1870–1917.* Port Washington, N.Y.: Kennikat Press.

Tocqueville, Alexis de. 1945. *Democracy in America.* New York: Vintage.

Troeltsch, Ernst. 1960. *The Social Teachings of the Christian Churches.* 2 vols. New York: Harper.

Tuma, Nancy Brandon, and Michael T. Hannan. 1978. Approaches to the censoring problem in event-history analysis. In *Sociological Methodology, 1979,* edited by Karl F. Schuessler, 209–240. San Francisco: Jossey-Bass.

———. 1984. *Social Dynamics: Models and Methods.* Orlando, Fla.: Academic Press.

Tuma, Nancy Brandon, Michael T. Hannan, and Lyle P. Groeneveld. 1979. Dynamic analysis of event histories. *American Journal of Sociology* 84:820–854.

Turner, Jonathan. 1980. Legal system evolution: An analytical model. In *The Sociology of Law: A Social-Structural Perspective*, edited by William M. Evan, 377–394. New York: Free Press.

Tyack, David, and Elizabeth Hansot. 1982. *Managers of Virtue: Public School Leadership in America, 1820–1980*. New York: Basic Books.

Unger, Roberto M. 1976. *Law in Modern Society*. New York: Free Press.

U.S. Bureau of the Census. 1927. *Children Under Institutional Care*. Washington, D.C.: U.S. Government Printing Office.

U.S. Bureau of the Census. 1965. *Statistical History of the United States from Colonial Times to the Present*. Washington, D.C.: U.S. Government Printing Office.

U.S. Census Office. 1895. *Report on Crime, Pauperism, and Benevolence in the U.S. at the Eleventh Census: 1890* (by Frederick H. Wines), part 2. Washington, D.C.: U.S. Government Printing Office.

U.S. Congress, Senate Committee on the Judiciary, Subcommittee to Investigate Juvenile Delinquency. 1973. *The Juvenile Justice and Delinquency Prevention Act—S. 3148 and S. 821: Hearings*. Washington, D.C.: U.S. Government Printing Office.

———. 1978. *Implementation of the Juvenile Justice and Delinquency Prevention Act of 1974: Hearings*. Washington, D.C.: U.S. Government Printing Office.

U.S. Department of Justice. 1974. *Legislative History of the Juvenile Justice and Delinquency Prevention Act of 1974*. Washington, D.C.: Office of the General Counsel, LEAA.

———. 1977. *Children in Custody: Advance Report on the Juvenile Detention and Correctional Facility Census of 1974*. Washington, D.C.: U.S. Government Printing Office.

Ver Steeg, Clarence L. 1964. *The Formative Years, 1607–1763*. New York: Hill and Wang.

Vinter, Robert D. 1967. The juvenile court as an institution. In *Task Force Report: Juvenile Delinquency and Youth Crime*, edited by U.S. Task Force on Juvenile Delinquency, 84–90. Washington, D.C.: U.S. Government Printing Office.

Vintner, Robert D., George Downs, and John Hall. 1975. *Juvenile Corrections in the States: Residential Programs and Deinstitutionalization: A Preliminary Report*. Ann Arbor: University of Michigan, National Assessment of Juvenile Corrections.

Vollmer, August. 1923. Predelinquency. *Journal of Criminal Law and Criminology* 14:279–283.

Vorenberg, E., and J. Vorenberg. 1973. Early diversion from the criminal justice system: Practice in search of a theory. In *Prisoners in America*, edited by Lloyd Ohlin, 151–183. Englewood Cliffs, N.J.: Prentice-Hall.

Walker, Jack L. 1969. The diffusion of innovations among the American states. *American Political Science Review* 63:880–899.

Walker, Samuel. 1977. *A Critical History of Police Reform: The Emergence of Professionalism*. Lexington, Mass.: Lexington Books.

Wall, Robert Emmett, Jr. 1972. *Massachusetts Bay: The Crucial Decade, 1640–1650*. New Haven, Conn.: Yale University Press.

Walzer, Michael. 1967. Puritanism as a revolutionary ideology. In *Essays in American Colonial History*, edited by Paul Goodman, 33–67. New York: Holt, Rinehart and Winston.

Ward, Lester. 1883. *Dynamic Sociology*. New York: D. Appleton.

Warren, Carol A. B. 1981. New forms of social control: The myth of deinstitutionalization. *American Behavioral Scientist* 24:724–740.

Washburn, Wilcomb E. 1965. Law and authority in colonial Virginia. In *Law and Authority in Colonial America: Selected Essays*, edited by George Athan Bilias, 116–135. Barre, Mass.: Barre Publishers.

Watson, Frank D. 1922. *The Charity Organization Movement in the United States*. New York: Macmillan.

Weber, Max. 1958. *The Protestant Ethic and the Spirit of Capitalism*. New York: Scribner's.

———. 1978. *Economy and Society: An Outline of Interpretive Sociology*. 2 vols. Berkeley and Los Angeles: University of California Press.

Weick, Karl E. 1976. Educational organizations as loosely coupled systems. *Administrative Science Quarterly* 21:1–19.

Wentworth, Edwin P. 1901. The origin and development of the juvenile reformatory. *Proceedings of the National Conference of Charities and Correction:* 245–254.

Wertenbaker, Thomas J. 1947. *The Puritan Oligarchy: The Founding of American Civilization*. New York: Charles Scribner's Sons.

White, G. Edward. 1980. *Tort Law in America: An Intellectual History*. New York: Oxford University Press.

Wiebe, Robert H. 1967. *The Search for Order, 1877–1920*. New York: Hill and Wang.

Wills, Garry. 1979. *Inventing America.* New York: Vintage Books.

Woodward, C. Vann. 1951. *Origins of the New South, 1877–1913.* Baton Rouge: Louisiana State University Press.

Ziff, Larzer. 1973. *Puritanism in America: New Culture in a New World.* New York: Viking.

Zimmerman, Jane. 1949. The convict lease system in Arkansas and the fight for abolition. *Arkansas Historical Quarterly* 7:171–188.

———. 1951. The penal reform movement in the South during the progressive era. *Journal of Southern History* 17:462–492.

INDEX

Abel, Richard L., 244
Abolitionist movement, Romantic influence on, 56–57
Adjudication: and distinction between criminal and noncriminal juveniles, 217–218, 220–221; separate, for adults and children, 168–171; and summary commitment of children, 94–95, 99–101
Alcott, Bronson, 54; association of, with Keagy, 82; on deviance, 66–67; influence of Pestalozzi on, 57; and Romantic view of childhood, 61
Allen, Stephen, 73, 79
Allison, James, 166
American Bible Society, 54
American Peace Society, 56–57
Anglican Church: in Massachusetts Bay, 20; in Virginia, 29
Anglicans, in Massachusetts Bay, 20, 22
Antinomianism, 36–37
Arkansas, juvenile detention laws in, 169
Atlanta, informal juvenile court in, 156
Auburn system: advocates of, and refuge movement, 74n.10; Calvinist influence on, 69–71; Eddy's influence on, 72; and humanitarian reform, 64; in southern states, 105

Baltimore, informal juvenile court in, 156
Banner, Lois W., 54
Baptists, and benevolent reforms, 54

Barnard, Kate, 178n.7, 179
Baum, Lawrence, 185, 226
Bayh, Birch, 213–214
Beaumont, Gustave de, 82, 87n.13
Beccaria, Cesare, 63, 70, 72
Bentham, Jeremy, 63
Bethune, Divie, 73
Body of Liberties, 19
Boorstin, Daniel J., 28–29
Boston Civic League, 156, 181
Bourbon Democrats, and convict leasing, 106
Brenzel, Barbara M., 9
Bullington, Bruce, 206

California: decarceration reform in, 201–202, 218; juvenile court law in, 157, 163, 179
California Club (San Francisco), 181
Calvinism: and concept of the calling, 16, 24, 26, 38, 57–58; covenant as model of social order in, 26; influence of, in Jacksonian period, 50–51, 69; and original sin, 57, 59, 61; and predestination, 5, 51, 52, 57, 58–59; and refuge ideology, 48, 88–89; social base of, in nineteenth-century United States, 54–55; and view of childhood, 57–59; and view of deviance, 61–65; and view of social order, 4, 26, 44
Cambridge Platform, 24–27
Canon, Bradley C., 185, 226
Carolina, colonial law in, 33

Prison Reform Association (Louisiana), 181

Probation: efficiency of, 135; enactment of, and juvenile court laws, 171–176

Probation Subsidy Program (California), 203, 223n.10

Professionalization: ideology of, 125, 131–132, 144–145; of juvenile probation, 145–148; political significance of, 131–132

Progressivism: and administrative reform, 123–127; and federation, ideology of, 128–131; and nonpartisanship, ideology of, 127–128; political significance of, 132; and professionalization, ideology of, 131–132; role of the state in, 130–131

Provo Experiment, 203

Puritanism: and concept of the covenant, 26, 255; and Congregationalists, 20, 24, 35; family authority under, 16; influence of, on nineteenth-century reform, 54; and Presbyterians, 20, 22, 24; and secular reform, 29–30; and Unitarians, 35. See also Calvinism

Quakers: in colonial Pennsylvania and New Jersey, 33; individualism of, 30n.11; influence of, on reform movements, 54, 56, 63, 64, 69; and "inner light," 64

Reconstruction, politics of, and convict leasing, 105–106

Reformatories. See Disposition; Houses of refuge

Reformatories, adoption of: and date of statehood, 104; in southern states, 104–107

Regional effects: on decarceration reform, 223–224; on juvenile court adoption rates, 186–191, 196–197; on reformatory adoption, 110–115; on separate trial legislation, 186–188, 191–193, 196–197

Remonstrance, 22–24, 28n.10

Rhode Island: and colonial law, 31; juve-

nile court law in, 162, 169; slavery, in colonial, 15; stubborn child law in, 11

Richmond, Mary, 139–140, 144

Robinson, George, 166–167

Romanticism: influence of, on reform movements, 50, 53, 88–89; social base of, in nineteenth-century United States, 56–57; and view of childhood, 60–61; and view of deviance, 65; and view of social order, 52–54

Roosevelt, Theodore, 180

Rosett, Arthur I., 235

Ross, E. A., 255

Rothman, David J., 47, 48, 107n.9, 122, 126n.1, 173

Rousseau, Jean-Jacques, 52

Safe Streets Act. See Omnibus Crime Control and Safe Streets Act

Sargeant, John, 73

Schiesl, Martin J., 126n.1, 129n.3, 131–132

Schlossman, Steven L., 9

Schluchter, Wolfgang, 246

Schwartz, Richard D., 240

Scott, W. Richard, 238n.1

Scull, Andrew T., 205, 207, 208–209, 210, 223, 224–225, 230–231, 244

Selznick, Philip, 247n.7

Sentencing. See Disposition

Servants, and children, in Massachusetts Bay, 17

Seward, Rudy Ray, 15, 16

Sidman, Lawrence R., 14, 17

Skocpol, Theda, 248n.8

Skowronek, Stephen, 129n.3

Slavery, in American colonies, 14–15

Society for Alleviating the Miseries of Public Prisons (Philadelphia): Enlightenment influence on, 63; founds Philadelphia refuge, 70, 74–77; refuge management by, 77–78

Society for the Prevention of Cruelty to Children (Louisiana), 181

Society for the Prevention of Pauperism (New York): ideology of, 62; reorganization of, 69. See also Society for

DATE DUE